Will Write For Food

J.P. Devine

Will Write For Food

Copyright © 2015 by J.P. Devine

All rights reserved. No part of this book may be reproduced or transmitted in any form or by any means without written permission of the author.

ISBN 978-1-943424-08-5

Library of Congress Catalog Number 2015915503

Cover design by Stacy Blanchet

North Country Press
Unity, Maine

For Kay, Dawn and Jillana

Acknowledgments

After over thirty years of writing for food and wine, a devoted fan of my weekly work, Earl Smith, former Dean of Students at Colby College in Waterville, and published historian, *Mayflower Hill: A History of Colby College*, and mystery writer, *The Dam Committee* and *More Dam Trouble*, took a liking to my work and brought me to the attention of his publisher, Patricia Newell of North Country Press.

She took me aboard, compiled the years of writings and published this book. I owe her and Earl for the fun of seeing the book in print. In addition, I thank my brilliant wife, former actress, dancer and educator, Katherine, the only woman in Maine to have kissed both myself and Robert Redford. That's her acting story to tell.

I thank my two sweet and brilliant and successful daughters, Dawn Marie of Alexander Street Press and Jillana, attorney and actors' agent in Hollywood. All three were my first editors.

You're reading this because the editors at both newspapers, the *Morning Sentinel* and *Kennebec Journal*, Stacy Blanchet, Maureen Milliken, and Managing Editor Scott Monroe kept me in print. All columns included here were initially published in these papers.

So why ARE you reading this book?

Forward

By 1983, musician Marvin Gaye had been shot to death by his father, producer-writer Dominick Dunne's daughter had been strangled by her lover, and the city of Los Angeles had been terrorized by Richard Ramirez, aka "The Night Stalker," who had broken into multiple homes in the middle of the night and raped and tortured 25 victims. We were still shaking from Charlie Manson and his crew's vicious murders in Beverly Hills back in 1969.

Crime was on the upswing in Los Angeles. My teacher wife and I had survived 7 earthquakes, a couple of riots and a slump in the television and film business where I made my living. We were in desperate need of a laugh.

"Why don't we sell this wonderful house for an enormous profit and move to my home town in Maine?" she asked with a smile.

With note and pad, she figured it out.

"With my Los Angeles teacher's pension, your Screen Actors Guild pension,"

"Wait....Maine?"

"Your social security, profits from the sale and our savings,"

"Maine?.....What will we wear?"

"We can pay for car expenses,"

"Maine? Isn't that like...way up?"

"There'll be plenty for heating, home repairs, new furniture, lawn care and clothing."

"Wait," I said. "Food?"

"What about food?"

"You forgot food."

She closed the ledger and without a smile replied, "That's where you come in."

WHY ARE YOU READING THIS BOOK?

This is a book of short stories. That's what a column is.

A little lady in line with me at the supermarket asked me if I made all of this up. Did I really have early morning chats with Fred Astaire and Groucho on Rodeo Drive in Beverly Hills? Yes. Was it true that I had coffee with writer and friend Ray Bradbury, lunch with actor Jack Nicholson? Of course. Did then President Ronald Reagan really read your column with his morning coffee? On occasion.

Did you really have a late night dinner with actor Ricardo Montalban and six tall dancers from the Dean Martin show at a Mexican restaurant on Christmas Eve? Sure, haven't you ever done that? And do you even remember Ricardo?

Did comedian Jerry Lewis give me priceless comedy advice on his show at NBC in Burbank? Yes, constantly, so did Bob Newhart and Johnny Carson. Did I make up that story about a late night dessert of chocolate truffles with Olivia De Havilland and Orson Welles behind locked doors in a bookstore? Just the part about the chocolates. No, and they were really chocolate covered cherries.

Was I really twenty feet from Bobby Kennedy when he was shot down at the Ambassador Hotel in Los Angeles on June 5th? Sorry to say I was. That's one of the columns in this book that isn't funny. There are more than a few others like that to keep you awake.

If you knew all those famous people, why didn't you become famous? Because they all died in L.A. and I didn't want to. So I left.

Shortly after I got off the bus in Maine, Bob Moorehead, then the editor of the *Morning Sentinel* in Waterville, read some of my L.A. columns and offered me a weekly place on the editorial page. And the rest is history.

Thus started thirty years of stories, fun, snow, laughs, tears, snow, ticks, deer flies, snow, weddings, heart attack, recovery, snow, great friends, teaching, theater, directing, acting, traveling Maine, snow, ice storms, mini-hurricanes, weddings, engagements, summers, snow, birthdays, anniversaries, snow, loons, skunks, weeds, and ice storms.

In the beginning there was darkness upon the face of the earth and God said, "WRITE!"

Summation in One Word
Maine's vocabulary expands with 'Yapowahon'

There is a new word in Central Maine's lexicon. It has replaced "Ayah" and "wicked good." It is a simple word made up of three words run together. It will be with us for all time. It is "yapowahon."

Wherever you go for the next couple of weeks, to the market, the Puffin Stop, Champions or the movies, someone will surely run up to you and ask, "Yapowahon?"

How you answer is very important. If yapowah went on sooner than theirs, you will merit a frown. If yapowah is still out, they will hug you and offer sympathy. But if yapowah never went out at all as with some fortunate souls, then you will have severed a friendship and probably be ostracized in your neighborhood if not the entire town. Just walk on.

Yes, Virginia, there is a fifth horseman and he is called Ice. He rides a mule at the rear, and when somehow you've survived Pestilence, War, Death and Famine, Ice drops the icy rain. Your driveway turns into Steuben glass and your city becomes Stalingrad, 1944.

Yes. For most, it is over. The blue sky has returned. The air is icy, but the threat is gone. This will be the last time I mention it. The event will be talked about for years to come but not by me. I'm into therapy.

I am about to start my 2 a.m. run of the house checking to make sure the lights are burning. They have not been turned off since they came on a week ago. The Teacher wants me to turn them off now and come to bed. I refuse. Sometimes I just stand at the switch and click on and off. Yes, I giggle. What's the problem? On and off, on and off. Aren't they wonderful?

I carry with me a supply of No Doz and a small basket of bulbs. I've got your 100 watt, 200 watt, a few 45 watts and a half dozen three-ways. That is 50, 150, and 200. I have done nothing else in days but replace burned out bulbs. I don't care. I'm happy. My dogs are hiding and She is wearing her sleep mask, but these lights are not going out again in my lifetime. Not if I can help it.

Yes, it's very warm in here. I keep the furnace running day and night. I have it jacked up to 95 degrees, so that in the event that it should fail again the house will retain heat until the year 2000.

When I do go to bed, I lie there listening to it the way I used to listen to my infant daughters breathe in the darkness of their nurseries. She thinks putting out offerings of Oreos, Scotch and incense in front of it is insane, but She's gotten over her night sweats.

Perhaps I'm overreacting. In the history of great disasters, our event would not be listed up there with the Titanic, Hurricane Andrew, or even Kevin Costner's "Water World." It will not be mentioned in the same breath with Dunkirk, the Hindenburg, or the loss of the Health Reach building to Oakland, but still it haunts me.

By Memorial Day the horror will have begun to fade like cheap jeans, like a knife scar, but we will know we were cut.

All in all, I think I handled it pretty well. I am an Irish child of the Great Depression. Rain is our natural condition. It is bred in our bones. It has been over a century since the Great Hunger and almost 70 years since the Big Crash, but we still eat with one hand on the plate because someone hungrier is always watching.

Yes, I handled it well. Yes, my hands still shake and I can't sleep without my Pinocchio night light, but I'm here. Yes, when the picture on the tube flickers or the lights dim, the palms sweat, the eyes tic, the mouth dries, but I'm alive, I'm a survivor, I have walked through the valley of the shadow of ice and my "powahison."

On/off/on/off.

A Californian Now and Forever

The score is on the board. I will never be a Mainer. Truly, one must be born here to be a native. No matter how long one stays, how hard one tries, the rosy nose and cheek look, the big white toothy cracked winter lip smile and hunters' orange cap are not for me.

God, and I am assured that God is a Mainer, knows I've tried. I have a complete L.L.Bean wardrobe, plaid shirts, one in Blackwatch, the other in Campbell. I have fully lined L.L.Bean trousers. I have J.Crew and Banana Republic sweaters, and a Ralph Lauren Polo red-lined, fully down-filled parka. See? Here are my Timberland shoes and L.L.Bean high-topped snow boots. Nice try, hun?

"Give me a child for five years and I will have him for life," the Jesuits and Californians say. Even though I've lived all over the globe, I spent the most time, 28 years, in Southern California – not counting two in San Francisco, which is not in California at all. This total immersion marks one for life. I've tried to escape with no success. You can take the boy out of L.A. but you can't get the stink of eucalyptus out of his tennis shoes.

In the deepest part of the night, I awaken to the sound of the rats rustling in the dry fronds high up in the Washington Palms bordering La Cienega. I hear the roar of the $6 million homes sliding down the cliffs to the Pacific Coast Highway, the crash of the roaring surf as it smashes into Burgess Meredith's living room.

I still miss hearing someone trying the front door, the screams down the street, the smell of gun smoke and pizza on Hollywood Boulevard, the visits to my mugged wife in the hospital. All of these are shapshots in my life book.

Paste all of these scenes against a tropical orange sky, towering ochre lamp streetlights, hooker-lined boulevards and famous murder scenes and it burns a permanent hole in a boy's soul. Ahhh, memory land.

I could become a Missourian again, or a South Carolinian, a New Mexican or Savannah, Georgian. These are my roots, but I could not and never will be a Mainer.

This is never more evident than in my total, complete revulsion and antipathy toward that favorite haunt of the born Mainer, The Basement Playroom, or as we call it in the South, "The Cellar."

The oil tanks are there. The furnace is there. It creaks, stinks, hunkers in the damp darkness. It has a quaint work bench. That the former tenant and others like him could spend evenings actually tooling around in that Budapestian gloom, milling happily about in a smog of wood dust, constantly amazes me.

Even more amazing, more mind boggling, is the habit of the average Mainer to make a play room out of this nether world. People actually carpet these places, wallpaper them, put bars in them with those silly little bar lamps with moronic blurbs like "This Bud's For You Dude."

I have friends, good friends, outwardly charming, seemingly intelligent, normal people, who have pool tables down there and game rooms with lawn furniture on hiatus from the summer winds. On occasion, these good friends, wonderful folk all, actually celebrate weddings in them. They sit down there. Sit in the cellar.

In California, cellars are for flooding, furnaces, wine storage and in some parts of Los Angeles, for burying fallen pets, friends, wives and body parts of unsuspecting travelers. These are tiny spaces, not meant for tarrying, let alone random outbursts of festivities.

The "cellar" as we always called it, was a place of refuge for my father who kept his best booze there away from the prying hands of his five sons. He went there dutifully in the long winter nights to Stoke the Furnace. Often, he would stoke the furnace for several days. It was then, as it should be, a damp dirt-floored place.

I can think of only one place in all of St. Louis where the cellar was used as a playroom. That was the basement of a family I knew, parents of the infamous, glorious, imaginative Rosemary. They called it a Game Room. Ahhh yes, those wonderful games Rosemary played.

The former tenants of my house, a strange family who now live in the barren, Siberian wastes of Northern Maine, as well they should, made a recreation center out of one large room in the basement. They paneled it. Paneled it. It has genuine moulding, Naugahyde benches and tar-leaking linoleum squared flooring. If only the light were better I would invite Better Homes and Gardens in for a photo shoot.

My teacher has never been down there, and she's a Mainer. My dogs refuse to go down there. If it were not that I had to go down once or twice a winter to kick the firebox into action, I would not go there at all.

Call it a rathskeller, family room, playroom, or rec room, call it as Adolph and Eva did, The Bunker, call it what you will. Paste up posters, paint the walls, play polkas on the piano, it will always be a cellar to me. Poppa? Are you down there?

Do me a favor and kick the firebox?

Left Coast Impressions
Hooray for Hollywood, now let's really go home

Thursday, July 29: We arrive. The city of Angels rears its cabled head above the metallic mist known as smog. We have spit in the eye of Thomas Wolfe and come home again. After three days of prairies, mesas, buttes and boredom, we have arrived.

Right off the bat, allow me to apologize to my readers and friends whom I've tortured over the past 15 years with my paeans to Los Angeles. You thought I was nuts. You were right. Can I come home now?

First of all, whatever I left behind is gone. Los Angeles did not wait patiently for me to return. It's like the room you left when you went off to college; mom and dad made it into a pool room.

THE REAL L.A. STORY

Impressions: There are no old people. I'm sure there are but none is in sight. I imagine they keep them out of sight until the sun goes down. This is no joke. Passing eight sidewalk cafes, we saw no one at the table over 23. The Teacher and I were afraid to pass, let alone sit down.

Everyone is thin—there are no fat people. Fat people live in San Fernando Valley with tiny stucco apartments that have rug-sized lawns in front. Fat people are not allowed to be tan. Only thin people are allowed to tan. I have disguised myself as a thin person by wearing a baggy Hawaiian shirt and baggy pants and keeping my cheeks sucked in. So far I have not been found out.

Cell phones are to people in Los Angeles as black flies are to Vassalborians. Every citizen has a cell phone.

I'm serious, this is no joke. I counted 63 in one hour as I stood in place in a local mall. In the city of Santa Monica I stood next to film director Joe Shumacher while he talked to his agent on his cell phone. While there, three other "cellers" walked by: a small girl, about 11, wearing braces, tight pedal pushers and sucking on a lollipop while she chatted; a stunning model had one; and an elderly woman held hers in one hand and her walker in the other—then someone came and whisked her away, it was too early for old people to be out.

There are no gnats or black flies here. As there is no humidity or real expanses of grass, there are no mosquitoes, unleashed dogs, loose cats or snakes.

I take it back about the snakes, while eating lunch, two boys on skateboards rolled by with real live snakes draped around their necks.

Rolls Royce automobiles, Jaguars, Ferraris, Mercedes and Bentleys are everywhere, but the car of choice seems to be the new Volkswagen Bug. They are the black flies of Beverly Hills.

If all of this sounds like a Hollywood television sitcom description of Hollywood, that's exactly what it is. Hollywood and Beverly Hills have become a self-fulfilling dreamscape. It seems to say, "This is what you thought we were; voila, we are."

Twenty-four hours into my visit it became apparent that I have emotional dementia. All the landscape I left behind has been torn down. Los Angeles abhors "old." In Steve Martin's "L.A. Story," he remarked to a girl he was showing around, "Some of these houses are over 50 years old." No one who saw the movie in Hollywood laughed.

A MISSING PAST

To kick up some nostalgia, I wandered the day and night streets, visiting the sites of old haunts. I say sites because the haunts themselves have vanished into the jaws of bulldozers. Old friends have gone on to their rewards or relocated to asylums, nursing homes or the New Jersey coast. I could find none. Burt Reynolds, Jerry Lewis and Johnny Carson, men I once labored with, didn't return my calls. One maid suggested that I not try to call again. Fame is fleeting.

At the famous Farmers Market, a collection of food stalls, shops and cafes where I once rubbed shoulders with colleagues, I ran into an old neighbor.

"Hi," I said, "Don't I know you?" She stepped back and held her sun umbrella in front of her as though I were Charlie Manson. "No," she hissed, "I don't think so."

"I'm Jerry Devine. I used to live next door to you." Her jaw dropped and she gasped, "My God, Jerry, you've put on weight and your hair is so white."

I never liked her. Her rotting avocados kept dropping in my yard.

As you read this, The Teacher and I will be crossing the Kittery Bridge, never to leave again. Bring on the ice storms and black flies. I will be back at my stall in Jorgie's soon. If you missed me, give me a call. I have a new cell phone.

Age Beckons One and All
We are what we pretend to be.
    — Kurt Vonnegut Jr.

"What do you think?" I asked her. "Do I still look like Tyrone Power?"

It was snowing outside, not that Christmas jingle bells kind of snow, but that Russian prison camp, waiting-in-line-for-watery-soup kind of snow.

I was wearing my old Mexican army officer's coat, Peruvian one-size-fits-all knitted cap, and new round 1930s-style glasses. They were steamed up and I was fighting a cold sore.

She was taking my money for a carton of Instant Slim Fast Chocolate Royale diet drink. She looked at me for a moment and squinted as she snapped her bubble gum. It stuck to her braces.

"How about Tom Selleck?" I asked.

She smiled. "I don't think so," she replied.

"How about Lionel Barrymore?" I asked.

"Who's she?" she asked. I knew in my heart she was right. Young and stupid, but right.

My worst nightmare is upon me. I have begun to lose my looks. And this morning's column is a public service announcement for all of you out there on the cold edge of middle age, saying goodbye to youth like a young soldier of fashion and charm bidding adieu to his sweetheart at the railroad station as he nears the 50-year mark. Sure, laugh if you will, but it will happen to you.

It's the glasses, of course. That's how it began, with the glasses. I had this pair of stylish wire-framed tortoise-shelled glasses I bought in the days when I was single and had money and was thin and tan and looked like Tyrone Power. I wore them in the '60s to pick up girls at peace rallies.

In later years I wore them with tweed jackets to Beverly Hills parties so interesting people would talk to me. I didn't know then that only Bulgarian shoe salesmen wore tweed jackets to parties in Beverly Hills in the summer.

Just before this past Christmas, I began to feel a bit dizzy after drinking bottles of low-cost Chilean wine I had purchased from a street vendor while watching the pre-war news shows on CNN. I was scared, I'll tell you.

The women of my family, bored with my dizzy spells, gave me a multiple-choice test: Throw out the Chilean wine, visit a doctor to see if it were a brain tumor or an eye doctor to see if it were my vision. Prudently, I opted for the eye doctor.

Luckily it was my eyes. I had dropped about 300 points. A hard blow to take at my age. The eye-care people at LaVerdiere's passed my prescription around and giggled.

I was told I would have to wear them only when looking at anything farther than 3 feet away, which of course, unless you're a professional lambada dancer, is most of the time.

I went to the eye-care center and shopped for fun frames like Tom Selleck wore in his latest movie. Mr. Hallee squinted hard at me and said indeed I did resemble Tom Selleck in my new frames. I bought two pair. No fool, he.

I bought another pair that makes me look like the late Joe Kennedy. It was fun. Most of my friends, not wanting to appear in a newspaper column in an unflattering light, squinted and agreed that I did look like Tom Selleck.

A caveat. For those of you near 50, I have a warning about new glasses. You can now see the white hair growing out of your nose that up until now no one else would mention.

Also you may be alarmed to know that (1) you have gotten grayer in the last few years and (2) the new razor does not shave as close as a blade so get your money back. One more thing.

You will discover that you have serious hair growing out of your ears.

I was convinced that that was the cause of the hearing thing. I was happy with my new glasses until the hearing thing started. A friend of mine, a very good audiologist named Lynn Sparkes, tricked me into a hearing test.

The test is painless. One sits in a soundproof booth similar to the gas chamber at San Quentin. It has ear phones and a microphone. You kind of feel like Barry Manilow on death row.

Sparkes proceeded to read words that sound alike and gave short electronic beeps in each ear. Some faded away too soon. The Selleck image was fading fast.

She told me I had a sort of dipping arc in the audio reception of one ear. That's something you can't get out with a Q-Tip.

I am sitting by the fire as I compose this. I am looking through old photo albums of the '50s and '60s and I am on my second bottle of Merlot.

I have another warning for those of you approaching 50, as I am. Do not look at the old photos while wearing the new glasses.

Turn Frank Sinatra up and drink deeply of the wine. Hold the snapshots at an arm's distance up to the firelight. Look at the black hair, that thin neck, the smile, the fashionable clothing of the time.

Yes, if I squint, I can see it around the eyes, the mouth, the hair ... yes ... Tom Selleck.

110 in the Dark

Christ was betrayed on a night such as this. I just know it. It was hot and humid like tonight, with a temperature near 98 degrees in Jerusalem and Judas was sweating.

It wasn't the money, it wasn't the devil that made him do it, it was the heat and humidity. One cold front down from the Allagash and Christ would have been hard pressed to find a betrayer. Music made by snow soothes the savage beast.

It was on a night such as this that they found the Black Dahlia murder victim in an empty lot in L.A. years ago. She was famous for haunting night spots on hot nights such as this.

She wore black with white dahlias. A hot desert wind was blowing in from the south, and they found half of her in an empty lot.

They never found her killer, but those hot Santa Ana winds made him do it. I just know it.

Pyros love nights like this. They sit in rented rooms waiting for it to get dark, and then drive out to the woods and toss a match in the brush. They return to their rented rooms and watch the blaze on CNN.

Cops dread nights like this. There's a full moon made hazy by tons of bat breath from the woods, and the hardware store has had a run on butcher knives.

Cops check their ammo and seat belts and sit in the wet dark waiting for the radio to crackle. Maybe nothing will happen tonight. Sure, and Lee Harvey Oswald was just up on the sixth floor having a Coke.

The 6 p.m. news: Zachary Taylor sat in the hot sun all day watching a bocce ball game or something. He ate a whole lot of cherries, they say, and drank some chilled buttermilk and died of a bad cramp. This lady says it was an assassination plot. Why didn't the CIA think of that?

The night Lincoln was shot was unusually warm and the Ford Theatre was not air conditioned. Booth had been drinking in a local tavern, and that combination of Tennessee mash, actor's ego and Potomac heat sent him over the edge.

C'mon, you know how he felt. You just got fired. You go to the fridge for a beer and they're all gone. You just want to take it out on somebody.

To my knowledge, there has never been a serious assassination during a snowstorm. Murderers, rapists and barn burners hate the cold. Evil hibernates like a bad news bear waiting for summer nights such as this.

We are in our third straight day of heat as I write this, African heat. Probably the hottest June night in 50 years. This, afternoon salesmen stood in front of Levine's taking the air like pall bearers on a coffee break while waiting for a 52 portly to walk in.

Turn on the fan because this day won't end. It crawls along like a gut-shot Bengal tiger that refuses to die.

A kitchen helper stands outside his door smoking a cigarette and watching a woman get out of her car. Her dress sticks to her flesh like colored cellophane on candy.

Everybody sweats and the day won't end. They say it's the greenhouse effect or all those volcanoes going off or the Kuwaiti oil fields or one of those meteorites heading this way. There must be something there you like. Pick one.

Night brings no relief—10 p.m. and it is day hot. Six thousand kids are milling around in the Concourse tonight like revolutionists waiting for a beheading.

They move in small packs of six to 20. They seem to have pack allegiances. Too far away to see if they have group T-shirts. Maybe they do. Maybe they say something like, "The Just In Front of Ames Gang" or "The South of the Villager Mob."

It's 11 p.m. and I park near a grassy knoll overlooking the river and the tracks. As I sip a large take-out orange soda and listen to Rosemary Clooney on the radio, I think of Marlene Otto and her Shalimar-scented throw pillow that read "Made in Hawaii." We had no Concourse back then and there. We had Mooney Hagany's rec room with blue lights and bullfight posters on such a night as this.

A long string of box cars are being pulled north by a dirty burnt-orange engine. They make a mumbling sound on hot steel tracks that have been sitting in the broiling sun all day. When it's gone, the crickets come back.

The heat makes me think crazy things. I think of the night such as this when the great dancer Isadora Duncan caught her scarf in the wheel of her lover's Buggatti as it tore off down the Riviera. It broke her neck as clean as a hangman's noose, and a great career was over.

A couple sit in a parked car in the hot cream-colored light of Mister Donut. He has a tattoo. She has tobacco on her tongue that she can't spit out. They talk of a high school reunion they won't be going to, and of money they don't have.

The bumper sticker on their car reads "Honk If You Love Jesus." You notice things like that on a night such as this.

Frame houses sit like loaves in a dark oven of a street. Screen doors squeak. Old men in undershirts and seersucker shorts with black socks and leather slippers get ice water in the kitchen between innings of the Red Sox game. Their wives and daughters and grandchildren are killing mosquitos on the porch.

The 11 p.m. news: A riot in Hartland. One hundred folks busted. Big bucks and all spend the night in the slammer. On a night such as this.

A Qualified Finalist...

Boy, I was feeling down. I was throwing out the Christmas trash and I was down there baby, but I'm smokin' now. This morning I got a letter in the mail with my name on it. It said J.P. DEVINE. IT'S TRUE. YOU ARE A QUALIFIED FINALIST.

That's right. As we speak, I have been informed that I am a qualified finalist. I am on the short list to win 10 million bucks. I am going to be on my way. I am going to be on EASY STREET.

I have big plans for that money. Now that I can afford the good stuff, I may take up drinking again. Not big, just a little hundred-year-old stuff now and then.

The day the check arrives, I am going to drive over to the school and escort my teacher out by the arm.

Oh, I'm not going to change with all this money. I plan to remain the same gentle soul, the same thoughtful and considerate human being I've always been. I'll just be harder to reach. I'll be traveling in the Caribbean a good deal and taking my teacher with me.

Don't get me wrong. I'm nothing if not realistic. I'm going to do simple things as well. I'm a basic kind of guy with simple tastes, but simple things cost more money than big things. A roof job is expensive. A new furnace is big bucks. I need a few of these things. Let's see ... new furnace ... five grand ... new roof. .. 2 grand ... yep ... I got plenty left.

Let's see. I don't need any more sweaters. I've got 12 sweaters. Oh, yes. I'll get my teeth fixed. I want all new front teeth like Robert Redford has. I want the fuses to blow when I smile like Julia Roberts. I'm running low on boyish charm now and sister always said you need a nice smile to get ahead in the world.

I want these trees around here cut down. I don't get enough sun on my house. My house is like Jeffrey Dahmer's laundry room all summer long because of my neighbor's trees. I will pay him to cut those suckers down. He says they give us oxygen. We're hard up for oxygen in Maine? Get real. There are enough trees across the street from me to supply oxygen for Jersey City.

With only this $10 million, I wouldn't have enough to loan the Sentinel enough money to get a new building but I could kick in a few bucks. Maybe they could even buy the decaying old dinosaur city hall. What with the law and order moving out to a new building, the Sentinel could move right in. With the press right downstairs, any future mayor would have to watch his beans very carefully.

I guess $10 million wouldn't be enough to build a new library but it would be thrilling to see that wobbly old antique come down and in its place find a new super glass structure with an elevator, garden dining area, film room library and state of the art computers for the new generation of kids.

I might donate a couple million to the Railroad Square kids so they could have one screen dedicated to showing only vintage films at my expense. Think of it. One movie screen with nothing but Preston Sturges, Frank Capra, John Ford, and Orson Welles. We could have week-long William Powell and Cagney festivals, "Worst of the '50s" festivals. Think of it. People would say, "Look at what that guy did with his life."

Wait a minute. Who am I kidding? I'm not going to win that $10 million. I'm ranting on like this because it's 11 o'clock at night, and I'm sitting here with a lukewarm cup of sugar-free Nestle's hot chocolate and staring at an empty Christmas tree, and I know damn well no matter how much money you win or what you do with it won't make up for what you could have done in life without any money at all ... and didn't.

I've taken off the ornaments and lights and put them in boxes. The kids are gone. There wasn't any sun today and may not be any until February. While I was stripping the tree, Ed McMahon and Dick Clark came on and suggested very strongly that I was up for some real money. I didn't really believe them, but you desperately need something to dream about while Christmas is shattered and packed about your feet.

Of course it's not going to happen. I'm going to get my residuals and actor's pensions and go shopping for cheap cantaloupes just like you. Still, I keep thinking about what Rick Russo's Miss Beryl said. You there on the couch. Have you done enough? Doesn't it bother you?

It's almost '95 and it bothers me, my friend. I have this bad dream. It's the year 2020 and my grandson checks on my gravestone and at the bottom; after the part where it says, "loving husband, devoted father, nice writer," it says "Qualified Finalist."

Next year is here . . . .

The teacher I live with is big on making lists. She still has the list from our wedding.
1. Take the bus to City Hall, St. Louis.
2. Get married.
3. Take bus home, pack and catch bus for New York.
4. Go back home and get Jerry.
5. Rethink marriage.

She taught me to make lists. Besides teaching me how to pronounce "Calais" the way they don't in France, it's the most valuable trick she's taught me. I taught her how to make beds with hospital corners, hang up the cordless phone and find "Nick At Nite" on the cable box. I figure we're even.

I made a list for things to do "Next Year" last year. I try to learn from my mistakes. Once burned is enough for me. I never make the same mistake twice. You don't see a Rolls Royce in my driveway, do you?

Now I can't find the list. I think I threw it out. I wrote it on the back of a menu from a high fat restaurant I don't eat at anymore. I shouldn't throw things out without checking them. I'll put that on my new list for next year.

I made this list of things to remember to do "Next Year." Now, as Sinatra says, "That rainy day is here."

I remember saying that I should renew my subscription to the Victoria's Secret catalog. It's so embarrassing to check it out in the library. Some people think I'm just lascivious and have an unhealthy interest in women in scant hosiery. That's not the case at all. I only get it for the articles.

I said I would have the house painted. I did that. I was very clever about that. I got the Republican National Committee to pay for it. It's simple. I don't know why I didn't think of it before. I simply had a mural of Richard Nixon opening China painted on the back of the house.

I remember saying that I must remember to have someone mow the lawn one last time. The idea from last year was that I left it too high, and raking the leaves out of it was like getting burrs out of my sheep dog's hair.

Why does grass keep growing in my back yard after the frost? I thought it was supposed to stop. I thought only my fingernails and nose hair kept growing after death. Why doesn't it turn brown and die like a natural lawn? Is it trying to annoy me? Do you think lawns think?

I know I made a note to remember to get those leaves raked up before the first October rain. If you remember, last autumn was a soggy one and it kept raining, and I kept putting off getting out there. Well, this was a dryer season, but the leaves stayed on the tree until it rained, and now they're out there waiting for me to come out with a spatula and scrape them up.

I'm one up on that count. I've arranged for some young studs from the high school to rake them for me this year. That back problem prohibits me from swinging a rake. Yes it does, it certainly does.

Then there is the snow list. Same back problem prohibits shoveling snow. Yes it does. The whole thing started when I fell off the couch reaching for the remote. I should sue. People get money for less anguish than that, don't they? Whom do I sue? The remote is made by Mitsubishi. My lawyer doesn't speak Japanese. Will I have to appear in Japanese court like Dana Andrews in "Purple Heart?" Will Richard Loo be there? That's scary. I think I'll let the whole thing drop.

I know I made a note to remember to turn off the hose lines so they don't freeze up. I

I need to hire someone very stupid to climb a ladder and keep the snow off the bathroom roof, so it doesn't ice-jam up and leak and ruin the bathroom again. I know I'm not going up there. Dr. Lawler doesn't want me climbing anything higher than the step into the car.

On that list is a reminder to have the driveway snow "blown" instead of plowed. I'm tired of having to have to re-seed the lawn because the plowman put my grass in my neighbor's mailbox. This driveway is a year-round problem. It's beginning to break up in the summer now. In the winter it's impassable. I'm considering having a North Korean demolition team come in and blow it up.

Oh yeah, I must remember to buy some more of that rodent poison. I had rodents last year. They got into the basement because I forgot to remind myself to put those big plastic things over the windows.

Last year I set those big wooden traps. That shows what I know. Nobody sets traps anymore. The hardware store still sells them, of course, for morons from L.A. like me who don't know better. All night long I could hear them snapping shut. I knew in the morning I had to go down there with little rodent body bags and do the wet work.

The Mafia has these guys who come in after a big hit job and "clean up." I wonder if they do rodent traps? Naw, I'll get the poison. They just eat this stuff and go away and die. It's like a fast food pit stop for mice. Very efficient.

Oh, there it is. I found it in the trash. Here at the top it says, "Buy oil." Soooo, that's why it won't go on.

At Last, Spring Has Sprung

Spring is here and Adam Weir of Palmyra says stop. He has this sign that says STOP perched on the top of a pole he carries in his right hand. Upon his head he sports an orange helmet. Adam works for the Waterville Water Department at the moment, and the moment is a pleasant, sunny one for Adam and other road workers. It is April and, inexplicably, it is not snowing.

Adam stands with semi-military bearing on the hot asphalt of West River Road as a truck rolls by. Country Western music pours from the cab as the driver scratches his beard, waves to Adam and disappears with his dog and gun rack into a cloud of dust like a Hank Williams apparition.

Big, smoking, grease-stained trucks full of memory dirt ripped from the once verdant lawns overlooking the river roar by. Progress rears its ugly head everywhere.

HEAVY EQUIPMENT

At the foot of Kennedy Memorial Drive, where once crickets chirped in August and pigeons perched on the war monument, huge orange and yellow machines tear at the earth like rapacious raptors, chewing up old trees and coating the big ice cream cone at Gifford's with dust.

The gravestones on Grove Street tremble and quiver with the booms of heavy equipment scoffing at the age-old mumble of preachers, "Rest in peace."

After a winter of frozen stillness, the work of building the bridge over the river is going full-steam. One only has to squint one's eyes and whistle "Colonel Bogey's March" and one can see Alec Guinness and Sessue Hayakawa standing on the steel spans.

It is spring in Waterville and signs of madness are everywhere. Mayor R. Joseph has abandoned her electric-Kool-Aid-neon-bright-cerulean-blue winter suit and the faded blue awnings of the Morning Sentinel hang listless in the warm breeze like Liston on the mat in Manila.

You Know Whose Pub owner Norton Webber strolls defiantly through The Concourse in new lawn-green walking shorts and the Rev. Ted Evertsen sports new spring-garden-green clerical garb as he strolls along. Ahhhh, the voice of the turtle is heard once again in the land.

The tables are out in front of Jorgensen's Cafe and shop owners and customers alike are peeping heads out of the doorways and squinting at the sun as though an all-clear siren had sounded.

We have passed another Earth Day successfully and we are still here. We were pummeled and shoveled, buried in the white death cream and resurrected. We were frozen into the ground like discarded Siberian wagon wheels and yet we have survived. We have survived the rumors and the dumping of leaders and we are here. Geez! Don't cha just love this country?

RENEWAL IN THE AIR

Look there. Courageous buds are popping their heads above the topsoil, eager to do combat with the sweaty crush of a yet another faux Northern New England summer.

Do we sense new growth? Dare we use the word? Could the Dream Team be right? Are we on the way up? Is there an "up"? The pulse quickens, the eyes flicker. Waterville is alive. It has survived failure, closings, despair – and yet the body stirs.

One only has to look at the stacks of barbecue equipment and mounds of charcoal in Shaw's KMD store to know renewal. High school kids with red noses and chapped knees stand bravely defying traffic with signs offering cheap car washes. And for what? Baseball. Beyond the listless Polish-like cinder block Cinema, the peepers scream into the night. Good Lord, man, could the flatlanders be far behind?

Our hearts skip a beat. They're singing songs of love in the land, and this time they are for us. Hope is afoot on the side streets. Two of my best friends have sold their houses, which were on the market for two long years. They are giddy with new cash and hope for the future. Of course, they dropped their prices to pre-war lows, but hey! Cash is cash.

Lisa M. Gerrie, a perky young blonde orthodontist assistant, is making plans for a May wedding. Would she be getting married if Main Street were dying? Not likely.

Berry's is freshening its windows. Railroad Square's Stu Silverstein is prepping a brand new eatery to rise on the ashes of the old movie theater and to be called Grand Central Cafe. Two cafes in the same pot-holed parking lot? Does that sound like bad times? No indeed.

North Street Ice Cream Parlor is open and large black migratory birds are bathing and supping in the greenish water of the public pool.

Look out, get out of the way. Colby students, preparing for next month's graduation, jam the boulevards, taking one last look at the town that has rimmed their home for the last four years. Many look eager to depart. One, in town to buy new shoes for the ceremony, stands in front of Levine's. "Man, bummer," he cries. "When did these dudes close?"

There's always one guy who doesn't get the word. Well. Spring is here. Take your heart out dancing.

Running From Cold Winds
In sunny Los Angeles, darkness breathes death

"What on earth brought you to Waterville?" This is a question asked of me almost daily. The answer is simple: I ran from madness until I could run no more.

It is winter in Los Angeles. In a town full of palm trees and taco stands, Mercedes convertibles and sandy beaches, winter comes like a rollerblading tourist, wide-eyed, bullying and uncontrollable, unfamiliar with the landscape.

Like a tourist, it sometimes behaves, sometimes not, but it never stays long. Year in, year out. Nothing changes.

Winter brings rain to LA. It brings quick early darkness, and darkness in LA brings fear. One night last week winter brought the cold wind of death up from the ocean and blew out a pair of candles someone cherished. One was a shot heard around the world because the bullet hit a famous son. He was not poor, or on drugs or probation. So we all paid attention. The other killed a poor inner city girl. Silence. Nothing changes.

Death in LA, unlike winter, is not a tourist. Death is a native son who knows the streets by heart and posh and poor hear his footsteps. A walk with your dog in the best neighborhood is a journey of chance, a balmy starlit crap game with loaded dice. Murder in LA is as common as a dog bark. The cold wind comes and candles go out.

EARTHLY ANGELS

Ennis Cosby was his father's candle, his mother's summer wind. He was a young black man in a Mercedes. Corrie Williams was a young black woman on a bus. She was her mother's heartbeat. A candle went out, a heart stopped beating.

Nothing changes. Taking my daughter to see a movie on Hollywood Boulevard some years ago, I took her hand and gently nudged her across the street.

In our path was a young black man on the sidewalk. He appeared near death. Two policemen, one white, one Hispanic, stood over him like space-age street cleaners waiting for a bus.

I did not know Ennis. But I had worked briefly with his father, a huge sponge of a man full of all the love and anger he had soaked up in a Hollywood that covers its racism with cashmere and chrome. He has given all of us more than most. He does not deserve this cold wind in his heart. But this is LA and nothing changes.

Young men of color die younger and faster than others in the City Of Angels. Cosby knows this. His beloved Ennis was only one of hundreds in the past year. But now Cosby's angel is one of the victims, and no knowledge of computer printouts will dry his face or cool his scalded heart.

STILL THEY COME

Each year they come, singers of songs, dreamers of dreams. They struggle and work and sacrifice to make it and create a life for their children away from the mean streets and fallen angels with dead eyes.

All of us who lived that dream and were touched by crime still have the bitter taste of sudden fear in our mouths. Some of us survived; some, like Ennis Cosby, did not.

Tonight the young of LA will hit the streets. Before the late shift is ended, more young men like Ennis, more women like Corrie, will die violently. People of all colors in all neighborhoods will walk their dogs with one eye on the shadows, an ear to crunching of leaves behind them. It's LA: "Only the paranoid survive" was written here.

Still, like Bill Cosby, they come. They come to do their work, to create magic, to be bright candles for us all, to find the big house on a quiet, safe, tree-shaded street in Pacific Palisades, to raise their children with a view of the ocean.

Here, up from that big blue ocean and the white sand, a cold dry wind came and blew out the candle in Bill and Camille's hearts. Miles away where the streets grow dirtier and darker, Corrie Williams' mother swallows her screams in the dark.

The pictures that once graced silver frames are now pinned to a marker board at Parker Center along with the images of dozens of other young black men and women. Drug addicts or honor students, they were all candles in some mother's heart.

Tonight, as you sleep safely with your candles nearby, when the orange sky turns purple, black and white cruisers will roll out to prowl the streets of the City Of Angels. Black and white, brown and yellow, the poor and unknowns, the rich and the famous will continue to live – and die in LA. Nothing changes.

"What on earth brought you to Waterville?"

"I'm a runner."

Rain on Roof, Drip in House
Maine's summer splendor lost below gray clouds

Just before I left Los Angeles in 1984 to move to Maine, I met an actor at an audition who had just moved there from Maine. He loved the warmth and the sunlight, the constant, unchanging sunlight and blue sky.

He asked me why in the world I was planning to move to his home state. I said I missed the seasons. He smiled and shook his head. "Which ones? The rainy season? The mud season, the ice season or the raking season?"

I had no answer.

Instantly I knew he was right, and it was too late to change my mind.

He must be happy now. It doesn't rain in Los Angeles. People only carry umbrellas to protect them from falling masonry in case of earthquakes.

Manhattan and San Francisco in the rain, are film noir, a Dashiell Hammett kind of atmosphere.

It adds romance and mystique.

Maine in the rain is Bosnia without the glitter, especially central Maine when the old factories get wet.

But the coast doesn't do much better.

Wiscasset, a lovely picturesque coastal village, is a "Kodak moment" when the skies are blue and the sun bleaches the boat decks.

But in a downpour, it's a bad Alfred Hitchcock movie setting.

The coast had a few good sunny days this season, but not enough to keep the shopkeepers warm over the winter.

CARE FOR A 'RAIN TAN'?

We are Vacationland. People come here from all over, mostly for the snow. They pay big bucks to ski the mountains, cross-country ski and nuzzle a vodka by the fire in mountain lodges.

Often they come for the turning of the leaves as if Wisconsin had no fall, Ohio no deciduous trees at all.

We don't complain, their money is as good as any.

But nobody pays thousands of dollars, stokes up the SUV and dusts off the canoes and kayaks to come and enjoy the rain. And rain is what they got this summer, Anton Chekovian, Moscovian rain.

Freeport this past week had no fewer rain-soaked visitors than sunburned shoppers.

But it was a depressing sight. Bunches of dripping visitors stood in doorways, waiting for a break to run from L.L.Bean to J.Crew.

A man sporting a soaked T-shirt that read "Macon, Georgia" stood under the eaves of Ben and Jerry's Ice Cream Parlor, rain dripping from his pale nose. I'll bet he wished he was back in the land of cotton, even with its 109 degrees.

It's sad to watch the camp families from away sloshing through the aisles in the supermarkets. They don't know where anything is, even if they knew what they wanted. It's just a chance to get out of the cabin, away from the drip, drip, drip of the pines and the mournful moan of the loons.

The old man fills the cart with Corona Lite and hot dog buns. You just know his charcoals are floating in rusty water by now.

The mother pushes the cart. She aimlessly plucks camp stuff from the shelves and drops it in the wire basket: chocolate milk, Cheerios, six different kinds of cookies filled with double cream and chocolate and lots of magazines.

The kids stumble along behind trying to con momma into some cheap water toys. They whimper and moan and cry.

(I'd settle for the loons.)

The father disappears and returns in a few moments with two more six-packs of Corona Extra.

It'll rain hard tonight, but he won't hear it.

DANK FOR THE MEMORY

I don't think this is what they planned on, this family from away. I think they were counting on Golden Pond. But it takes a sun to make the pond golden. And the sun is in Arizona this year.

It has been a summer for the books. We haven't had a summer this lousy since the mid-90s when it rained every weekend.

My grass got cut two weeks ago. Now it has grown more than 3 feet in some places. It will take Agent Orange to get those weeds down.

Nights are the worst this year. I only recently replaced my flannel sheets with summer cotton. I never took off my electric blanket. I grew up in warm climates. I don't like to slip into sheets that feel as if they were just shipped in from the local morgue.

This afternoon, the sun broke through the mountains of dark clouds for a moment and startled the birds; it made my dog bark at the shadows it created. Then it was gone like a familiar face in a crowded street.

A few minutes ago, I saw that Maine actor on the tube. He was playing an admiral in a disaster movie. In one scene he looked at the camera and our eyes met.

He had that question in his eyes; I still don't have an answer.

View From My Bridge

I could see Alcatraz from his office. It was somewhere up on the top of Polk Street in San Francisco and it was 1954 and it was raining.

It's always raining or snowing when I have to go to the dentist, always. I can't remember ever seeing a sunny day from the windows of a dentist's office. You've seen those big wallpaper murals of sandy beaches and waterfalls and mountains you can buy for your home? Well, dentists buy these murals of rainy days and glue them to their windows.

I could see Alcatraz from his waiting room windows. He was Chinese, this dentist, and I was going to him because I was on leave from my air base and was terrified of the base dentist, a fat man who chewed on a toothpick while he drilled teeth.

In the '50s, military dentists believed in the direct approach to dental problems: Pull it. I had a toothache and I was about to be discharged and was thinking about going to Mexico. A friend sent me to the Chinese dentist.

"Hold tongue over, please," he screamed. "Don't move mouth ... hold tongue quiet ... Now you spit." He screamed everything. I was terrified and he knew it and was annoyed by my Western lack of courage.

I will be going to the dentist again sometime this year. My current dentist is relatively nice, a short man with kind eyes and a cowlick. He laughs at me a lot, which makes me nervous. I think he is laughing to put me at ease to prepare me for what he has to tell me.

Dentists now wear rubber gloves and multi-layered masks and look like heart surgeons. New dentists' chairs go all the way back like operating tables. These are designed to make it easier for the dentist.

Never mind how you feel. Never mind that what blood isn't coming out of the hole in your mouth is draining from your brain. It is bad enough to have to go to the dentist without feeling like you are undergoing lung surgery.

The mask gives him a sinister look. Eating lunch at the Silver Street Tavern, my dentist looks like a drug store soda jerk and a close aging friend of the Beaver.

Every few moments he will look up and over at his assistant, a woman who seldom smiles and when working on me, never. They exchange arcane glances.

There is some comfort in the design of his waiting room and office. Pastel prints soothe, the magazines are updated regularly and are interesting and eclectic. The assistants are charming and pleasant for the most part.

I feel sorry for my dentist. It isn't his fault. He has to deal with my panic and fear because of Dr. Death.

Dr. Death was my childhood dentist. His office was downtown on the Broadway Street Car Line, one of the worst in the city. I always had tooth problems in the winter. I never had a toothache on a nice day.

My mother was more terrified of dentists than I, so she arranged for one of her sisters to take me. Aunt Winnie always won.

Aunt Winnie was a woman who believed in bravery and had little patience with wimps. She kept saying things like, "Little men don't cry," and "Little men don't shake and tremble and scream." Little men don't try to jump out of the streetcar window either, so I guess I didn't qualify as a little man.

Dr. Death's office was in a building copied form a KGB model he found in a Soviet magazine. It was liver-colored with buff trim. You went up on an elevator with an iron cage door that was operated by a black man who sat on a fold-out stool and asked you how the little man felt today. Like vomiting, I said.

The hallway to Dr. Death's office was 17 miles long and the carpets smelled of ether and mold. His waiting room had brown wooden venetian blinds that had been paralyzed into a half-closed position since the Spanish Inquisition.

It's a good thing, too, because the window looked out on the loading platform of what I think was a glue factory, where horses waited in a long stall to die.

Dr. Death always made you wait. You waited while a cold rain beat against the leaded windows and moans and drill sounds came from behind the frosted glass door pane. You sat there and inhaled the smell of blood and chemicals. There was always this pounding sound from the glue factory like the music from "Jaws."

The magazines were varied. *Police Gazette, Popular Mechanics*, back issues of *National Geographic* and dental equipment catalogues.

His receptionist was a refugee from Krakow with a Novocain mouth and dead eyes. She wore a nurse's cap and a cardigan sweater with a blood spot on it.

I can still remember the streetcar ride home sucking on the piece of bloody cotton and reading a newspaper someone had left on the seat: "Man Dies in Electric Chair." Lucky him.

I am due to go to the dentist again sometime this year to have a partial bridge replaced. It will require lying on my back for a couple of hours trying to hold my tongue still while the blood drains from my brain. It will cost several thousand dollars and many sleepless nights and panic attacks.

At least you can't see Alcatraz and the glue factory from there.

The Postman Slips Twice

It's a nice day. You're feeling spiffy. You think maybe it might be nice to have your picture taken on a pony.

When Roosevelt was in the oval office, a guy would come around the neighborhood with a pony and a big camera with a black hood on it. Mothers dressed their kids up in their best clothes and waited on the curb. This guy would come down the street with the pony that had a little bell on it.

This photographer, probably some former banker who was too chicken to jump off a building, got himself a pony and a cheap camera and went into business. He always called the kids "Pal." He would hide under the hood and ignite this flash powder in a hand-held trough. It lifted me out of the saddle but it didn't seem to bother the pony. I guess he was used to it. I still have the picture on my den wall and the tic from the explosion.

Nowadays, you take your kid to Sears or J.C. Penney and have some guy in cheap slacks and a bad tie take the picture. It's OK, but it's not a pony ride.

It's Tuesday and it's raining. You're out of milk. You have to go somewhere in the car and get it. When you were a kid, the milk was delivered. A guy in a white suit and matching cap came while it was still dark. It would be on the doorstep when you woke up. My mother would let it sit out there until I got up so I could get it. Sometimes there was a quart of chocolate milk and another of orange drink. It was like finding Easter eggs.

You didn't have to go out in the car or walk to an ice cream parlor. This guy in a white suit and a truck that played "The Band Played On," with bells, came down the street at the same time every day in the summertime. He had so many choices it took several minutes to make up your mind. He was very patient. While you scanned the list he read comic books. His name was Herman and he had a pencil mustache and breath like Vick's salve.

Paddy Carr and I would sit on the curb with a dime clutched in our sweaty palms waiting. The same time every day. If Herman was late, you knew he was probably dead.

At night the tamale man came. He came up the street with his lighted cart. He rolled it by hand, no motor mind you. This was during the war when tires and gas were rationed. Still, the world was a square, block. You didn't have to go anywhere, the world came to you.

Yes, the world beat a path to the consumer. Doctors made house calls, even the priest came for the last rites. I was told recently that they don't do that anymore.

The insurance man came around, had a cup of coffee or iced tea and flirted with your big sister. The neighborhood grocery delivered. A kid would come to the back door with a wooden box and there it was, supper.

The paper hit the porch twice a day and now and then a friendly cop would bring your brother home from a fist fight. Everybody delivered.

The postman, we called him the mailman, really did ring twice. He put the mail in your box outside the door, twisted the little bell and walked away.

Now I have to walk down a slippery hill, cross a street that is quickly becoming a super highway and get my mail out of a rural box. I pay Bel Air property taxes, and I get my mail like Li'l Abner. In the winter I get a little note from my mailman asking me to clear the snow in front of the mailbox. What happened to "Rain nor sleet, nor hail nor Hurricane Andrew"? Lindbergh flew through hail and fog to deliver my letters. This guy wants me to shovel snow? Would Lindbergh ask me to sand the runway?

I'm thinking how nuts and lonely you get when you grow older. Nobody comes around anymore, not the mailman, Herman and the ice cream truck, the tamale man, the grocery boy, nobody. Kids write their parents from England or China but they don't get the letter because they forgot to plow the mailbox.

Maybe that's how it ends. Nobody comes anymore except God. God comes for you in the morning with jingling bottles by his side or in the middle of the day in white pants and shirt with six flavors for a dime, and his name is Herman or even better. He comes late at night offering a last tamale and a beer. Don't get your hopes up. The priest won't come and you'll get a letter saying deliver the corpse after 9 a.m. or before 5 p.m. That is if you plowed the mailbox.

Garage Sale From Hell

At first we thought it was just some little field mice, tiny screechy sounds in the night like far away elves screaming. Being from Los Angeles, we're used to hearing elves scream in the night.

No, we said it's just field mice, the kind you see in illustrated children's books. You give them names and imagine them living in little nests like humans, with a momma who wears a tiny mouse apron and a daddy who smokes a mouse pipe and reads the Mouse Sentinel. How deluded we are by that pubescent propaganda.

So my permanent stay-at-home daughter who is kind to small creatures suggested those small traps that ensnare but don't kill. They're called "Katch-But-Won't-Kill-Mouse Houses" and they're biodegradable. I bought 85 of them. Save your money. They sat there untouched for a week while "The Rat" ate the Rangeway.

It didn't occur to us that something the size of Danny DeVito was too big to get into one of these things.

So I bought 600 of those boxes of sure-kill pellets. This morning I found him in the basement, the George Steinbrenner of rats, deader than the Yankee's chance of winning the pennant. In fact, everything in the basement was dead.

Now that we're rid of him, it's time to get on with spring. It must be spring, all the teachers are bald.

This has been one for the books. This winter has been the rattlesnake of winters. My snowmen of Stalin, Freud and Vlad the Impaler are melting, a sure sign of spring. I will drink Pennzoil before I live through another winter like this one.

I have survived three months of suicidal thoughts, thoughts of divorce, therapy, homicide and unwarranted sexual advances on my blow up almost-life-like Jane Fonda doll.

People are stumbling into the sunlight downtown like survivors of the firebombing of Dresden, looking around, hugging each other, weeping on their knees as they blink at the sun, forcing their kids to look up.

"Look Billy, look Jane, that's the sun. Remember mommie and daddy told you about that?"

It's been that bad. Ohhhhhhh yes it has, don't give me that yuppie "You oughta learn to ski" crap. For the very rich, winter is three months with Michelle Pfeiffer. If you're broke, homeless, and living in two rooms with 16 kids in a tenement, then winter is three years in an elevator with Ernest Borgnine.

Ohhhhhh don't start with that "Why'd-you-come-here-if-you-don't-like-winter" stuff. I told you why I came here, I won a Sears Roebuck executive search contest.

I'm up here in the attic. She sent me up here to start putting things together for the first annual "we're moving" garage sale. I have quite a lot already. She has promised me my own card table in the driveway. You can come right to me for the fun stuff, things we won't be needing in Charleston, or Key West. That's right, Key West, that's a possibility.

Yes, that's right, they have 37 gay bars, a crocodile petting zoo, a 16-screen cineplex that shows only Yugoslavian porno films and a Serbo-Croatian take-out or eat-it-here drive-in. I know you don't like gay bars, but what could you possibly have against Serbo-Croatian food?

I have some priceless stuff in case you want to get here early. I have some old Sen Sen wrappers. You probably don't remember those. What we smoked in high school, you could cover with those. What your kids smoke you couldn't cover with napalm.

I have a giant jig saw puzzle picture of the White House when Eisenhower was there, a paperback copy of "Love Story," 300 books of Green Stamps, a gift certificate to Stern's Department Store, the old one, and a portable typewriter with K and L missing.

I yell down to her that I can get 50 bucks for that, she yells up that my K and L are missing.

We need money to move. We would like some extra, of course, to take a side vacation to Europe. I'm not set on Europe. I mean, in case I don't get my asking price for the green vinyl La-Z-Boy; I'm keeping it, man.

This will bring in some big bucks, a complete 8-track recording of Charlton Heston sings "Songs of The Bible."

Here's an old wallet my Uncle Pete got for Christmas but never used. It still has the plastic insert, an unwritten-on ID card and a three-color picture of Rhonda Fleming and George Nader hugging.

How about a Nehru jacket? Here are some 45s, the Carpenters, Sonny and Cher, "Arthur Godfrey Sings Soul." Here's a great paperback, "Pee-Wee Herman Movie Reviews." Here's an old magazine that has a picture of J. Edgar Hoover walking out of church with Clyde Tolson. The caption reads, "This time it's for keeps."

Well, it's almost the day. We'll be open early that first hot morning and everything will be on the lawn. That's right, 85 biodegradable "Katch-but-won't-kill-mouse houses" for only a buck fifty. Is that the smallest bill you've got?

Five Things That Went Bad

You think you're bored with local cultures, don't you? You crave wild cherries from the vines high in the Greek mountains, coffee in a toilet-sized cafe in Morocco. Local food and entertainment, like the British Museum, has lost its charm.

So you decide to look elsewhere. This is your first mistake, not to be confused with "Five things that went bad."

The former redhead who owns my house thought it would be a fun idea to celebrate my upcoming 54th birthday by spending the weekend before it at a nice hotel in the Old Port in Portland and eating at a very sophisticated, elegant restaurant called Raphael's. I agreed.

The hotel chosen was the highly recommended Regency Plaza in the Old Port in Portland. It has been touted as being one of the finest 200 small hotels in America. Remember that Bush's place of residence in Houston is probably 194.

Bad Thing No. 1: It was here that I discovered that she had made the reservations for the following week ... after my birthday. She goes by a school calendar and you know how they are what with snow days and all.

Bad Thing No. 2: The room. We were assured that even though we were less than a year early, there were a couple of rooms still left.

"We will be able to squeeze you in," was what someone said. That always makes me nervous. They said that to Rocky Sullivan on the way to the chair.

The room was down a long, well-lighted hallway filled with interesting pictures. So far so good. Once inside I put my bags down in the tiny anteroom and waited to be shown the bedroom. Imagine the hilarity I experienced when we were told that the "tiny anteroom" we were standing in was the room.

This room was well appointed. It had that "New Englandy" look so popular with Californians. I guess I still smell of smog and taco oil. The bed was very close to all four walls.

The wallpaper was low keyed, very tasteful but very, very stripey. The stripes seemed to be closing in on me. My mild case of claustrophobia is a condition I share with Woody Allen. Let me stress here that it is the only condition I share with Woody.

I explained that it seemed a bit small but with the window open ...

Bad Thing No. 3: I was told that none of the windows open. All windows in the hotel were sealed on the outside. We would be breathing packaged air courtesy of the Regency Hotel. That means lying awake listening to a constant hum while you watch people outside your window move their lips soundlessly. One would feel like Beethoven at the end.

We were shown another room on another floor. It was considerably larger, but still with the stripey wallpaper and KGB prison windows.

We decided to try another hotel. The old and venerable Sonesta on the other side of town seemed the ticket. As I am somewhat old and venerable, that seemed to be the right choice. As it turned out, it wasn't at all.

We were given a wonderful room on the ninth floor with a spectacular wrap-around view of Portland. This is not right up there with Verona or Gstaad, but it was better than the sealed window view of two drunks trying to catch a waterfront bird in total silence.

The room did have a damp feeling and a slight odor, but we suspected it would go away as the day warmed up.

Bad Thing No. 4: The damp feeling of the carpet did not go away. It was as if the Bruins team had thrown up on it and it had just been cleaned. Also there was the matter of the sound of running water from a grate high up on the wall over the beds. It gurbled and gurgled like a running toilet. She said it reminded her of a soft rain. To me it was more like a running toilet.

After a splendid meal at a super elegant Raphael's in the Old Port, we returned to the hotel where the former redhead insisted I visit the penthouse nightclub where I was promised there was a spectacular view of nighttime Portland.

This is best described as a graveyard with lights. Very few lights. We returned to the odorous room where the soft rain and running toilet lulled us to sleep.

Bad Thing No. 5: We were jolted awake at 1:30 a.m. by what appeared to be the entire United States Merchant Marine fleet christening a new supertanker in the suite above.

We spent the rest of the night listening to 37 seamen belch, relieve themselves and flush the toilet.

We met them in the morning at the complimentary breakfast in the lounge.

They were indeed the entire Merchant Marine, to whom table manners are as ancient Greek to Dan Quayle.

I will pin this column on the wall above my typewriter to remind me that, on my 56th birthday, to stay in town and dine al fresco in The Concourse.

Taking the Short Goodbye

Before he jumped from the 15th floor of the Sunset Strip hotel, he must have had a great view.

As he stood there waiting to take the jump to Jesus, he must have seen the ships corning into San Pedro Harbor, the lights of Warner Brothers in Burbank, and the neon snake of traffic slithering up from the Mexican neighborhoods of East Los Angeles.

It was a clean, clear night in L.A., a travel-video-ad night rich with the smell of lemons from the backyards of the valley and the sugar-sweet expensive perfume coming from the bare arms dangling from the passing Mercedes. A hard night to leave.

Think of your favorite moment – sunset, sunrise, raking the leaves, biting into corn on the cob, kissing those lips, sipping that wine, holding that child. You wouldn't leave for the world.

Not all of us are that lucky. A whole bunch get tired of the movie and walk out just before the best moments.

He hit the tops of two cars only 65 feet from us. "Us" was a pack of would-be stand-up comics waiting in the parking lot next to a Sunset Strip comedy club.

He hit with a dry sound like a hundred pounds of sugar hitting a warehouse floor. No one moved for a long moment. The traffic kept flowing and the comic on stage inside never missed a laugh.

I never knew his name. He was a comic who had gone too long without a job or a laugh. He had taken the short goodbye. One Fourth of July night the following year, I was invited to a party at a beach house in Malibu to watch the fireworks over the water.

There was a sweet young girl there who sat next to me at the piano. Her parents were there, but not for her. She talked about Freddie Prinze, the Chicano comic who had blown his dream machine away only weeks before. She held my hand as we watched the fireworks. At the end of that summer, someone told me she had killed herself.

People take the short goodbye a lot in our society. In 1988, 30,796 Americans killed themselves. According to the National Center for Health Statistics, there are more suicides in this country each year than murders.

A doctor even invented a machine to make it easier. It's kind of like one of those comb and condom machines in men's rooms in cheap taverns. You put in 50 cents and out comes death.

Some cases present a good argument. Maybe you're a retired and widowed cop living in two rooms over a bakery. Your friends are dead and your kids are gone and the piano player doesn't know your favorite song anymore.

You've just discovered you have stomach cancer from years of living on hot dogs and chili burgers on late night stakeouts. Why stick around just to have some ugly nurse who couldn't care less walk by your room every night on her way to life?

I know you don't want to read about suicide this morning. It's raining. People are getting engaged, married, pregnant. The Red Sox are winning and we're reading about why Nancy was smiling during the Iran-Contra hearings. It's hard to imagine, but some can.

There have been more than usual lately and closer to home. It's one thing when you read about a famous writer or old actor taking the easy way out, people who live on wealthy moons light years away from the rest of us. But when it happens down the street, you pay attention.

Not long ago, a local priest, who seemed to have lost his faith, or maybe found it, walked off the Winslow bridge. Scandinavia has a very high rate. Winters are long there and the wind is cold. Sound familiar?

In Japan it's blamed on peer pressure and school failures.

It hits all kinds of people in all walks of life – high school kids, teachers (understandable), cops, and priests. It occurs to strict Christian parents when their son moves in with another guy.

Actors at the bottom and stars at the top do it. Ernest Hemingway did it. Hart Crane and Socrates did it. Cleopatra and Charles Boyer did it. William Holden did it in his own way and so did my own brother.

Professionals tell us that out of 10 people who did it, eight have given countless warnings. We have to pay attention to each other. Listen to the words but watch the eyes. We've become a nation of fear. We fear each other. We've stopped talking and listening to each other.

Walk up to a stranger in the market sometime, smile and ask them how they're feeling. They leave tire marks.

Most of us have thought about it. Not seriously of course, just in the passing of a bad rainy Monday when we're hit with hospital bills and taxes, Christmas in a rented room, the death of a partner. You know them. Pieces of daily lead dropped into our hearts until we sink.

Maybe you're the one I'm writing this for. Only you would know. I can't change your mind; all I can do is make you laugh. I saved a life once that way, I really did. That's why I still do it, even on those days when the piano player doesn't know my favorite song anymore, and I can see the ships coming into San Pedro Harbor.

It Ain't Heavy, It's My Tree
Bring on the eggnog, it's time to decorate

There it is in the corner of the garage where it's been since last year. I had it covered with plastic for a while, but it scared the hell out of me whenever I pulled in at night.

This is the Devine family Christmas tree. Yep, it's a fake. I know, it's Maine and we have all these real trees, so why am I using a fake? Because it won't make my dog sneeze, it won't drop needles and it won't catch fire and burn my house down. Next question?

In 1939, my father, in a whiskey glow of nostalgia for his childhood, insisted on real candles for the tree. I can still see these five men of the family throwing a burning tree through the front door into the yard. I grew up thinking that was an Irish Catholic tradition, like throwing up on the side of the church at Midnight Mass. I cried the next year when they wouldn't burn it.

Irony. In Los Angeles we always had a real tree. It was quite an ordeal doing that. You could go to one of the lots dotted around the city and buy one for 60 or 70 bucks. In Beverly Hills they have custom-grown trees for about $100. Some were sprayed silver or gold, just like in an MGM forest.

An actor buddy of mine tipped me off to a cheaper way. We had to drive down past East L.A., avoiding drive-by shootings and anti-Vietnam rallies, to the railyards. Here the trees came in daily during the month of December. They were about 30 bucks cheaper and they were gorgeous. Jimmy Stewart got his there.

GETTING REAL

Living in Hollywood, you need things that are real. It's important to teach your kids that Bing Crosby wasn't a real priest and that palm trees are too high to decorate. When it's 82 degrees and above on Christmas, you need nostalgia. You need the smell of a dying tree in your living room. People would say, "Smellllllll that tree."

Relocated to this winter wonderland, I caved and got a real one. I sat up all night watching it like a staked-out cop. I was terrified one of the bulbs would heat up and burn us out. What was funny in '37 loses its charm when you own it.

Three hours after Christmas the needles start to fall. I don't care how much water you put in it, those suckers drink like the ushers at an Irish wedding. You wind up with water-stained rugs and six inches of needles. My college educated daughters never studied Broom 101. Guess who sweeps?

So I bought this beauty. It's six feet tall and perfectly shaped. It's fireproof and carefree. No water or sweeping is required. It comes back every year like Uncle Pete, only sober.

AWKWARD

One problem. It's very heavy and awkward. Getting it in the front door is no easy trick. It doesn't bend like a real tree, there is no give. On the way in, it breaks glass and scratches paint and rips up rugs. It's like dragging a condemned man to the electric chair.

Decorating. I hate this part. Every ornament is like a dagger to the heart. It requires lots of eggnog to get through this and I don't mean Shaw's eggnog.

There is this one ornament we bought when my youngest was born. It's hers. She just called me on her cell phone from a Delta flight somewhere over Florida. Time flies when you're having fun?

There is the angel made of a Dixie cup with paper wings. It has no head now, just the cup and one wing. It was made by my oldest. She checks every year to make sure it's up. I need more eggnog.

I should have the fake up and lighted by Sunday night. I put it off longer every year, as though it were a root canal appointment. Christmas, as one grows older, is like Aunt Mamie's fruit cake, tougher and sweeter. Maybe someday I'll have a son-in-law and he'll put the damn thing up. He'll probably want a real one. Let him sweep.

But at the end, it will look real. It will glow and sing and tinkle and smile. Everybody will go "oooh" and "ahhh." Some will even say, "Smellllll that tree."

I'll have to watch them play around it, these two grown women who made the paper angel. Funny, ain't it, how the glow of colored lights wipes 20 years away? Now I know why my father drank so much eggnog.

No Other Place but Here
Waterville beats everyplace else in final analysis

Don't count on it, but I think winter is over. Winter is a club in the teeth. For six months it keeps smacking you in the mouth with oil bills, plow bills, chilblains and ice storms. Then suddenly it stops. You're afraid to look up, in fear you'll take one in the eye, but you do and you find it's spring. Well, maybe not spring, but end of winter.

Usually about this time, unable to endure yet another winter, I start reading the travel section of the New York Times to find another place to live. I've lived almost everywhere in America and some places in Asia, so I have a pretty good idea of what it would be like to relocate. I've got the bag packed and have withdrawn my savings. Let's see:

Japan is out of the question. My Japan was 14th century. Now it's New York with noodles and everybody is broke.

Hong Kong was fun when I was 19, but it belongs to China now — and there was that matter of Korea.

I'm thinking of Los Angeles again. I think of the swaying palm trees and remember that sometimes it's a 6.8 earthquake making them sway. I also remember that those same palm trees have palm rats in them. I think of the doves at twilight and remember the sirens, the screams you hear driving through certain neighborhoods. Tacos and terror. Maybe later.

There is San Francisco. I loved San Francisco with the cable cars and the smell of hot crab sandwiches on Fisherman's Wharf at midnight. But San Francisco has earthquakes and sirens, too. And when you're 75, walking home up one of those hills that look like the North Face is impossible.

BIG CITIES

New Orleans. It's nice and warm most of the year. It has the Mardi Gras, fabulous restaurants and river boats and jambalaya.

It also has some of the most polluted river water in America and from what I read, the most corrupt police department outside of Bosnia, and that Mardi Gras carnival features wall-to-wall pickpockets.

My hometown is St. Louis. I've considered going back. I've thought about how nice it might be to spend my twilight years back in the old neighborhood with Moo Moo and Billy and Sonny Gerber. But I'm told that they've all left town. Nobody knows where they are. They say my neighborhood has gang problems now, and Skeeter O'Neal's saloon was bulldozed long ago for a trailer park. The worst news is that Rosemary DeBranco had six kids and is a perfect size 52. Thomas Wolfe was right.

San Diego is too Republican, and Santa Fe is too high. I endured Seattle for three years as a kid. We called it a graveyard with lights. But I hear that's changed. Microsoft's Bill Gates has cleaned and brightened it up. It's a major city now, with a ball team and 6,000 coffeehouses, but it still rains 324 days a year.

SAFETY

I spent six days passing through North and South Dakota. That was without stopping. You don't ever want to stop in the Dakotas. Custer found that out and it hasn't changed a bit since he got in a drive-by with Sitting Bull.

Manhattan. Now that's a possibility. I love New York. I spent 10 fun years there. But then everybody's twenties are fun years. You're young and stupid. Being broke is fun, hungry and locked out of your apartment is fun, a small part in a garage theater at 15 bucks a week is fun.

But sadly, my old apartment now rents for two grand a month and dinners cost more than the rent. Movies are 10 bucks there and when you get old, the urine perfume of subways loses its charm.

Should I break new ground? North and South Carolina get blown away at least once a year. Georgia and Alabama have been leveled, Boston is boring and all the girls in Little Rock really do look like Paula Jones.

Then I remember why I came here. It's the last safe place in America. OK, face it, unpack the bags, put up the screens and call the boy about mowing the grass. It's going to be another summer in Waterville. But this is definitely the last one. Let's go down and see if Faye Nicholson is making any progress on that gazebo.

Oh Baby, It's the '50s Again

Don't wipe those ketchupy fingers on your jeans yet baby, the second order of fries and cherry Cokes is on the way. Who's that in the back seat with the neon cherry pink eyes and apple blossom white skin? Oh baby. It's the '50s. Wow Archie, the '50s are back. Oh Gawd, I forgot. I can't call women baby anymore. I'm being politically incorrect. That will go on my permanent record.

Yes ma'am, the '50s are back. My high school class had its 40th a year or so ago. I didn't go. I said the '50s are dead. Besides what would I have worn? Now everywhere I look it's deja vu all over again.

Are you ready? The '50s are in again. Hula hoops are for sale again in every store from Filene's to dusty windowed two-for-a-penny mom and pop stores in Tupelo, Miss. Except now they glow in the dark like Russian teenagers.

Sears is showing pink and charcoal sport shirts. Graceland has booked extra tours. Hear them black leather thighs rubbing together? Yes mama, Elvis walks again tonight.

Yes, baby, (Gosh, I wish I could quit that.) the '50s are back. "Grease" is back on Broadway, and "Damn Yankees" and "Guys and Dolls" and they're hits. Do the time warp. Do it now.

I think I loved the '50s. Maybe it's memory. I personally packed more living into the '50s than any other decade, perhaps more than any other living being.

They're bringing back 3-D. Can you imagine what it would have been like if we had had to watch that whole Tonya Harding/Nancy Kerrigan thing in 3-D, or worse, Cinemascope?

Hey, we're not ready for this. We're not ready to time travel back to high school — not unless we get to change those annual things. I got "Weirdest Sense of Humor." I wanted "Best Smile" or "Best Dancer." I got "Weirdest Sense of Humor." I wonder if that's on my permanent record?

Don't kid me. Most of you couldn't wait to get out of the '50s. When they weren't dull, they were scary. There was a draft. People were shooting people. Russia had the bomb, and the Melba always ran out of frozen Milky Way bars on Friday nights. Is Red Carr still waiting behind the mail box to trip me?

Movies were so wonderfully politically incorrect. Jeff Chandler was "Cochise," and Rock Hudson was "Taza, Son of Cochise." Debra Paget was always the "Native American Princess." (We used to call them "Injuns.") Debra wore white leather dressed with red and blue beads and kissed with her eyes closed. Neat, man.

Doris Day pretended Rock was straight. Jayne Mansfield did a cheap impersonation of Mrs. DiMaggio and teeny idols like Tab, and Touch, Tony and Troy made Marlene's heart pound.

While we were having cherry Cokes with Rosemary De Branco, Dien Bien Phu was falling in Vietnam. MacArthur was flying home from Korea with Harry Truman's blue card on his permanent record. Katy Hawkins stood us up at the station, married a Marine and had five kids. They'd be married now with five of their own.

While we were wintering over in Japan, Norma Jean DiMaggio and her husband Joe honeymooned in Tokyo. She entertained the troops. She was great. We wanted to go home with her. We would have gone home with Ernie Borgnine.

Five families on each block had a small round television. Sonny Erb had one in his rec room. I met Martha Wright there. I gave her my letter sweater. She gave me her cold sore.

The '50s were an illusion like pink and charcoal short sleeved sport shirts. You can see them on "Nick at Nite" for insomniac small town folks and big city rock star heroin addicts.

Last night I had this dream that I was having breakfast with the Nelsons. The Nelsons were so comforting to those of us alienated from our own families.

Unlike my own dad, Ozzie was always home. Harriet had supper ready every night, and they ate in the kitchen. You could sit there and smell that meat loaf and mashed potatoes, Jell-O and spritzed-on whipped cream. The boys had crew cuts, freshly pressed khakis and alpaca sweaters. They're all dead now, like Betty Furness and Dwight Eisenhower and Mamie. I went to a wardrobe warehouse in Hollywood once and saw Ozzie's alpaca sweater. I cried.

I was no fan of Lucy and Desi, but in retrospect, they were much funnier than their '90s counterparts, the sickly cowgirl Roseanne and her Porta-Potty hubby Tom Arnold. Lucy and Desi are dead too. If God is Irish, we'll outlive Rose and Tom. Hey, we've already outlived Jimmy Dean, Natalie Wood and Betty Furness. We're on a roll.

I think that the future makes it easier to die. I mean, the "grunge" look is acceptable on a certain existential level. I can live with it, but you can't look CRISP in those things. Call me a fogey, but I don't really want to live in a world without seersucker slacks, white buck shoes, crisp white shirts and Milton Berle. It's bad enough I have to live in a world without Audrey Hepburn.

I'm not going to the next reunion either. Look at these jeans. They have no cuffs. I can't roll Lucky Strikes up in this T-shirt sleeve, I don't even smoke anymore and hold on baby. I can't wear these socks to the hop. They're not white wool. But still Rosemary might be there ... in that apricot ... oh baby. I wish I could quit that.

One Flu Over the Nest

It looks like a woman at a black and white beaux arts ball in 1930's New Orleans Garden District. It's not. It's a driveway lamp post all black frozen iron, waiting for the summer heat to come back.

Only through fevered eyes does it look like anything else, or does it seem to sway in the wind when there is no wind.

It's snowing again. It's past Valentine's Day now, and all that red-box candy and "I'm gonna love y'all till I die" greeting card crap didn't stop Mr. Winter death-breath from coming back and bringing Cousin Flu with him, now did it?

It's snowing again. In the booze-induced pre-Christmas hysteria, all that white stuff is like fallout from a fast-food junkie's marshmallow dream, but from January on, it comes as a slaver's whip across the small of the back.

The Writer has the flu. The flu comes like a letter bomb. The flu has names like "Shanghai" and "Hong Kong." Old Mao's ghost got even with us after all for trashing his dreams in Panmunjom.

Flu brings delusions like six cups of bad saki on an empty stomach. One sees carnival lights on the walls and ceiling of the sick room. One sees the lips of old girl friends and hears giggling in distant rooms and phantoms quietly turning the screws.

Three in the morning on the bathroom floor the Republican Guard part of the flu has taken over. The powder-blue toilet bowl yawns widely. The water one dares not to drink sits in the bowl looking like an oasis.

See the dark-blue wash cloth soaked in hot water for the fevered face, feel the steam. One peers through the blinds at the backyard woods where the African daisy roots sleep like vampires waiting for summer.

The trees don't move without winds. There are twenty-three pines, cold edged, tall, black with white-trimmed limbs, looking like a bevy of Cole Porter beauties waiting for a cab outside the Ziegfeld Theatre in 1929, or a whole mess of pall bearers at a piano player's funeral.

A flu night moves slower than an outward-bound freight train through Georgia swampland.

Black plastic garbage-filled bags are waiting curbside for the big orange garbage hearse to come coughing up the street. They sat all night in the cold and the snow and have white tops now, body bags for dead Grape-Nuts boxes and Shaw's own 1 percent low-fat plastic milk cartons, discarded Kleenex tissues and wine bottles.

"I can see the lights of the city from here," Jesus once said from the Mount of Olives. One can see them from the Rangeway.

Winter comes to the city like a telegram announcing a death. Winter doesn't like the city; winter likes the woods. The woods cover up with snow and sleep, hum, snore, belch and shiver deliciously under the snow, like a sodden Irish uncle on New Year's morning. Winter is a harlot who dresses for its best customer.

The city cringes from winter, like a street person cringes from a mean cop. The city is a spoiled girl who likes hot front granite stoops and neon light and party sounds from way upstairs.

City sidewalks like spilled ice cream cones and cigarette butts and melted Hershey chocolate bars, not snow, not clean snow and ice without footprints. The city cries out in winter, rattling its garbage lids, steam grates and window shades in the dead of night.

Two a.m. A flu night. Peter Arnett does his stand-up routine for Saddam for the last time of the night. The boys of our summers are slouching towards Baghdad, bearing the banner on a javelin. One watches Larry King ask silly questions of a KGB agent posing as a "journalist," or an "embassy official." Kafka would be so happy. Orwell would be giggling.

Twenty-four-hour flu, she says, it'll pass. Twenty-four-hour flu is like a twenty-four-hour tumor, there ain't no such thing, Harry. That saying is one of those your mama used to embroider on guest tea towels.

The flu is a winter's cruise on the North Pacific. It has a menu for you. Stand by. Cream of Wheat and Rice Krispies and apple sauce. You can have weak tea or flat Diet Coke or hot lemon water but no chardonnay or merlot or chablis.

That's what Hell is gonna be like, brothers and sisters, a big ballroom-sized bathroom with six bowls, no waiting. A flu room with a view of dark trees and cold city lights, no wine, no salsa, no Mexican music or refried beans.

Forget what the priest said. He had all the naughty thoughts you had as a kid, only he got the flu and almost died and begged forgiveness and made a crazy promise, and now he's telling you that Hell is going to be fire and pitchforks but it isn't, it isn't at all.

Hell is going to be perpetual winter, 12 dark months of ice and snow. There's going to be wind and a view of the palm trees in Heaven. There's going to be round-the-clock CNN reports on the unending Third World Wars and Cream of Wheat and flat Diet Coke every night for supper.

Take it from a sinner, come to the Lord and change your ways. Heaven is a winery in Jamaica, and Hell is a New England winter.

And then God said, "Hey, that's pretty good stuff...got any more?"

California Dreamin'

"There is a natural tilt to the North American continent, and sooner or later everything loose rolls into Southern California."
— H.L. Mencken

It was New Year's Eve 2013, and we were sitting on the bench in the Santa Monica mall, waiting for the shuttle to take us back to the Motion Picture Home in the San Fernando Valley. I had just finished my seasonal job, the last one since retiring from television acting, as Santa at the mall.

She, who had retired from practicing law, had been Mrs. Santa this year. I had fallen asleep on the bench. Suddenly I jolted awake.

"OMG!" I gasped. "I just had the weirdest dream."

"What on earth was it about?" She asked.

"You won't believe it. I dreamt that we were living in Maine. We'd been there for years." "My Maine?"

"What other Maine is there?"

"In Waterville?"

"Of course," I answered. "It was winter."

"But you've never been there in winter."

"But it was so real," I said. "We were older, I had hair as white as the snow, not like this fake Santa stuff. I guess we were older."

"How did I look?" She asked.

"Pretty much the same, but your hair was golden and curly."

"Curly? You're really stressed. I told you to ask the mall manager to let you be an elf this Christmas. You're getting too old to be carrying all of those kids on your lap."

"You're just jealous," I snapped, "because there were more twenty somethings visiting Santa this year."

She lowered her sunglasses to the tip of her nose and peered over at me.

"So tell me this crazy dream, Santa."

"Well, we were living in this big house in Waterville, on a hill with the longest driveway you've ever seen. It was the middle of the winter, and it must have been a bad one because there was ice all around, ice on the driveway, the lawn, the trees were thick with it, and they were toppling down into the street. You were home with me because it was a snow day."

"Snow day? What's a snow day?"

"In the dream someone said it's when they close the school because of snow. You were a teacher."

"A teacher? In Waterville, Maine? Were we poor?"

"I don't know, maybe we were, because I was wearing these old heavy coats and scarves and dirty sneakers. I was working for a newspaper, and I was coming out of a bar and slipped on the ice."

She sat up, pale as a ghost. Her mouth dropped open.

"A newspaper? You were delivering newspapers in my home town?"

"No, I was writing a column for the paper."

"Oh boy." she gasped. "You were writing for the paper? We really were poor. Were the girls in the dream?" she asked.

"No, they weren't in Maine. They were living in Los Angeles."

"Oh good," she said.

"That was the sad part of the dream."

"Sad?"

"They hated the snow and ice and refused to come to Maine to visit us anymore."

"This was all in the dream?"

"Yes. I'm sitting at the bar in this run down tavern, and someone called me to the phone, and it was the girls, and they said they weren't coming anymore because they came at Easter last year and got snowed in."

"They came to Maine in the winter? Both of them?"

"Easter."

"Same thing. What a crazy dream. You've been asleep for an hour, is that all of it?"

"It was so sad, they agreed they weren't coming, and I said how sad that would be for you, so they said they would hire two actors who looked like them and send them."

"That must have been the youngest, the actor's agent, she was always coming up with crazy ideas like that. So was that it?"

"No, there was more. It went on and on in color. It was like watching HBO. We went boating on this big lake."

"You're afraid of water."

"Not in the dream," I said. "I went boating and water skiing and everything."

"Go back to sleep why don't you," she said. "See if there's a happy ending."

"Kind of," I beamed, "I became a famous journalist and won a Pulitzer."

"Okay, Santa, the bus is here. You can sleep on the way back and come up with something less preposterous."

I guess there's no point in telling her how in the end of the dream they made a movie out of one of my columns about her, and they cast Scarlett Johansen. I'll save that part for the guys at the New Year's party tonight at the home. Happy New Year, old girl.

A Last Room

It was the stairs. Three weeks before Christmas, 1967. There were more lost moments, the forgetfulness. Then the stairs became an issue. Once they were twelve, now they seemed to become 14 or 15. She would stand at the top some days staring down at her front door, as if preparing to dive into an unfamiliar sea. As the days went by, she descended more slowly, and coming up seemed to take longer.

The family offered to find a safer place but she refused. She had her "lady friend" next door. They shared a small balcony together that looked out on the busy street. She and her friend would sit out on their balcony on summer nights, watching the comings and goings, gossiping and laughing at the parade of strangers. It was better to them than television.

At Thanksgiving, the family noticed new and disturbing things in her speech and her manner. She had always been feisty and argumentative, but now it grew sharper and darker. When her next door lady friend died suddenly, she sat on the balcony, even though it was dark and cold, and watched them take her body away.

After that, it was as if a window shade had been dropped across her eyes. Her smile faded, and she sat for long times staring out the window. She stopped answering the phone. The family knew something had to be done.

Three weeks before Christmas a meeting was held. Here were two of the five brothers who had remained in the city, who had not, for reasons only families can understand, spoken to one another for over two years. There were the three daughters who couldn't agree on what to give for Christmas let alone what to do with mother. Finally an agreement was reached. A nursing home was in the cards.

The others were far away, there was no time. So it was decided that her favorite son would handle the situation, and they all knew who that would be. He had always been her favorite. During the war she could get four letters a day from the others, and if there wasn't one from him, she would sit and cry and worry that he had been lost.

He was the most like their father. He even looked like him. He made her laugh as her late husband had. They had had their fights and long weeks would pass before they spoke, but he was her favorite and they knew it. Besides, he had only one daughter, and it was snowing now and his house painting business was slow.

So one day, three weeks before Christmas, he came and spoke to her in soft tones about it. She protested, cried and threw things across the room. But eventually, she came around and it was over.

A week before Christmas he and his wife and daughter came for her. They took her across the river and folded her into her new world, a bright room with a view of the river she had grown up on and where she remembered how her father had built river boats that rolled by. That seemed to please her.

The next day, her favorite son came and collected the objects she loved most. There was his first communion picture, a menu from a restaurant in New Orleans, photo albums and letters. She had kept all of his letters from the war, a box full of them, and she had tied them with an orange ribbon. This, he said, was the hardest part.

Six years later when she gave up the breath of life, he was the one who came first to fold her arms across her chest and close her eyes.

Today, three weeks before Christmas, down the block, across the street in every home, millions of sons and daughters are faced with a morning of sweeping up the memories of a parent's life, collecting letters and photos and folding a beloved figure, a childhood icon, a keeper of all the flames that lit their lives into that last room.

A Life in the Movies

This is the week of the crunch. The Maine International Film Festival, held each year in Waterville, Maine, is about to convene. It is my job as the lone film critic/reviewer for Maine Today Media, to sit up and pay attention. I must view ten films and write about them each day of the festivities.

So I sit here in the twilight of my days, doing the one thing I'm good at, writing, and that would be about the one thing I know most about. Movies. How did this happen you ask? How did I, a formerly handsome boy from the streets with so much promise, arrive in this place and this task, you ask? Okay, you didn't ask, but I will tell you anyway.

One warm March afternoon when I was nine, my father shattered my normal boyhood by slipping silently and slowly to the sidewalk, only six blocks from where I sat on the front porch, waiting for him. It was the end of his life and the beginning of my new one.

Suddenly I was the only kid on the block without a father, a confused outlier. I had brothers, of course, all much older. A brother can pretend to be a father, but you both know that it isn't the same. Slowly and silently, I slipped away from the pack. I became someone else. No one seemed to notice.

It happened like this. After the formal funeral, there was the traditional wake at the house, where someone, a sister or brother, worried about me. I was sitting in the corner, fiddling with my collar and tie, so I was given a quarter to go to the neighborhood movie house, the Michigan Avenue Theater, where I bought my popcorn and soda, and settled into my seat in the second row, and watched Walt Disney's "Pinocchio."

It was the first time I had ever gone to the movies alone. There I was, surrounded by a soothing darkness and so stunned by the color and light that all pain and shock vanished. I was part of the movies. I never left that movie house. I packed it in my heart and took it to Chicago, New York, New Orleans and San Francisco, to Hong Kong and Tokyo, almost always alone in the dark but never lonely. It was a movie house, and the dark was light enough.

At least three times a week, after my homework, after supper, I went to the movies, the way kids today turn on the television. I saw every movie Jimmy Cagney made. He was my favorite, my hero.

It cost a dime. I always found one, on the floor, in the sofa, in my brother's old coats. A dime. A ticket to the comforting darkness of the Michigan. My old buddies on the block weren't allowed to go to the movies as much as I could, and many didn't have the dime admission. So by some quirk of fate, I became the neighborhood movie reviewer and critic.

On summer days, after seeing a movie, I'd run home and line up the other kids on my front porch steps and tell the entire story, acting out all the parts, male and female and animals. The actor was born.

One summer night, I heard my pal Alan on his porch next door, begging his father to take him to see a Tarzan movie. His father, a cop, said he'd heard it was terrible. Alan said, "No, Jerry says it's great, and Tarzan almost dies." He took him. A film reviewer was born.

When I was grown, after a life in the theater, I drifted into small parts in big films and little ones. I watched the stars and the name directors work. I had seen the magic, now I was watching the magicians.

One hot August day in Burbank, I was on the back lot at Warner Brothers, shooting a scene in "The FBI" with the wonderful Efrem Zimbalist Jr. When we were finished, I walked out onto the lot, and a big limo stopped just in front of me. A short, aging man got out with his wife. It was Jimmy Cagney. I glanced, he smiled. I looked away. When a hero smiles, the light can be blinding.

A Very True Story

Yes. I seriously considered running for mayor of Waterville. Not that I'm crazy about the job, but if I ever wanted to be governor, that seems like the necessary first step. I like Waterville, but I like Falmouth, Freeport and Camden too. Okay, I'm partial to the south and the coast, but that's beside the point. I live in Waterville, and it's a nice town, but I have serious problems with it and the most serious would be the streets. Small cars and children have been known to vanish in the pot holes of this city's streets. If I were mayor, I would make them my raison d'etre. That's French for "The only reason I'm mayor."

So I considered it. I thought maybe I could run on the Tea Party ticket. There are a lot of those out there, and I don't think they have a serious candidate. They're so serious. There isn't a comic in the bunch. America needs laughter. I don't much like the Tea Party. I don't like broccoli either but I eat it. I don't like super-dark chocolate but I eat it because of the flavonoids. I'm not sure what flavonoids are but I hear they're important. Then it hit me. I can't find my birth certificate. This is very serious. This is 2011. We all know by now that if President Obama showed HIS copy of his birth certificate, all the Tea Party folks would vote for him. So If I'm going to get their votes, I'm going to need my birth certificate. I don't want Birthers swarming around my campaign demanding proof that I was born in America.

This is the problem. I had two of them. The first one was from St. Louis City Hall. My Irish immigrant cousin, Rosie Chambers, was sent by my father down to city hall to record my birth. Rosie had lost the slip of paper with my name on it, so she just said, "I think it's Jerry." So, forever and ever in black and white, it became Gerald Joseph Devine. Rosie made up the middle name on the spot. This is a true story. I know, because my Uncle Pat told it at every Christmas party for years, even when he was sober.

My mother, of course, was horrified and banned Rosie from the house. That wasn't the name she wanted. Sister Amilda, a friend of the family from the convent across the street, said, "Don't worry, the only true name will be the one you give him when Father Keating baptizes him." That's a true story.

So when they doused my head with holy water, the good father intoned, "Jeremiah Patrick, do you renounce Satan and all his works?" My brother Jug said that I actually smiled for the first time. My mother made the sign of the cross in fear, but Aunt Mamie said it wasn't a smile, it was only gas. I didn't find any of this out until she, who renounced Satan and all his works in French, and I got married. True story.

I digress. I can't find either of these documents, and this Birther movement has me worried. This could bring me down and crash my political career. Rosie is long dead as is everyone who was there that hot September day. I guess I can write city hall in St. Louis and the church where I was baptized, but the election thing is getting close and just in case I really do want to challenge Dana Sennett, I have to hurry.

Okay, this breaking news just in. She, who thinks she's funny, just handed me both documents. She was hiding them just in case it wasn't the wine that made me talk about running, and that I might be serious. OMG. Am I really that old?

Man In An Orange Suit

Once upon a lonely Christmas Eve back in 1952, there was a tiny bar atop a hill in wintery, foggy San Francisco, where I heard a story that stayed with me for years before I lost it in the fog of my own aging mind. But every once in a while it snaps back. The taste of it comes right back to me like the froth of the beer we drank there, and the sound of the juke box that played Eartha Kitt's "Santa Baby."

I heard it from a one-eyed Chinese man who tended bar there and liked to sneak free beers now and then to men in uniform. He was a sad little man who had lost his eye in a fishing accident. He spoke little, but when he did, he was full of stories about growing up in that magical city.

From the big bay window of that bar, festooned with cheap colored Christmas lights, one could see the fabled penal island of Alcatraz that floated out in the bay like a corpse.

That Christmas Eve, as we were preparing to ship out to Japan and Korea, some one of us mentioned it. As he gave us our free going away drink, our Chinese friend told us a story about a man who had spent twenty years on "The Rock." It was during the war, he said. "When he was freed he just stayed in the city. He came in here every night until he didn't no more."

"He said to me one night, the saddest thing. He said, the worst time on The Rock was evening, when you could see the lights of 'Frisco go on and when the wind changes you can smell the hot crab from the stands on Fishermen's Wharf. That was the worst thing." We all looked out at the island. No one said a word. Somehow, even as young as we were, we knew what that must have been like.

On the late news last night I watched two Marines bring a man down a line of steel fence. They led him down a sandy path through a tunnel of razor wire and mesh fence, this hooded man in an orange jump suit.

You've seen this act before. It's the daily run at Guantanamo in Cuba. We're told that they are terrorists, evil Muslims, dark princes of death. Some really are, but all? Who can know? We can only take our government's word for it. We could do that.

But that's a discussion for politicians. It's not on my mind today.

Today, I only think of this man, a boy really, a prisoner snatched up from a land far away and thrown onto an island prison far from his home, his mother, the sandy streets that smell of roasting lamb, the spices and scented smoke from hookah cafes.

The guards took him to a cage overlooking the sea, where he joined other men in orange suits who sat staring out at the water. They can't see when evening settles on Baghdad or Kabul from there. Home for them is a long way away, a lot farther than San Francisco from Alcatraz. They became warriors and are suffering the consequences of losing. Guilty or innocent, they may never see their homes, their mothers, wives, children again. These are not the Saudi Arabian men who flew the planes into the World Trade Towers. Many of these men were caught up in a net like tuna, by men who were fishing for sharks.

They were recruited, probably in religious and patriotic fervor. They can't see home. They can only remember, and when you're lost, truly lost, remembering is the cruelest torture.

I went back to San Francisco years in 1975 to find that the bar, the colored lights, the juke box and my bartender were gone. Alcatraz is still there as a tourist attraction. Perhaps, now that things are changing in Cuba, that may one day be Guantanamo's fate.

And a Leaf Fell

It fell like a bird shot from the sky. It made no sound of course. Just before twilight as I sat on my deck, only half an hour before the uncorking of the new wine, a leaf fell. I hoped it was an old leaf from last season, part of a cluster on a dead limb that had been dislodged by the June monsoon season.

Maybe, I thought, it was the first leaf of autumn, dropped prematurely, not by accident but sent ahead as a sort of advance scout to measure my feelings.

A Buddhist ballet dancer once told me that trees think. She was right. As I sat there on the deck, they've been taking my measure. There's the big city boy, they whisper to one another. He probably doesn't know what we are. To his kind, we all look alike. He wouldn't know a birch from a pine.

When I first came to Maine over 24 years ago, June was a hot sweaty month, humid like Manila or Singapore.

People got married in June, they had picnics and ice cream socials, rode on bicycles and stood fanning themselves in long lines at the ice cream stands. They stayed out late until the sun was gone but had left enough glow to walk the dog. It reminded me of my childhood in the Mississippi Valley, where each June day was a two, maybe three shirt day.

It's July 2009. June has slipped away in the night like a small town embezzler. My linen suits and shirts hang in morgue cool darkness waiting for 85, 90 degrees to strut their stuff. The white shoes sit under the bed waiting. In Georgia, I'm told, the lawyers are all seersuckered and white shoed, sipping bourbon and branch water as their daddies and granddaddies did under the Casablanca fans at the Mansion Hotel on Peachtree Street, while I sit here on the frozen lip of North America having a panic attack about a single oak leaf...or is it an aspen?

Autumn? In the middle of July? I can smell it, yes. When the breeze switches direction I smell it. Woodsmoke.

Woodsmoke in July? Yes. And then the breeze grew stronger and brought that leaf down closer to the deck and it spoke to me and said I am here and I am the first of millions to come, yes, and not one of your prayers can stop us.

I went to it, picked it up and dropped it across the fence into my neighbor's yard. Let it talk to him. Let it find him and get him all depressed.

Autumn in July and I'm pathetic. I stand in the middle of the garden in wet Crocs and damp linen and search the sky for a patch of blue, hungrily, desperately, the way a drunk tries to find a bar on Sunday in a dry town.

I can tell you from experience that an Irishman can find a bar the way a cop's hound dog can find a corpse. But blue sky? They say that rain is the natural condition of the Irish and that blue sky, even a patch of it, is harder to find than slippers in the dark.

And then it happened. The breeze grew stronger and the clouds vanished and the sun, the very sun the Mayans and Egyptians worshiped and sacrificed virgins to and built really cool monuments in honor of, poured over me like baptismal holy water. Yea, I am renewed, born again. A month of rain seems to have passed and the darkness has lifted.

I felt joy seeping back into my soul. I reached over and took the leaf back. I was convinced of its innocence now. This was no spy, no advance scout. Each thing, Sister Rosanna told me, has a time and place, and this was the time for it, and my garden was its place.

Awake and Sing

I miss John Boehner. I miss Harry Reid, "Plan B" and Eric Cantor. I even miss Donald Trump and Mitt. I miss the terrible anxiety of the fiscal cliff, and the push and shove of the hordes rushing through the mall. This week I pulled back the sheets to reveal that I am not only a political junkie, but an unabashed stress junkie.

I had thought that stress was what gave me my little heart attack two years ago. It wasn't. I know now that it was the calm and peace of summer, the lazy charm of soft breezes by the lake and chirping of flocks of the state bird.

Once the tsunami of election tweets started coming in, I began to heal, take deep, delicious, tortured breaths, and arrange my pile of newspapers. Each morning I started my daily run through of political shows, both from the crazy Right and the furious fist jamming Left. I was healing, and I was excited and joyful. The true meaning of being pure Irish began to break back through. We are a people for whom rain is the natural condition. When things get peaceful and calm and when all men join together in harmony, we start a revolution, running in the streets, handing out pamphlets calling for the firing of one, the impeachment of another.

We like strikes and tension, songs of revolution. We like building bronze statues of political losers and angry poets. Nirvana.

For weeks now I was thriving on the fury of the Secretary of State appointment, the chaos in Egypt and Syria. There was the tension of the last minute gifts, the horror of finding a bill that had gotten tucked away with Christmas cards and had to be rushed to the mail box.

Rushing to Portland to meet the kids before their plane landed, and left them standing alone sipping cold Starbucks filled my veins with crisis juice. My hair stood on end, my eyes glittered with passion. I was cooking and pulsing through the cold December days, leaving plumes of steam behind me. Sweet days.

Then the calm of the final moments descended. People began singing carols. Santa went into hiding before his journey. Everyone began whispering. It was almost Christmas Eve. The soft light of evening fell on everything and everyone. They were all so sweet and gentle. Good will and peace on earth. I started biting my nails.

What was wrong with these people? Didn't they know the Mid East was burning down? Had they forgotten the ancient Chinese warning, "See the man who is laughing. He has not yet heard the news."

"Isn't it nice?" they chimed. "No traffic, no crowds." No traffic? I love traffic, the thicker the better. I love the crowds, the long lines, the screaming kids and blaring horns. I needed that. I needed anxiety.

I've always been like this, from childhood on. The weeks leading up to Christmas were bustling, noisy and full of tension. Christmas Eve was a jamboree of shouting, drinking, hugging, kissing, tearing of paper, spilling of drinks. Sometimes there were tears, and then forgiveness, chewing and sometimes vomiting. But it was big and powerful.

Then Christmas morning, it was all over. A silence fell on the house. Even the snow looked gray.

I have always hated what I considered the "boring" holidays: Easter, New Year's Day, Thanksgiving. Those days when everything closed, even the movie theaters where I lived, especially the movie theaters. The saloons were shuttered, groceries locked. Yes, I know, I'm nuts. We've already cleared that one up.

Even today, I love waking to the sound of traffic hissing by, the music of buzz saws, the pounding of hammers, as workers dress up old houses down the street. It seems to annoy neighbors. Not me. To me, it's the heartbeat of commerce,

America's pulse. I love slamming store doors, customers shouting out orders, cash registers chiming away.

Now it's back, it's all back. Fox News is pounding the right wing drums, Chris Matthews is screaming, Rachel Maddow is chanting the liberal carols.

The fiscal cliff looms. Taxes might go up or down. Pandemonium hovers over Wall Street, a maelstrom threatens the House, bedlam creeps along the floors of the Senate like fetid smoke. Will there be a free for all? Bedlam? Havoc? My deadlines threaten me, as I waste time Facebooking my political daydreams. The earth is awake again. Oh, joy! Oh, jubilation!

Gimme My Toaster

Citigroup? Wells Fargo? Bank of America? Lehman Brothers? Does this mean I'm not going to get my new toaster? Bummer. I was counting on it. I'm sure many of you alive out there can remember when banks still gave away a free toaster to anyone opening a new account. Those days are gone forever, along with dish night at the movies. You wouldn't remember that, but dish night was big. You got Bogart and Bergman and a soup bowl.

In the Great Depression, no, not this one, the other one, the one your parents and grandparents told you about, give-aways were the norm, and it was a common event for banks to hand out free toasters to young couples just starting out. All you had to do was come in and fill out the forms. This was a problem for us due to the fact that we never actually had a bank account. My brother Jim said that when my father was in the navy, Mama spent his checks so fast there wasn't time to actually put it anywhere. Willie Sutton once robbed a bank in St. Louis, but I can tell you he didn't get any of our cash. My mother loved spending money. And when my father retired and became a civilian engineer, nothing changed.

My sisters said that there was a legend in the family: If all the department stores in St. Louis gave all their money to my mother at supper time on Friday, it would be back in their registers by Monday morning.

So we never counted on a free toaster until my cousin Bill Brady became a Vice President of the Mississippi Valley Trust during the war. Then we all got free toasters. Because Mamma wouldn't be seen dead walking out of a bank with a free anything, she sent me down to get ours. She gave me car fare and fifty cents extra, so I could get a waffle ice cream sandwich at Woolworth's lunch counter. Woolworth never gave anything away.

Cousin Billy met me at the back door. He put our toaster in a Kroger's Market bag, and I took it home on the street car.

I went through some old catalogs recently, of Depression Era toasters, and I think I found ours. It was really cool. It was the Sunbeam Silent Automatic Toaster, the one that came out in 1938. It had this little glass button on the side that glowed orange while it was toasting the Wonder Bread. I checked it on line and it's now selling for $435.

Actually the practice of toaster give-aways is alive and well in New Mexico where the Bank of the West is giving away shiny new toasters from April 2nd to May 11th to any new customer who signs up for a checking account and debit card. The car fare to New Mexico is not included.

I've been a household husband now for almost 48 years, and I have some advice for newlyweds. Buy the most expensive toaster you can afford. She and I have been through probably 48 cheap toasters since we got married, not counting the one I threw out of the window on 72nd Street.

A toaster is very important to this woman who supports her writer, as she toasts everything. If she could figure out how to get her lasagna into a toaster, she'd do it.

Our current toaster is okay. It's not the Sunbeam Silent Automatic with the little orange glass eye that you can watch as it toasts, but it works fine if you slice the bread really thin.

I'm thinking this is the year we go for something cool. Williams Sonoma has a terrific new model, the 4-slicer Breville Di-Cast Stainless Steel Toaster. But it goes for $179.95. Unless it toasts lasagna, that's a deal breaker. Willie Sutton always said he robbed banks because "that's where the money is." I wonder if Willie ever copped a toaster on the way out.

Is Barney Home?

I can get my house painted inside and out, new windows put in, complete roof remake. I can get my lawn mowed, raked and seeded. I can have a new boiler put in, basement redone, floors polished and my dog groomed. But I can't find anyone to fix a drawer.

The drawer is in the upstairs bathroom. It's part of an oversized vanity, much like my own. It has two big drawers, hers and mine. Wouldn't you know that it's mine that's broken? It appears that the sliding fixtures have detached somewhere in the back, and the drawer sort of hangs there like Quasimodo who has forgotten where the bells are.

I tried fixing it myself and for a piece of time, it worked, then like everything else I've fixed in life, like my daughter's tricycle, it came undone and it's hanging there.

The problem is the once ubiquitous "handyman" has faded from the American scene.

There was a time when I was younger, back around the time Roosevelt defeated Wendell Wilkie, that the landscape was sprinkled with handymen. It was an honorable profession almost like being a bus driver or school janitor. Every American neighborhood from St. Louis to New Orleans to Waterville, had one or two.

When not working fixing porches, bannisters, window sashes and cellar doors, you could find one up on a ladder somewhere or sitting in a corner table at the local diner, sipping soup or munching on the daily blue plate special. He had a universal costume, old blue jeans or work khaki pants carried over from the last parts of his First or World War 2 uniform.

Maybe he had a worn leather fading bomber jacket worn over a denim shirt, and he looked like an older Tommy Lee Jones, wearing that stained old fedora, slumped over a bowl of soup or standing on the corner trying to light a Camel cigarette in the wind.

In my childhood, I knew such a man. His name was Barney, and he lived with his mother on the top floor of a two-family flat across the street from the Catholic church.

Barney walked with a slight limp favoring his right side. One of the firemen at the firehouse said it was because that's where he carried his tool box. Mr. Schneider at the drug store said that he had lost the lower part of his right leg at Pearl Harbor, and that was sad, he said, because he had been a great baseball player in high school.

In the late thirties, when I was old enough to start being aware of things like that, there were men and boys everywhere to fix things. But then my father died without saying goodbye, and Pearl Harbor was bombed and suddenly the family handy men were gone. Then somewhere around 1944, Barney was there, limping down Soper Street with his tool box, and all the widows and blue and gold star mothers were hiring him to patch up their neglected homes.

It worked like this. If my mother got tired of stepping over the broken board on the back porch, she would send me up the street to Barney's house. I would knock on the door, and his mother, who worked for Father Keating across the street, would come to the door, wiping her hands on her apron that had pictures of autumn leaves on it. You remember things like that when you're a strange lonely little boy with no brothers around.

I would ask her then, "Is Barney home?" He never was. She would tell me where he was working in the neighborhood, or that he was having chili for lunch at Auel's cafe on the corner. Then I would go there and find him and tell him that my mother needed him.

He would listen to me and nod, and say he'd be over.

Sometimes he would give me the extra oyster crackers that came with his chili. So here I am some hundred years later with a broken drawer and no Barney and my brothers, who were always good at fixing things, are all gone to the other side.

I asked around today and everyone said they were all busy plowing snow or painting a house or building one. If you have a Barney in your neighborhood, let me know. I'll walk over and see if he's home.

Don't Let the Bed Bugs Bite

They're coming. They haven't been sighted locally yet, but if you don't have them now, you will, or at least that's what conventional wisdom is telling us. Who is CW? That would be almost every news outlet out there: CNN, NBC, CBS, MSNBC, FOX, yes, even Right Wingers are being infected. Yes, they're coming: BED BUGS. If you haven't heard or God forbid, been bitten, there are things you need to know.

You may not get this information in your regular paper until it's too late. If you go online on your computer, Michael Colongione, President of "GotchA! Bedbugs Inspectors" has some clues for you.

Let me break it down to save some time. This is no joke. This is not some cheap Bates Motel plague. Bedbugs are now officially ubiquitous in America, affecting rich and poor alike. They're in many of the big chain hotels (they're not admitting it yet) and retail stores. It's being alleged that hip trendy Hollister and Victoria's Secret are infested, but it doesn't end there. What could be next? Starbucks? OMG.

Colongione's list is frightening in and of itself. What if you find one at a friend's home or in a restaurant? OMG. You get home and "Shazam," there's a bed bug on your couch, your bed or bathroom rug. Don't panic. Experts are saying you should have a certified inspection team visit your home to check for bedbug eggs. Check your local listings. BEDBUG EGGS? OMG.

Apparently they can arrive via the mail, arriving in a package from an online store. OMG! You buy that Christmas sweater or sweat suit, open the box and OUT JUMPS A B.B.! What you do here is to close the box immediately and return it. (Be sure to put the bedbugs back in before sealing it.) These are not pets, remember. You can't housebreak them or train them to sit up or fetch. These are BED BUGS!

The internet is jammed with experts, semi experts and faux experts all giving advice. One solution is an over-the-counter bug spray that you can carry in your purse, and use anywhere. It's called "Pronto Plus." Be sure to spray your purse first, then your bed, your dog's bed and if local laws allow, your neighbor's bed. Be sure to call first before entering. With new laws on the books, your neighbor may be carrying a weapon. Everyone is jumpy, so knock before entering, then hold up the spray so they can see through the peephole that you're not some progressive, distributing literature.

If you find one in your house, there are probably more there. Ask yourself important questions. Where did I eat last night? Was it at the Smiths? Jones? Call them at once, warn them that they are carriers and that they are no longer welcome at your place. Then call all their friends and warn them not to go to the Smiths/Jones. Put them on FaceBook. They should have known better.

We're being advised to purchase a spray, such as the above, or one that is certified by the Environmental Protection Agency. If the EPA has been shut down due to budgetary concerns, call your mother. She always had advice about these things. Wasn't she right about cooties?

It's important that you kill the eggs as well. This is not to be confused with the latest egg salmonella thing. That's about chicken eggs. Don't go spraying your eggs.

There are also services that provide a K-9 bedbug sniffer. I'm not kidding. They're being used in major city hotels. You can Google that. To save money, I'm trying to train my sheepdog Jack to sniff out bedbugs. So far he's only come up with some fleas and an occasional caterpillar. Sheep dogs are notorious for their weird sense of humor.

If you're traveling, we're told, keep your clothing inside your suitcases and don't open them. This could be a problem, so make sure you're wearing cute clothes that work for day and night. They advise us not to put our clothes in the hotel closets or drawers, and that includes that one with the Gideon Bible.

Before going to bed, check the bedding, including mattress seams, headboards, pillowcases, box springs and comforters. If you weren't sleepy before you started this, you will be by the time you finish. Thank God, bedbugs have yet to be found in the complimentary bar.

It is not clear, at this printing, whether or not bed bug bites are being covered by the Obama Health Plan. Stay tuned.

Tuesday With Heph

Tuesday morning: He's down there now. The Sturm und Drang of installation is over. He's all shiny yellow, not a lemon yellow, but a futuristic yellow, the yellow of the dawn of a new day. His appendages are silver and metallic gray with coils and dials and little digital numbers black against storm sky gray tucked into silver frames.

He's a wonder of twenty-first century technology. He's "Hal" from "2001: A Space Odyssey." He cost more than any other single item in my house, more than the flat screen or my computer. He makes no sound, save a quiet whisper much like a breeze from Long Pond. I think I'm in love.

It is our new boiler.

Yes, I know. It's unseemly to feel such passion for a piece of machinery. But this is no ordinary furnace. No, this boiler is very much on the cutting edge of the new space age technology. It's where the future is, a mystical blending of Deepak Chopra, Steve Jobs and Stephen Hawkins. This boiler is what our President meant when he said, "Our time is now."

Don't laugh, but I think I can hear it talking to me in the night. So I put on my slippers, took a flashlight and went down to the basement. This is a gloomy place that could be a KGB holding cell. Were it not for HER I would have had it installed in the kitchen.

I dusted it softly and spoke to it. (I dust it every day.) I know it hears. There was a soft hum from within, a kind of spiritual/mechanical purr as one would get from a dog or cat. Then it came to life and hot water began pouring through the baseboards, cascading out of the shower and the dishwasher. Hot water, gallons of it. Oh joy! I brought a folding lawn chair so I could sit there with my decaffeinated tea and just watch him.

I hate calling it "It." So I've given it a name. This is why She Who Supports Me keeps the nursing home on her speed dial. But she doesn't understand these things. I've decided to call it Hephaestus, after the Greek god of fire. Heph for short. And the best part? The installers put a small sticker showing an American eagle against the flag, on Heph's chest. "Made in America, by American workers" it says. My chest swells with pride.

This now, is the final touch to the house She owns. First were the roofs, then the new energy efficient windows. Our carbon footprint grew greener with every move. We felt confident we were doing our part, participating in taking back the earth while all the while falling into penury. "Thank God," I shouted up to her, "that we didn't return that Bernie Madoff fella's persistent calls." She never answers me.

But down in the KGB room, the old boiler, rusted and coughing like a wounded lion, tried valiantly to keep us warm for twenty-five years. It died a hero, but it had to go. The house was like the guy in the $4,000 suit but with torn underwear. Now the house is ready for sale. We're asking $400.000. No offer will be refused.

So I'm down here now with Heph. It's late I know, but I had to come down and say goodnight. Heph knows I'm here. I can almost see him smiling, his little LED lights blinking in the soft darkness. I wonder if I should have him baptized. You think that's too much? I'll have her call the rectory.

Three Little Chickens

She's beautiful and well educated. She's the product of the Marlborough School for Girls in Los Angeles and a graduate of Colby College in Maine. She studied and lived in Paris and London and speaks French fluently. She's an account executive for a prestigious international publisher operating out of Los Angeles.

Then why, one asks, is she on her knees outside a chicken coop in 103 California degrees, with a handful of meal worms, making chirping sounds to three little chicks? Full disclosure: She's my daughter. Next question?

Later, she will clean the coop and then set about weeding the organic garden aside the house she shares with her partner Rick, on a quiet street in South Pasadena. Rick is busy picking arugula for their dinner salad.

These two unlikely urban Angeleno farmers fell in love over a simple salad of arugula, tomatoes and feta cheese. Now, they grow these vegetables together in the shadow of a brand new chicken coop. A father could not be happier...or more jealous, not of a house in South Pasadena or the 108 degrees, nor of the organic garden, but of the chicken coop, and their three lovely hens.

Last year, when the rumor that one could actually raise chickens right here in beautiful downtown Waterville, was being bruited about the halls of the City Council, those of us of a certain age who grew up in a more agrarian time of life in America, were suddenly swept up in a big coop of nostalgia. I, for one, am still planning a coop on my property should I have the requisite dimensions as demanded by local law. As I reported in this space last year, I have talked to various other chickenistas as to the problems, joys and demands of the art. Now that it's back on the front burner at City Hall, I'm excited.

My passion for the eatable feathered friends goes back to my early childhood. We had a big house on the corner across from the convent, where the landscaping nuns, yes there is such an order of sorts, raised not just chickens but rara avis of many colors. They were free range, of course, and during the quiet years of the war, would drift across the street to our yard and peck around. Adding to this group, Haag's Market, owned by the protestant Haag brothers up the alley, had a big pen of chickens in its back yard who would get out and wander down to join the Catholic chickens to form a sort of ecumenical cluckster in the late afternoon.

Somehow, during the mid-thirties, when box car tops full of wandering, jobless Americans rolled through town two streets down from us, several of the birds began to disappear. The Haag brothers put the clamp on their flocks' fraternization with the Catholic birds, and the good sisters posted a sentinel. So much for feeding the poor.

I guess my stories infected the imagination of my daughter and her new love. Rick, ever the green citizen, built a superior coop out of recycled wood, and my Dawn, ever the Hollywood child, set about naming the birds:

The Rhode Island Red is named Rita after Rita Hayworth, because she has a reddish hue. Her eggs, I'm told, will be light brown.

The "Buff Orpington" is named Jean after Jean Harlow, because she has a blonde tint. Her eggs will be beige or blue.

And finally, Myrna, after Myrna Loy, who is the darkest, is an Araucana who will lay colored eggs just in time for Easter.

Now that the city of Waterville is reconsidering giving the birds a hand, I've formed my three choices. The Silver Sebright Bantam, because I have a sport jacket that matches her plumage. The Araucana, because I look good in black, and finally, the Barred Rock. A political move. Where do I buy chicken wire?

The Taste of Freedom

It is raining. It seems that it has been raining since Memorial Day. I sit here in my car outside of Bolley's Famous Franks on upper College Avenue in Waterville, peering through the windshield wipers, two long black fingers humming like two insane metronomes. Outside my windows, sodden clusters of American working men and women dash from their trucks into the shop. Bolley's is the quintessential eatery for local workers of blue collars and white. There are cops, lawyers and judges, CMP pole climbers, roofers, house painters and newspaper writers.

Outside under an overhang, two huge men in yellow helmets and matching vests munch on their dogs, two at a time and share a paper bucket of fries.

It's lunch time in Central Maine, and the aroma of chili dogs and French fries floats in and out as the door opens and closes. I'm waiting for the downpour to become a trickle. I know I shouldn't be here. I should be eating a salad somewhere. There is no calorie counter pasted to the window. None of these workers need to see a calorie counter. These are hungry, wet, working people just hanging onto their jobs and the fat content of what they're eating is exactly what they want. This is America. Cholesterol is our natural condition.

As I wait I read a magazine story about four Chinese Muslims who have been released from Guantanamo and dropped off in Bermuda. Isn't this that pastel island where "Bermuda shorts" were invented, and tourists get to ride little pastel colored motorbikes and go snorkeling? There is a picture here of someone offering them food that looks suspiciously like hot dogs.

The magazine says these four boys are Uighurs (pronounced Wee-gurs) and were picked up in Afghanistan and Pakistan in 2001. Then we found out, seven or more years later, that they weren't really enemy combatants at all and should be released.

So I'm thinking. Imagine that you're from this terrible, stinking lost place in the world and fate tosses you into a cage in Cuba where, when the wind changes, you can smell those great rice and bean suppers. Then they take you away to this place where someone hands you something else to eat, and it's a hot dog. Maybe it's got mustard and relish on it, maybe sauerkraut. This is a life changing event.

I have an idea. Let's say we bring the remaining thirteen Uighurs that they're thinking of sending to the nation of Palau, and welcome them to Maine. We outfit them at L.L.Bean or Reny's and then bring them here to Bolley's Famous Franks and hand them this thing, this American thing, this work of art, this chili dog, with a basket of large fries with vinegar or catsup.

After a couple of weeks, we drop them back in the mountains of Pakistan. Don't you think they're gonna go down to the market place where folks are maybe reduced to eating a neighbor's horse, and tell the local homeboys all about this wonderful place in America where they were given the most magical piece of food, a large chili dog with extra chili and large fries? Now we send these four guys and the new thirteen Uighurs home to the Pakistani sticks with a couple frozen crates of Bolley's hot dogs and the recipe for the chili. How long would it be before the Pakistani government requests a Bolley's Famous Franks franchise be opened in Islamabad and Punjab?

I'm inside in line now. One of the guys with the yellow helmet is back in front of me, ordering two more chili dogs. Bolley's chili dogs with extra chili and large fries. The smell of America. The taste of freedom.

Coffee With Andre

We were the only two tenants on the fifth floor. I was the struggling actor, with a view of a street bordered with colored discarded doors where they were tearing down our neighborhood, just down from West 67th and Columbus, a space that would soon become Lincoln Center.

Just down the hall from me was Andre, (always tell your kids your stories when they're 8, and they will never forget a name).

Andre, an ancient black man, a retired hotel door man born in Haiti and raised in New York, had a view of the alley. We became friends. Because he had a working coffee maker and I did not. A visit to Andre's cluttered kitchen revealed three distinct items: framed pictures of Jesus and Franklin Delano Roosevelt and a calendar from a funeral parlor. An Irish Catholic boy felt right at home.

Whenever I came home late from work at the Waldorf Astoria, he was always there at the top of the steps, looking down, chuckling at the way I cursed each flight on the way up. He was waiting for me like I was his son or younger brother.

At first it was annoying, unless I had lost my key and buzzed Andre to let me in. After a bit, I kind of looked forward to seeing him up there waiting, like a father or mother leaning on the old dark brown scarred bannister. New in town, I had few friends and, like Andre, no family.

When I had a cold or flu, Andre would come over with soup or a peanut butter sandwich wrapped in a paper napkin from the Dew Drop Inn on 86th and Broadway. Andre seemed to have no one else. He said all of his friends had died long ago of booze or old age. Of one, he said the funniest thing I had ever heard, "He just lost the use of his self."

Andre, in his wisdom, taught me two things. The first was how to protect my larder from the ever present roaches and their storm trooper friends, the rats, by always putting everything edible in the "icebox." Rats and roaches increased every time another building came down.

Cereal and bread went in there, cupcakes stolen from the Waldorf kitchen, breadsticks stolen from the Italian cafe on Second Avenue. Everything.

The second lesson was how important America and its traditions were to him. When it came to Election Day, November 6th, 1956, (which I had to look up again) it was cold and miserable. I had the day off and had no plans to get out of bed. But Andre had been talking about it for months, and I knew how deadly serious he was. Luckily, I was a registered voter with absolutely no political sense at all.

I was reluctant to walk the eight or nine blocks to the voting poll, but there was Andre in his cap, looking to me like a hundred years old. Guilt won out, and I cast my vote for Adlai Stevenson, who was trampled by Dwight Eisenhower.

I've voted in every presidential election since, and like Andre, would never consider not doing so. Romney? Obama? Your business. Sitting it out? Remember the pictures of the Iraqi women who proudly held up their purple fingers in the Iraqi 2005 election, when polling place suicide bombings took the lives of 44 people who dared to vote. Think of 108-year-old Joanna Jenkins, a black woman from South Carolina, who most of her life, had been denied a chance to vote and just gave up. This year, 2012, Ms. Jenkins will cast her ballot for the first time, for Barack Obama. Think of Andre in his rainbow cap walking eight blocks in the snow with a dumb young actor. Vote.

Come Down With Me

A devastating tornado in Springfield, Massachusetts? Springfield? And this week, one spotted in Maine? What's going on here? Last year I wrote a column called "They're Coming," in which I predicted a mass diaspora of storm weary pilgrims from the Midwest. I predicted that huge numbers from California, weary of fretting about earthquakes, would soon seek solace in our green forestland. I proudly called New England the last safe place in America. Now I'm forced to eat those words with fava beans and a nice Chianti. I'm afraid New England has lost its glitter of safety. With El Niño and volcanic eruptions in a country I can't spell, it looks like this isn't going to be our father's summer.

With fear of tsunamis and nuclear crashes in California, plus the dreadful tornados in Alabama, Arkansas and my home state of Missouri, Americans don't know where to turn. In St. Louis, where the last of my living relatives still abide, a tornado ripped dangerously close to the ancestral estate, which I'm told now houses a new micro- brewery. These turns of events are particularly alarming because I fear long forgotten relatives will soon arrive "just to see the leaves turn" and stay the winter. Egad!

This fear was triggered when my baby sister emailed that cousin Owen, who has eight cats and collects swizzle sticks from bars to arrange them by color, asked her, "How is little baby Jerry and does he take cats?"

None of that is of concern today. Today I have to take action in the event that this week's mini-tornado is a portent of serious weather freak-outs to come. It can happen here.

We have in our spacious basement, and this is a true story, an actual root cellar. Neighborhood legend has it that the original builder meant it as a bomb shelter, constructed in the 50s. This was when we were all being taught how we could survive a nuclear blast by simply hiding under a wooden desk. This was at a time in America when our old Catholic school listed on the blackboard instructions for under-desk-hiding. Tools for survival included one orange, a diary, paste made from flour and water and a rosary. That may or may not be accurate.

This root cellar/shelter is at the end of a long dark concrete-encased hallway directly under the garage. It has a dirt floor and currently serves as a shelter for discarded building materials. I believe that this could survive a number 5 on the Fujita scale. This is not to be confused with the Toyota scale.

She, who scoffs at my fears, refuses to consider taking refuge down there, even though I said I would set up a chair and reading lamp for her. She has only been in the basement once or twice since we moved in. Once, when she came down to see the new state-of-the-art boiler, and once before when she came down to help me up when I stepped on a nail.

Jack, the dog, is a problem. He doesn't like going down there, even with me. Strangely, he will go down with a stranger, like the plumber or oil man. We need to book one of those in advance so that we can save Jack.

How long we might have to stay down there is a concern. What to bring down in terms of survival gear? I suggested canned goods, like baked beans that can be eaten cold. Should the hurricane strike at cocktail hour, I suggested to her that a nice brie and a couple of bottles of pinot noir would be a good idea.

At this point, she has taken to ignoring me. She even refuses to nod. Okay. She'll see. When the big one comes and sends our house to the sky, she can choose to play Dorothy- in-the-cabin with Toto, or survive to join me in welcoming Owen, his cats and swizzle sticks, after the deluge. Her call.

Got Your Permit?

I pride myself on always being the first to warn you, the reading public, when things are getting darker. Well, things are getting darker.

What with the Pope giving up his red shoes, the sequester threatening to bring down the economy, Anne Hathaway having problems with her Oscar Prada dress, and OMG, another near miss from a space rock, what's next?

Is it true what we hear, that murderers and drug addicts are at the door and under the bed? Is it a fact that there are modern perils Pauline never imagined? (If you're under 60, you can Google her.)

Things have gone so badly it seems, that thousands of Americans are applying for permits to GASP! carry a concealed weapon. Does that mean that some of those smiling folks I pass each day in the market place, neighbors down the street and teachers who teach our heirs are actually carrying concealed weapons?

So I gave myself some early time last afternoon, to stand in the produce section of my favorite market, and try to spot one or two of those who are "packing a Gat." That's Jimmy Cagney talk for gun, in case you're still in school.

I went about dropping a banana and the occasional avocado in my basket, while peering around the flower baskets to see if I could spot a "packer."

I'm old enough to have street creds in these matters. I learned from Cagney and Bogart how to spot them. In one such movie, Bogie said to a girl, "See that guy to the right? See how his coat hangs longer on that side? He's got a gun in there. A big one."

So as I drifted around the market, I kept my eyes open. There was a man with a big, baggy coat that hung unevenly to one side. You see? Bogie had it right. But I knew this guy. He's a florist. Florists don't carry concealed weapons. Do they?

Little things caught my eye and gave me a chill. The checkout lady, sweet, maybe in her fifties. I never noticed before, but she had a suspicious bulge in her left pocket. A cell phone? A handy bottle of Pepto Bismol? Who knows? It could be a collection of keys, or a .38 or a Glock, I don't blame her for being nervous and up to date. Some of these customers can be scary. She couldn't possibly know when one of them, outraged at the elevated price of a tomato, will suddenly "pull" on her.

There was a suspicious woman in the cereal aisle. But then I recognized her as a local retired nun. Yes, I could dismiss her based on that. But what if she's outraged at the Pope abandoning her? What if? Who knows what little thing could break her, and the next thing you know, she "pulls," and everyone in the cereal aisle starts diving into the oatmeal rack?

They've got a new customer at my favorite coffee shop, who keeps patting his pocket as his eyes flit from customer to customer. Is he waiting for someone he's terrified of? An ex-girl or boyfriend? What happens when they walk in? Will there be blood and extra venti double shot upside down skinny caramel macchiato, all over the place?

My barber appears nervous. He keeps a drawer near him slightly open. He keeps cash there. Who knows?

Driving home, I devised a plan. I'm going to apply for my concealed weapon permit. Just in case this newspaper or any paper prints a list of permit holders, I want my name on that list, so that any miscreant afoot will know, or think, which is just as good, that a gun lives in this house, a really big gun.

Absent the list, maybe they could make up some signs like those BEWARE OF THE DOG signs, only that say, "GUN PERMIT OWNER LIVES HERE." I would think that that would be enough to scare off the bad guys or girls. We could buy decals for the car, DON'T DRIVE SO CLOSE, DRIVER HAS GUN PERMIT."

Paranoia aside, do you think those red shoes will pop up on eBay? I'm just asking.

R.U. There, God?

There was a crack in the bottom of the Blessed Mother's blue dress. From that, on the small piece of stained glass inside the confessional, a thin piece of late afternoon sunlight broke through and fell directly across my face. Mary Lister told me that if you sat back away from it, Father Keating couldn't tell who you were as you recited your sins. Paddy Carr told us he thought Father had done that deliberately.

I went along with this for some time, right up until the day, after he absolved me of my sins, he said, "Tell your brother Jimmy, I want to talk to him about Mary Villa." So much for the security of darkness.

I always liked the confessional, and up until I started dating Rosemary DeBranco, she of the one thousand and one pastel-colored angora sweaters and simple strand of pearls, I really believed that God forgave my sins. All things pale in time.

I liked the box in a way because it was the coolest place in the church on hot St. Louis afternoons. I liked the way the velvet curtains soaked up and retained the smell of incense long after it had gone from the rest of the church. It was a peaceful place until the little sliding wooden door between myself and Father slid back with a chilling crack, much like the sound of a guillotine.

I even liked that stained glass picture of Mary and Jesus until I found out about the crack.

I'm told that most modern churches don't even have confessionals anymore. I find that sad. I've also heard that some parish priests don't even give last rites any longer. I find that scary. I was counting on that.

But despite the chaos that has gnawed at the edges of the church these past few years, I'm happy to tell you all that some churches are moving into the electronic age.

Harriet Barovick, of *Time* magazine, comes bearing good news for those too weary, too busy or afraid of Father Keating. Harriet tells us that we may all soon confess....on line. That's right, you heard it here. No more little shutters or broken stained glass windows, no more waiting in line in the aisle while other penitents watch you wondering what sins you will spill today.

Soon, you may check into sites like DailyConfession.com or GroupHug.us, and bare your soul to the lord or a reasonable facsimile. Now, these are, of course, secular sites not affiliated with the Catholic Church, but can Rome be far behind? Can the Holy See afford to isolate Catholics from the world of the internet? For the time being, Mother Church is staying clear of online confessions, declaring that the rite of confession demands a priest to achieve absolution. Still, the illustration heading Ms. Barovick's article features a woman holding a Catholic rosary draped around a black computer mouse.

I'm not sure any Catholic would be comfortable confessing to an online priest, even with assurances of privacy, even with a back and forth web camera. But stranger things have happened in the church since I sat in the confessional those many years ago. So don't count it out. We're busier and busier, working two and three jobs, saving on gas. Before long, the devout, facing icy streets and snow bound parking lots, may well succumb and power up for redemption. My advice to you all is to sit way back out of the light, wear a mask and disguise your voice. Repeat after me, "Forgive me father, for I have downloaded *The Wall Street Journal*."

Death Comes as a Friend

Dying is a very dull, dreary affair. And my advice to you is to have nothing whatever to do with it.
W. Somerset Maugham (1874 - 1965)

She was the ultimate professional. Bone thin, soft blonde hair tied back, fashionably dressed in a brown pinstriped suit, she ushered us up a long flight of carpeted stairs into a small office. She was cool and polite and nervous as though this were her first funeral arrangement. But it was obvious as she whispered out a long list of options, that she knew what she was doing. My wife listened carefully and glanced at the details on the paper in front of her. She looked at the numbers and words as if in a dream, one finger tracing the figures.

Knowing that I wasn't going to be making any financial decisions, I drifted off as undertaker lady talked. I kept staring at this small triangle of dappled sunlight seeping in from a corner window. It kept coming and going as small clouds passed over the sun. I kept thinking of something funny to say and when I did, undertaker lady did not laugh. It was not her place to laugh. This was serious business and no place for an old standup comic trying to get a laugh out of Death in the front row. And so I looked at the triangle of light.

How nice of God, I thought, to provide me with a metaphor for life here in a place where those deprived of it come to rest. This patch of sunlight, bright, thriving, full of solar energy, filling the wall with beauty, then suddenly gone. On the wall above it, there was a faded patch where a picture might once have hung.

As she spoke, her voice faded in my head and I thought of this old movie, "On Borrowed Time," where Cedric Hardwicke played "Mr. Brink," in fact, Death in human form who had come to collect Lionel Barrymore. He was so dapper, and had a soft soothing voice. But Pudd, Barrymore's young nephew wouldn't let go and trapped "Death" up in a tree. While he was up there, no one on earth could die. When Mr. Brink explained that all over the world people were suffering and waiting for him, Pudd let him down.

Yes, all over the world and right here in this room, people were suffering. My wife was suffering with a loss, but her pain is only one microscopic drop of the world's pain.

Unlike in the movies, where Death, usually portrayed as a suave, handsome Cary Grant Angel or Brad Pitt hunk comes in fast, Death often takes his time. It doesn't matter if he has been waiting in the shadows down the long, antiseptic halls of a hospital or nursing home, Death is in no hurry. Too often, there is too long a period of suffering, terrible pain and depression when the family has to watch and wait for that door to open, for that man with the soothing voice to arrive. But then, to their disappointment, he arrives like an angry hungry tiger, ravaging, scourging, leaving chaos in his path.

When my mother sat in a hospital room waiting to be allowed to see my father who had dropped on the street, she told me of watching a janitor mop a floor. She watched him as he went about his work, mopping and buffing while she waited for Cedric Hardwicke or Cary Grant to come in the door. All at once, she said, a door opened somewhere, and there was this sweep of cool air and then a doctor came down the hall. And it was over. Death as cool air.

And then when it seems we can't take anymore, it's over. One moment life is there like a triangle of late afternoon sunlight on the wall, and then Death arrives like a cloud, even a small puffy white cloud like those that hang over China Lake. Things go dark and then quiet and the patch of sunlight that is life is gone.

Undertaker lady's voice pulled me back. This was no movie. This was life. Death had been there and gone. There was no soft voice, just the sound of a dog barking next door, a siren far away, children playing in the park. My wife sat across the table going through the business of burying her brother. Her face looked drained and absent light, her shoulders slumped. An icon was being taken down from the wall of her life and put away. There would always be a faded patch where that icon once hung.

We would go to the priest and pick out a tune and the proper prayer. Her brother's name would be inserted in the appropriate place like one of those vanity children's books with your kid's name.

There would be the service with a church full of friends and relatives all wishing they were fishing or watching a movie or eating lasagna in Chicago, anyplace but here. This was not a happy place. A happy place is full of life. A happy place is a ball park on a hot day, a box full of sheepdogs, kids running through a hose in their back yard, not in church with an urn full of ashes on the altar.

But it happens. It will happen to all of us just like in the movies. To paraphrase Max Von Sydow in "Three Days of The Condor," "It will be a warm spring day...you will be walking along...a car will stop, someone will get out...someone you trust, a friend..." Yes. That would be nice. Death coming as a friend, stepping out of a car and smiling. Wouldn't it be pretty to think so.

An Apple a Day

Monday, March 1st. It is cold and rainy with heaps of dirty snow. I am sitting in the outer office of my new doctor. This is the typical doctor's office. The furniture is non-descript, rural Vermont with hardwood walls. The magazine rack contains lots of dog-eared magazines like *Arthritis Today* and *Your Liver*. I don't have arthritis, and being Irish, I avoid looking at my liver. On the wall there is a framed picture of the gastric system. I avert my eyes.

The receptionist is scary. Not that she is Nurse Ratchet or anything, she is just very business-like and suffers no fools. I made a doctor joke; it fell on the floor like someone with a brain seizure.

I had already gotten on her nerves by forgetting to bring in the proper insurance cards. If this all sounds like I was frightened you're right; in fact I was terrified; there's a reason for this.

Twenty-five years ago, I was having lunch with The Teacher and my daughters. I ate, no, wolfed down: two chili dogs, a slice of pizza, a dish of onion rings and a large Pepsi. On the way home I had a severe attack of what seemed to be a major combination heart attack-panic attack and alien possession. The Teacher rushed me to a doctor.

I was then tested; every test in the spectrum was given to me, including blood tests. I passed. That afternoon, the doctor called and said there were some things in the blood he didn't like and I would have to take them over. This was Friday. He said come in Monday. I was in a coma the entire weekend. I prepared a will; I was convinced I had two months to live.

It turned out that the abnormalities were "lab errors." But the damage had been done. I didn't see a doctor for another 25 years; whenever I was cast in television as a doctor, I declined.

JANUARY 1999: My daughter wakes me to say she has had a dream in which I die because I didn't go to the doctor. In addition, it seems that my age is a cut-off phase between robust devil-may-care good health and 76 life-threatening diseases. I call for an appointment.

I am ushered into his office. He is wearing The White Coat. I take deep breaths. He is pleasant; I try to make him laugh; he only smiles. I'm thinking he is related to the receptionist. He talks for forty minutes and then turns me over to a nurse. She gives me the first run-through. I find I am two inches shorter than I thought I was. This morning I was Gregory Peck; now I am Danny DeVito. I weigh ten more pounds than I thought. Scratch DeVito; make that Marlon Brando.

She wires me up like the monster in "Frankenstein" for the EKG. I ask her how it looks; she says the doctor has to look at it, she can't tell me. Swell. To somebody like me, that can mean only one thing: two months to live.

Doctor White Coat is back. He listens to every vein and checks every orifice I have. So far so good. Then he puts on the rubber glove. I know this part; I have been primed for it by every guy I know who has gone through this. This is known as the digital prostate examination. It's over in a minute and I'm thinking, "Gee, that's not so bad, all my fears of imprisonment were unfounded."

Now we're back in his office where we go through the list of questions I answered. Most were "No." He seems surprised that I've never been hospitalized. I explain that not only do I take eight vitamins a day and eat well, I don't ski, run, snowmobile, swim, fish, bungee jump, bowl or play any sports at all. I didn't learn to drive a car until I was 40 and almost never leave the house.

I added that as a precaution, I never shake hands in the winter and kiss only The Teacher. On New Year's Eve, we always leave the party early so as to avoid unnecessary smooching. As a rule, I haven't had a cold or a hickey in years. He looked at me like he wanted to call some attendants.

The next morning, I had the blood tests. I joked with the nurse by asking if she was going to use a clean needle; she was obviously related to the doctor and his receptionist. No laugh.

The doctor called me that evening and assured me that I was "just fine." I hope that's true. I suspect that no matter how I checked out, he and the receptionist weren't going to risk my coming back. Oh well, here's to the next 25.

Send in My Clown

I stopped reading the Google hits after about 15 pages. There were more than 900,000 of them. They came from all over the planet, from virtually every newspaper and television outlet in the world. His face was on the giant television screens in Tokyo, in Manhattan and Germany. On the blogs, there were pictures of him with the Clintons, the Bushes, and almost every major star in films. Dom DeLuise was dead.

Dominick DeLuise, a Brooklyn boy, son of Jennie and John, was born to a tradition he knew little about until he was a grown man and became part of that tradition.

The pages in the history of entertainment, of show business, are filled with funny men, comics of all sorts. But they are not all alike. There are the ironic comics like Dave Letterman and Lewis Black, who capture the zeitgeist of the time. They do the headlines, the scandals and news flashes.

There are the standup comics like Jerry Seinfeld, Chris Rock and Katt Williams, the late Rodney Dangerfield and Bill Maher. This kind of comedy, the kind that laughs at pain, grows out of the rich tradition of Jewish humor, the humor of the lost and defeated, beaten up and reviled but still standing humans. Henny Youngman was one of those, the great Lenny Bruce, Shecky Greene and Jackie Mason followed.

But Dom DeLuise came spilling out of that fabulous tradition of the Italian "Clown." Dom was the epitome of the clown, much like the late Red Skelton.

Dom's ancestors were the Italian clowns who entertained the Medici family, the popes and the poor, the Commedia dell'arte, Pantalone and Pulcinella.

Dominick DeLuise comes from these people.

Yes, the whole world knew Dom DeLuise, presidents and kings, movie stars and millionaires. But I own a little piece of that life, a piece that goes back to 1955, when Dom and I were young and funny and poor and hungry. It was at the Cleveland Playhouse where I had come to study under the GI Bill. It was there, scared and lonely and broke, that Dom DeLuise befriended me, taught me what he knew, loaned me money that he had borrowed from other people and gave me a corner of his dinky little apartment to sleep in. We lived on his spaghetti, onion rings and Carling's Black Label beer, cheap wine and love of the theater. I started writing a bit then, sketches and short plays. Dom always insisted that that was my real game.

We performed in dozens of plays together and went to Manhattan and started our careers.

Then our lives came to a fork in the road, and we went separate ways. Dom got a part in a movie and went to Hollywood, while I stayed in theater.

When I got to Hollywood, Dom was in the hands of the great Mel Brooks and skyrocketing to fame. We met from time to time, at parties and movie premieres. He was famous now, beyond famous. He was a comic star, a great clown. But he was always my friend. Dom never had an entourage like other comedians. He had his family and his friends. I was one of his first. He would always ask, "Are you writing yet?" The last time I saw him, he asked the same question.

Dom DeLuise has passed, but he is not dead. In this dark time when the world seems to vanish in smoke, I would add this stanza of Stephen Sondheim's great song for two old friends,

"Isn't it rich
are we a pair
me here at last on the ground
you in mid-air...where are the
clowns?.. send in the clowns."

Goodnight Dom wherever you are. I'm writing now.

"Vamonos," he said.

I turned left at his insistence, pulled up over a shady on ramp. On ramp? What was an on ramp, I thought. Suddenly, there in front of me was the Santa Monica Freeway, the Autobahn of Southern California, Death's Highway. I crawled to a stop, saliva dripping from the corners of my mouth. "Drive," he said. "Vamanos."

Fear of automobiles is in my DNA. My mother never drove a car. As a family, we never owned one. As a navy officer, my father had no use for cars and hated them.

I guess I inherited my father's fear, and grew up without one. We were a bus community, who needed one?

In high school, of course, this became a problem.
It's kind of embarrassing to take a girl to the movies on the bus, expensive too, you have to pay her fare. So I made a practice of selecting close friends who had access to family cars.

This is not as bad as it sounds. Rosemary DeBranco, she of the one thousand and one pastel Angora sweaters and simple strand of pearls, always had the back seat where moonlight became her and went with her hair.

I proceeded to grow up in large major cities with great public transportation. No problem. No one in Manhattan had a car. Dating was a subway thing. No problem.

When she, who had her license early on, and I got married and moved to Los Angeles, things got stickier. We bought a cheap white car of suspicious origin. I'm not sure what make it was.

When, inevitably she grew weary of driving me from studio to studio for auditions and jobs, she insisted on teaching me to drive.

First day out in the San Fernando Valley, with myself behind the wheel, feeling exhilarated, I cruised down a side street. I got confused. I hit the wrong pedal. "Stop," she said. I hit the pedal. Wrong pedal. In desperation, I ran over a curb and broke a small tree in half. An entire Mexican family of about twelve siblings rushed out. I had killed their tree. My semi-Spanish-speaking wife explained to them that I was a beginner. They seemed unimpressed until the father spotted my St. Genesius medal. With the mixture of her Spanish and my brazen display of faith, the situation was resolved. But that was the deal breaker.

We bought a new car and she, who now feared for her safety and that of her children, insisted I get professional help. This was the Southern California School of Driving.

For weeks before my first lesson, I would sit in the very back seat of the bus and mimic the moves of the driver, left turn, right turn, etc. I was 43 years old and playing "driver" like a child.

The morning of my first lesson, I could not eat or drink lest I throw up in my instructor's lap. At 9:00 a.m. he arrived, a courtly Mexican gentleman named Jesus. A comforting sign. He was patient and polite, smiling and gentle. He seemed stunned at first that a healthy man of my years had never driven, but assured me that he had had students much older.

He put me behind the wheel, and off we went, cruising down a busy La Cienaga Boulevard. With his encouragement, I executed perfect lane changes, gave proper signals. I felt so secure.

"Take your next left," he said. I saw the big green and white sign that I had seen many times before, but now it was personal. HOLLYWOOD FREEWAY.

"That's the freeway," I said.

"Good," he smiled, "You know how to read, that's a good sign."

"I'm not ready for the freeway...am I? We'll soon know."

I paused at the edge of a rushing blur of cars all at which seemed to be going 800 mph.

"What are you waiting for?" he asked.

"A break."

"There are no breaks," he laughed. "Vamonos."

"What?"

"Drive," he said, and then he made the sign of the cross.

There we were, flying through the smog, both laughing and screaming "Vamonos." At last, I was a driver, excited, a bilingual new middle-aged driver. Thank you, Jesus, both of you.

Third Mass of the Year

I'll be in church this morning. Behold this silver-haired devil in the pink checked shirt with blue summer blazer and pale blue tie dotted with pink flamingos and thin titanium-framed, violet-tinted shades propped up like a corpse in a western saloon display, still waiting for God. Style is everything, is it not?

That would be me in one of the pews at the back of the theater. I always arrive a bit late as I've long ago memorized the opening act. The lighting leaves something to be desired, but I won't complain lest I anger the producer. It's a Lebanese Maronite church full of the descendants of "Men of Sidon," a Semitic people the Greeks called Phoenicians because of the purple dye they sold at market. I repeat: Style.

I will be dozing next to she who still closes her eyes when she prays and occasionally bumps her knee against mine when I keep mine closed too long, which means I'm dangerously close to letting my head fall back with my mouth open. That would put an end to my attendance.

There are three masses a year I never miss out of respect for she who enables me to buy pink flamingo ties at Brooks Brothers, Easter, for the reasons noted above, Mother's Day, for the same reason, and Christmas, because, well, it's Christmas.

I stopped going to church as a weekly thing, years ago. It happened like this: One bright Sunday I was walking to a local church and as I approached the door, something snapped in me, and I threaded my way through the pilgrims and kept walking. No one tried to stop me or even seemed to miss me, so I kept walking. And that was how I recaptured my childhood compulsion to walk.

Now, in the twilight of my years, I walk two miles a day except for days full of big wind or freezing rain or after an ice storm. My friends who have meaningful jobs keep nudging me to join a gym, one of those places full of nubile creatures with lots of exposed flesh. I refuse. To me, a treadmill is a spiritual dead zone. There is no real air around it, and what there is smells of perfumed sweat from the nubility. They provide big television screens, but they're too far away to see and hear.

I need to be out in the air where I can pick up vibes from the creatures who are sprinkled along my route. It's the same route I've walked for 27 years, and some would think that would be boring. It's not. Depending on the season or the way it changes the time of day and the play of light on the street, it can be mesmerizing.

I walk through a village of older ladies, widows mostly, who check their mail three times a day and wave at me from their tiny windows. I've sort of adopted one whom I call "Meme" out of respect for her French accent. One day I startled her when her back was turned as she plucked a tuft of weeks.

"Oh! It's just you," she gasped. "You're early...I wasn't expecting you." Imagine. She expected me. I had become part of her day. She only knows me from these pages and my passing her door each day. I knew then that love from proper strangers is a perfumed joy that only an aging spirit can smell.

I won't walk this morning. It's a nice day, but it's Easter, one of the three days. This morning I get to dress up like a Manhattan dandy and listen to the Mass recited in Aramaic, the language Jesus spoke. I don't understand a word of it of course, but when the entire Lebanese congregation sings in those words, I sing along with gusto. Sometimes I imagine Jesus himself standing in the corner applauding and commenting, "Nice try."

In a Magic Castle

Once upon a time there was a magic castle where everyone laughed and no one cried. It was full of magical people in great clothes and makeup. There were dancers and comics, artists and writers, big bright lights and halls full of music and musicians. It was called the NBC studios, a big complex out in Burbank, California, a slumbering, smoggy town over the hill from Hollywood. The NBC studios at that time housed The Tonight Show, Dean Martin's show, Laugh In Comedy Hour and the Jerry Lewis Sunday Night Comedy Hour. Everybody laughed, nobody cried.

Long before I, young and skinny, with lots of black hair and bravado, went to work on all of those shows in comedy bits and even writing comedy in the basement, I landed the best possible beginner job you could have. A friend got me a union card with the International Alliance of theatrical stage employees as an all-around "grip." Grips do everything. They handle lights and move furniture, supply props. They work with lighting directors and sound men. They do everything. It's a great job for struggling actors, because you're always around the people who can make your career.

My first job was buffing the floor of Johnny Carson's Tonight Show after hours. So at one in the morning, after I had finished the buffing, I found myself all alone on the Tonight show set. I sat in Johnny's chair and then moved to the guest seat and pretended I was the guest. Then I moved to the dead microphone and did a few minutes of improvisational jokes. It was fantasy land. I could hear the laughter and the applause of the audience. Then there was this chuckle and big booming voice. Out of the darkness came Ed McMahon, all made up with a makeup towel around his neck. He had a drink in his hand and a big warm smile on his face.

"Hiya kid, you the guy with the buffer?" he asked. Oh God, I thought, I'm going to get fired. "Could you do me a favor and hold off a second? We're finishing shooting a promo spot over in the corner, we'll be out of your way in a minute," he said. Ed McMahon, the best second chair in the business was willing to be "out of my way in a minute."

I watched from the shadows as he shot a last minute Budweiser commercial. When he finished, I clapped for him, and he lifted his glass to me and he and the crew vanished.

Six months later, I had my first NBC gig as an actor. I was hired, honored really, to be one of the "Mighty Carson Art Players," a tiny comedy support team for whatever skit the writers came up with. With a cast that included the late Peter Lawford, I played a pirate on a mock-up ship that "Captain Carson" took over. I had one line, a feeble one about how a lobster bit my toe off, but it got a big laugh from the audience and one of those laughs came from Ed.

Afterwards, he came up to me and complimented me on my laugh and said, "You look so familiar, haven't we worked together before?"

"I think we did," I answered. "It was...." and then someone called him away. I was glad I didn't have to tell him the truth, that I was the buffer boy who did him a favor once.

I saw Ed many times after that when I was down the hall working with Dean Martin and then Jerry Lewis. I would pass him in the hall or see him in the makeup room. He always laughed and asked, "How's the toe, kid?"

Everything you read about Ed McMahon this week is true. He was everyone's buddy, a down to earth all around good guy no matter what your job. And he had a big generous laugh for everyone, no matter how great or small.

Once upon a time there was a magic castle where everyone laughed and no one cried. That's changed today, but just for today. Goodnight Ed wherever you are. Thanks for the laugh.

Fat Fat Fat

Having watched Paul Newman, a man a decade older than I, move about with a spider's grace in the recent "Empire Falls," I took to reading health magazines that all asked these questions:

Feeling run down? Is it getting harder to make it to the fridge? Is the indention in the sofa permanent? Does the little woman look away in disgust when you emerge dripping wet from the shower, resembling nothing less than an East Indian water buffalo?

Have you a stack of slacks in your closet that just won't snap together anymore?

Perhaps you've taken to wearing your shirts outside the belt? (I know you see pictures of models in New York doing it, but you're not a model, and that's not why you're doing it, and you know it.) You're fat. She's fat, we're all fat.

You're wearing stretch pants year round and velour "leisure" mob suits, even to church. When people stop to chat, their eyes go immediately to your gut. You wear a lot of black, even on tennis courts, which makes you look like a Ninja player.

Every major magazine is after you to change as though you were a felon of some kind. You've become a social misfit. Even McDonald's doesn't want you anymore. They're trying to sell you fruit salads. McDonald's for pity's sake.

All the health magazines run articles now about the BMI (body mass index). Anything above 25, it tells us, is considered overweight. Anything above 30, is (gasp) OBESE. In a recent test, I was shocked to find that I had put on a few pounds. In fact, I am dangerously close to...well...unattractive.

Once, I could look in the mirror and see a young Cary Grant looking back. Now, I see Tony Soprano. All I need is the navy velour leisure suit, Velcro snap sneakers, some gold chains and I'd be a "made" man.

This is an American obsession that stops at the border. Mexico's obesity is growing. Russia is said to be the worst, with Germany close behind in pounders. Italy could care less and France it seems, despite its fatty diet, is the thinnest in Europe. That doesn't carry over to the French in Central Maine which is another story we won't go into.

It should be of small comfort to us that we here in Maine are not the fattest people in New England. The "summer people" from away are here on our beaches and in our markets, and I'm here to tell you, they're big, REALLY big, with tsunamis of flesh cascading over pink shorts as they waddle down the bread and cake aisle. You won't find these flat-landers in the veggie sections. They're here for killer carbs, filling their baskets with that camp food, ravioli stuffed with chocolate and jelly, lots of meat, white bread and take-out slabs from Dunkin' Donuts.

In a small unscientific poll I conducted by listening to accents and following them out to their cars and checking plates, Massachusetts is the heaviest on the BMI register.

Rhode Island and New Hampshire come in second, and New York is varied. Queens is high on the seismic table, Manhattan is lower. (You have to check dealer's decals to get to the truth.)

So I have set myself the goal of losing 25 pounds by Halloween. At that time, I will emerge from this chrysalis of flesh, tanned, trim, and Cary Grant-ish. Stay tuned for my leisure suit and Velcro sneaker lawn sale. Paul Newman, watch out.

One Wafer - Hold the Wheat

We were all dressed in sparkling clean white suits and dresses, as clean as our immortal souls would ever be again. It was First Communion Day at St. Mary and Joseph's on Minnesota Ave. Roosevelt was in the White House. God, we hoped, was in Heaven.

Sister Rosanna repeated the words of Jesus at the last supper, "This is my body and my blood, do this in remembrance of me." This was a big deal. It was even bigger to Mary Lister, the girl who gave me my first Valentine, who took everything, except me, very seriously.

Haley Waldman, an 8-year-old girl from Brielle, New Jersey, takes it seriously too. You may have read about Haley recently. This is the little girl who suffers from Celiac disease, a serious condition that hits the small intestine and kicks up a fuss when the body ingests the tiniest bit of wheat. It affects 1 in 133 people. There is wheat in the communion wafer and there the story begins.

Haley's diocese has steadfastly refused to offer her communion.

Catholic Canon 924, for those of you who may not have read it, says communion must be celebrated with bread and wine and that "the bread must be made of wheat alone." Was the original host, a matzoh, unleavened bread made with wheat? Who knows?

They say they're sorry about Haley, but as one priest said, "Rules are rules and they're coming from Rome." Another priest in sublime arrogance said, "I get the sense this mother is a little stubborn."

You bet your collar she is, Father. She is an American woman and she doesn't care what Rome has to say about her daughter. This is an American woman who didn't abort her two children and has raised them in her faith and is trying to live a good life, even without the total support on this matter, of her ex-husband, who claims she is "doing this partly to get attention for herself." What a guy.

Last spring, Mrs. Waldman got Haley all dressed up in her little white dress just like Mary Lister's. She got wheat free wafers from a Seattle company. But the priest, citing the Vatican's rules, said he could not offer the sacrament. No soy or tofu allowed.

So tough little Mrs. Waldman got a good priest "just down the road," to perform the ceremony in private, but word leaked out and Bishop John M. Smith of the Diocese of Trenton declared little Haley's first communion invalid.

Now remember, this affair went all the way to the Vatican where the Pope sleeps, and back. No deal, was the word. Even though nowhere in the bible is wheat specified.

This from the Catholic Church that is hemorrhaging communicants, losing priests and property. This from the church with hundreds of its priests indicted for heinous acts against its children going back decades, with some priests in prison and a once noble faith shamed.

This from the Pope who is about to canonize the late Emperor Charles 1st of Austria, whose troops used poison gas on the allies in World War 1. The miracle attributed to him? The healing of a nun's varicose veins. Are you screaming yet?

So little Haley, a tabula rasa in white linen, is barred from sharing that which in her faith is considered a sacred rite. Her church is telling her that what Jesus meant was, "This is my whole wheat body and blood. Thou shall not use any other bread." Christians are fond of asking, "What would Jesus do?" Ask again. Operators are waiting.

Book for a Buck?

Never mind the cicadas. They only come every 17 years. Forget earth warming, climate change, Benghazi, the IRS, those are Obama's problems. In time the Rockies may crumble, Gibraltar may tumble, they're only made of clay, but garage sales, like our love, are here to stay. Unlike our love however, there is no sweetness there.

From Gardener to Hallowell, Sidney to Fairfield, we pass them on a Saturday morning, they look like fun, like miniature carnivals or European street fairs, sans the Ferris wheels and carousels.

Look at the smiling faces, the tinkle of their laughter. It's all fake, an evil facade. Garage sales are the work of Satan.

See the "antique" bird cage. They probably got it at TJ Maxx in Bangor and then the bird died. They're asking more for it than they paid. Sales, like love, are for the very young.

Once you are on the far distant shores of Medicare, garage sales are nothing more than pre-heart attacks, slipped discs, hernias and headaches.

She, who snubs garage sales and never allows us to stop on weekend mornings, sings quite another tune when it comes to her. All winter, through the long night storms and dreary ice bound driveway days, she chortled about our forthcoming spring/retirement/final garage sale plans. She has been planning this for years. She genuinely feels that the twenty bucks we'll get for a mirror will see us through to the nursing home.

Through the year, whenever she's between books or finished with paper grading, she drags me from room to room pointing out future sale items. Her favorite line is "People are looking for these all the time," or "You can't find these anymore and watch how they sell." Right.

Of course they won't, or at least nowhere near the price she writes on the little yellow tags she bought at CVS.

She's started hauling out books. She seems to think that just because she paid twenty five bucks for a best-selling novel, that someone will pay five or ten bucks for it. They won't, I explain. It's an old book, just an old book to them. People who go to garage sales want big bargains, they won't pay more than a buck for a book, unless it's autographed by Stephen King or someone dead.

We've had garage sales in the past, and they always turn out the same way. The day before, I am dispatched to nail signs on light poles all over the neighborhood. We have already paid to put an ad in the papers that say "Starts at 9 a.m. No dealers."

At 7 a.m., the first dealers arrive and sit in their cars blocking the driveway, so that the average Joe looking for a dollar best seller can't get in. So we have to get up, because Jack won't stop barking until we do.

Then, in my robe, I open the garage doors and start hauling out the assorted junk I spent the day before setting up.

Throughout the day, providing it doesn't rain, the hordes of bargain hunters will come and go, including a best friend who gave us an item ten years ago, and that I will have to rush to grab and hide when I spot him coming up the driveway.

When all are gone, I'll drag the junk back in, despite her pleas to stay open for one more hour to catch the "late comers." The only "late comer" is always a large woman in Kitty pajama pants and slippers who comes back to see if we reduced the price on the used slippers. I give them to her for free, without mentioning that I could not get all the doggie poop off the bottoms.

As I close the garage doors, she, the Garage Sale Queen for a day, will be sitting in an unsold antique chair, reading a twenty five dollar best seller everyone passed up for the five dollar tag. This night we will go out to dinner and spend the fifty two dollars and 87 cents we made. The 87 cents was for a best seller.

A Gathering of the Bans

Q: If two city councilors leave Waterville City Hall at the same time, walking at the same speed but by different routes, which one will get to You Know Whose Pub first? And if they arrive at the same time, does that constitute a meeting?

A: Not if they wear sunglasses and sit at separate tables. Tapping out Morse code on drinking glasses would not be permissible.

It seems that while I was distracted by the vigilante lynching of Bill Clinton in Washington, our city has slipped subtly into madness. Has this something to do with La Niña? Is it the humidity or lack of it? Is there something in the water?

Apparently this all started when local real estate tycoon Charles Kellenberger charged that some councilors were meeting illegally at a local restaurant and pub. Kellenberger is clearly a local boy and has never lived or experienced politics in a big city, like Boston, Chicago or St. Louis.

All of these cities, and many like them, have bistros and assorted watering holes that are like second homes to the local pols. Lawyers and cops, councilors, judges and defendants, sooner or later wind up noshing ribs and cole slaw elbow to elbow in these digs.

In a few of the cities that I'm familiar with, where the pols are all Irish or Italian men and women of high moral standing, officials would never dream of discussing the public's business. And Nicole Brown Simpson was murdered by Martian underwear salesmen.

It was suggested that it would be a problem if the councilors met in places that discouraged the public from attending, such as in a restaurant or pub. How about a Lions Club production of Parsifal?

A church or school would be appropriate City Solicitor William A. Lee suggested. I've seen the lunch fare at a few of these schools, and it would discourage me I'll tell you.

A bar is out of the question as the public is expected to buy something. That definitely leaves the entire South Side of Chicago and most of Brooklyn off limits.

"You could go and have sandwiches together as long as the public's business is not discussed," Lee offered. Well, now we're getting into James Bond country.

"What'll you have?"

"I'll have the pastrami on rye."

"I'll have ham on whole wheat."

"Now about that bridge thing ..."

Fingers fly to lips. Eyes circle the room. Shoulders hunch and pencils scribble on napkins.

"Good idea ...," it's whispered," but do you want fries with that ... off-ramp?"

Councilor Carol Ann Olsen, R-Ward 3, suggested that many of the councilors are friends. Former Mayor Ruth Joseph would certainly attest to that. This is why, Olsen claimed, they met for sandwiches after council meetings. Olsen also wondered if they could order out? Now we're talking.

So the councilors could order Chinese takeout and discuss business right there. Olsen orders egg roll from column B and Halle opts for chow mein from column A but hold the peanut sauce. Why not pizza you may ask? Good question. Meanwhile the citizen viewers sit there salivating while acting Mayor Tibbets and City Councilor Dana W. Sennett, D-Ward 4, split an extra-large pizza with anchovies. I'm liking this more and more. I may run in the next election.

To add a Perry Mason flourish, Councilor John M. Fortier, R-Ward 5, pointed out that he could not have been at the contested meeting at the Pub because he was vacationing on St. Martin with his wife.

So now the locals, who can't afford an extra-large pizza or Chinese take-out, are sitting there nursing grumbling stomachs, while being told that their elected official is getting a tan in the islands while they shovel snow. The Bolshevik Revolution started over something very much like this.

It is January and slippery slopes are not uncommon. This is one of them. Pretty soon, glee clubs and theater groups will have to sneak around to discuss their business. They used to all gather at the Pub. But it's clear that politics and pommes frites don't mix.

"I don't know why she got the part...I was so much better."

"Shhhhh, there's the director and his wife."

"That's not the director ... that's Joe Blow the city councilor."

"Is he having a meeting?"

"No ... and that's not his wife ... that's his girlfriend."

"Thank goodness ... I wouldn't want that mess started up again."

A Day to Remember

It's here again. As I write this it's here, and as you read this, it's over. It's Saint Patrick's feast day, that day when the first born on American soil celebrated by cooking up corned beef and cabbage, and when my grandfather slammed his beer glass down on the bar at Skeeter O'Neil's and shouted, "Tell me again just exactly who it was who could afford corned beef?"

Yes, we're an angry lot and cynical. No matter how happy we are, we know tears are to come. No matter how happy the story, we know it's going to have a bad ending. Daniel Patrick Moynihan wiped his eyes at Jack Kennedy's grave site and said, "There's no point in being Irish if you don't know the world is going to break your heart eventually." And then there was Bobby and then there was Teddy and we knew he was right.

The present generation of Irish, the connected, the wired, the smart phoned, sun glassed, big screened descendants of O'Casey, Behan and Beckett, have mostly lost their purity. As for myself, there were nine of us once with this ancient name, blessed or cursed with nothing but green blood in our veins and lots of song and beer in the house. It was an old house built by old men, one full of singing and fighting, crying and laughing, and one by one we passed along until there are three of us left with that ancient madness in our brains. The great Edna O'Brien said it better than I can.

"You are Irish, you say lightly," she said, "and allocated to you are the tendencies to be wild, wanton, drunk, superstitious, unreliable, backward, toadying, and prone to fits, whereas you know that in fact a whole entourage of ghosts resides in you." Gimme an Amen.

The Irish, as America came to know, love, hate and pity, are gone now to their Irish Jesus. O'Neil, Cagney, O'Brien, Tracy, Fitzgerald, Crosby, Flaherty. All gone.

This new generation, blood thinned and blessedly washed clean of these ghosts, knows nothing of what Moynihan said. Few read the history of their blood if they read at all, and they have no one left to remind them of whence we came, of the floating caskets that washed us up here and why we left.

There is no one to remind them of the women who died on the way to Cobh, with grass stained lips and babies dead at their breasts, and why should they? It's Saint Patrick's Day-2012, a day to celebrate.

There are parades somewhere and green beer and river water and the occasional Mass for the dead, and you can see that there are few who will get up this morning for Mass after "the day," with swollen heads full of Celtic thunder.

There are no more of those old men who put on the funeral suit and joined their families in the pews and lay their foreheads against the polished wood, pretending to say their beads while simply fighting sleep. Those were men who brought the bacon and potatoes home, who walked the streets with badges and night sticks, who fought fires and worked long hard hours in breweries and coal mines and only wore on Sundays, the clean white shirt.

I was born just as the old ones passed on the memories to the first generation of American children. I was lucky enough to hear their last wishes and write them in my heart, promising their ghosts never to forget what it means to be pure Irish. My mother once had a list of family names to recite at Easter mass for the dead, Devine, Brady, Conlon, O'Reilly, McNamara, Kelleher, McCann and Egan. Bits of all of them float in my veins and inform the way I view the world. This day I lift my glass to them all and thank them for the memories. Slainte.

God's House for Sale

The late great departed American comic Lenny Bruce, famously said, "Every day people are straying away from the church and going back to God."

I'm reminded of Lenny's prophecy this morning, upon learning that Catholic churches in Central Maine are closing faster than storm doors in a blizzard. Some say, "It's the economy, stupid." That's ironic considering that it's the economy that drives most Catholics to grab their rosaries and fill the pews. Lack of attendance is the biggest reason. At a local church I attended on Mother's Day with she, whom I suspect knows all the names of the twelve apostles and their cell phone numbers, I counted roughly 48 heads, mostly grey and nodding. There were two young kids there, but they were altar boys. If a movie drew that size of a crowd it would close on opening night.

It comes as even sadder news for the aging French Catholics in Waterville, to learn that their ancestral church, St. Francis on Elm Street, is not only closed, but is being torn down. At least it will be replaced by a new building housing low income elderly. Low income elderly? It's 2011. Is there any other kind?

A shortage of priests is mentioned. A study by the National Conference of Catholic Bishops claims that there are more priests over 90 than under 30. We always knew that. That's why we say "Father," and not "Buddy."

My old friend Sister Jane Behlmann, archivist of the Sisters of St. Joseph of Carondelet, emails me that the church where I was baptized, and where an entire generation of Devine boys and girls confessed their sins, memorized the act of contrition and got married, is now officially out of business. It's been adopted by another parish, St. Stephens, and will be run only as an oratory, i.e. "a small chapel for private worship." This is a punch in the heart for the sisters there, because it comes on the 175th anniversary of the order.

All over America, many churches, particularly Catholic churches, are closing their doors. We noticed this trend coming a long time ago. When I first came to Waterville 27 years ago, I stopped by the Sacred Heart Church on Pleasant Street to "pay a visit." This is a nice old Catholic tradition treasured mostly by the old folks and actors. Actors, being natural sinners and forced to spend a good deal of the day on the street making the rounds of casting agents in search of a job, found it comforting to drop in at St. Patrick's or other neighborhood churches to "pay a visit," catch a nap or rub the sore tootsies and get warm.

But when I tried the doors of Sacred Heart, I found them locked. Locked? I was told that all the local church doors were locked now because of vandalism and theft, and that someone had once tried to start a small fire at the altar, some poor soul, I imagine, with a skewed sense of karma. So if Lenny got it right, and God, like Elvis, "has left the building," the faithful will be forced to converse directly with God at home, work and on the streets of the agora.

When I gave up jiggling the handles on church doors in vain, I dropped away. Now, when she, who'd rather chew olive pits than miss Sunday Mass, drives off, I stay home and do the housework, keeping in mind what my beloved Sister Rosanna used to say when I balked at cleaning the blackboards, "Offer it up to Jesus," she would say.

So here I am this Sunday morning polishing the furniture and cleaning the bathrooms. Hello God? It's me, Jerry, and I'm out of Comet cleanser.

Smile, You're Googled

If I had known they were coming, I would have had the lawn cut earlier. It looks shabby, the trees look under trimmed. Thank God I brought the trash cans up earlier, the ones with my number and name painted on them in big white letters. Actually, the new roof photographed well.

Too late. Nobody knows when they're coming. They're just...there. It can be at any time, any hour. I thought I was safe here. Now my castle in Maine is on Google. I'VE BEEN GOOGLED.

You probably didn't want to know this. But here it is. Smile, you too are on Google Camera.

There is a new player on the street, literally on the street, with a new toy. It's called "Google Street View," a feature of Google Maps and Google Earth, and it's taking your picture, well, it's taking your house's picture and hopefully, you're not out there in your underwear. Did you wash the windows? It's too late. The system was launched in May of '07 and only in five American cities. You thought nobody saw you sneaking that Big Mac at McDonald's? Sorry, you've been Mac-Googled. You know that suspicious Chevrolet Cobalt you saw on West River Road a couple of summers ago when you were parked with your best buddy's girlfriend? Remember me warning you about the Toyota Prius with the camera mounted on the front and back? That's the one.

Google Street View is a sister of Google Maps and Google Earth, providing 360 degree horizontal and 290 degree vertical panoramic street level views of your neighborhood. That's right. Check it out. But it's too late now. Whatever you've been doing out there, Google may have it all on the internet. You've been busted.

This stuff has long-term ramifications. Imagine you're on the Government Witness Protection System. You've changed your name from the gangster handle to an Irish one and you're feeling safe. Then one day you're out on the driveway in your Tony Soprano white terry cloth robe and CLICK! You're busted. Remember what Butch Cassidy asked Sundance? "Who are those guys?"

They're Googlemen. Yes, the Googlemen are coming, and you and your front porch have been...GOOGLED.

This has not been without its headaches for the billion dollar company. This year, one of their street view camera cars hit and killed a deer in upstate New York. Before long, the street level pics were mysteriously lifted from the site.

If you're curious and wondering how that new paint job looks to the rest of the world, and I mean, the entire rest of the world, you can go on Google Street View right now and download your street, follow the white arrows all around everywhere and cruise right past your house. Whoops! What's that? Your dog is dumping on your neighbor's lawn. Sorry. You've been busted. Don't worry. Google doesn't care. To Google, you're just another Googelite, a Googled nobody, a face in the Google crowd.

Yet, a couple in Pittsburgh tried. Poor saps. They claim it diminished the value of their home, and they sued Google for $25,000 for "grossly reckless invasion of their seclusion." Sadly for the couple, a judge ruled against them. You can't boogle with Google. Forget it Jake, it's Googletown.

Don't worry. It's been completed. But, like crab grass, they can come back. So, keep the lawn mowed and the house painted, and whatever you do, keep your dog tied up. You've been Googled.

Haunted Home Room

We were walking by the old Waterville High School in falling snow, growing darkness and a high wind. My walking partner, an ancient graduate, sniffed, pulled his woolen hat down over his ears and grumbled, "They can call it Gilman Apartments, Gilman Plaza, Gilman Tropical Gardens, it's still the old Waterville High. I couldn't wait to get out of there. Why would anyone want to go back?"

I listed the virtues of living in-town and how people loved the splendid accommodations and fabulous views. He would have none of it. "I heard that it's haunted," he said. Most would scoff at this idea, but then most don't believe in ghosts and haunted buildings. I do. He said a passerby had seen a crying boy in a basketball uniform looking out of one of the top windows.

"Probably that kid in my class who blew the tying basket shot and lost the championship."

She, who is a practiced and I suspect, licensed "scoffer," leaves the room when I try to tell her about this. I pointed out to her that I read somewhere on line that there is an old haunted high school in Austin, Texas, where a Spanish teacher roams the halls late at night. I thought this would be of interest to her as she is a Spanish teacher.

She informed me that if it's late at night, "she's not a teacher, unless she didn't get her papers done before she died." She went back to correcting her papers and refused to consider it further. I knew she was going to say that. Before she fell asleep last night, I asked her if she would like to have one of those swell apartments down there. "Not if it's haunted." I knew then that I had made a dent in her "Scofferness."

My sister in St. Louis emailed me that they're talking about doing the same thing with my old school down there. She said that if I decided to really retire instead of playing at it, and if I got tired of the cold, I could come home and get a swell loft there. "It's up where you used to sneak out with Rosemary DeBranco," she said. I wrote and asked if she had heard anything about the school being haunted. I got an out-of-office reply.

Curious, I researched on line, and it's a fact that paranormal occurrences happen all the time in "re-fitted" buildings, like former schools, convents and churches. This leads me to worry about Waterville's plan to tear down the old French St. Francis Church and build low cost housing for seniors.

Urban planners, not always a paranormal-sensitive bunch, don't realize that just because the building is gone, nothing changes. The ghosts are still hanging around. To those in my clan, we know it's because they now have nowhere to go, no rooms to haunt or dishes to rattle.

The ghosts are now homeless and in all the world of the supernatural, there's nothing worse than a homeless ghost. They're going to float around and make trouble.

In New York, many years ago, while waiting for a personal reading in a fortune teller's shop, I came upon an article about this small town in Mississippi that had "floating" ghosts. Urban renewal had torn down some old "haunted" mansions. The "homeless" ghosts went about extinguishing streetlights, "flickering" marquees and disrupting traffic lights. Homeless ghosts. I'm just saying.

I wouldn't be surprised that before long tenants of the Gilman Apartments begin hearing basketballs being bounced in the middle of the night, seeing chalk dust on the floor, and hearing running in the halls. They may even hear sobbing in those areas where the locker bays once stood. Many hearts were broken in those halls in days gone by. No matter how swell those apartments are, they will lose their charm when tenants begin smelling that awful lunch time cooking. Those lunchroom ladies die hard.

Heroes in the Shadows

It's my favorite line: "Why don't you go back to Hollywood and your rich movie star friends?"

How often I get this. As if that was what my life, or any working actor's life in Hollywood was about.

The truth is I never had one "rich movie star "friend" in my entire life in Hollywood. Yes, I drank vodka with David Jansen, coffee with Burt Reynolds and Dennis Weaver. They did not invite me for Thanksgiving and haven't returned my calls yet.

You know the Oscars. You know Clint and Uma, but the Hollywood nobody knows is much different. It's about 98 percent of The Screen Actors Guild who are unemployed at any given time.

But it's also about the real workers, the grunts behind the scenes, the men and women the movie makers depend on to get the daily job done.

These are members of a strong American union, the International Alliance of Theatrical Stage Employees, local 80, with a membership of over 105, 000. I was proud to be one of them.

That union card saved my butt more times than I can count. The Screen Actors Guild provides many benefits. Employment is not one of them.

At the bottom of my career, with a small family to feed, a good friend of mine got me a job as a grip on the old Dean Martin show which led to another and another at $50 bucks a day. In l970 that was gold.

I became a "grip," a job description that covers a lot of sweat work.

There are all kinds of grips, those who hold the mic booms, adjust the lights, build the sets, cart the costumes from truck to set. They work long hours building scaffolds and flooring. They create gardens in the desert, spray sweat on Leonardo DiCaprio.

They earn from $19.00 to $23.00 hourly and I mean they earn it. Long timers make as much as $1,374 and often the jobs are handed down in the family like antiques or houses. As a grip, I've worked with grandfathers who worked next to their sons and their sons. It's a hard union to break into.

Their hands are callused, sometimes bleeding. They stand on 75-foot structures in high winds holding a boom. It's not for sissies.

These are working Americans, not pampered movie stars and I was proud to be one of them. I have huddled in the rain and the snow with them, drank coffee in the back of trucks in freezing temperatures.

With big strong union men and women, I unloaded trucks and ran for props and waxed floors and delivered last-minute script changes.

These are not liberal elitist personalities. They are never invited to be on "Hard Ball" or "60 Minutes." They have families and they save their money. They don't live in Bel Air or Beverly Hills, but just like you do, in mortgaged homes with big electric and medical bills.

Some of them, lucky enough and talented enough at their jobs, become favorites of big directors. They spend off-hours like blue collar workers everywhere, on bowling teams, playing poker, barbecuing and taking their kids to Disneyland. Without them, and the background players, hopefuls who work as extras or "color," there would be no entertainment.

They are of all political colors, red and blue. They voted for Bush and for Kerry. They're in the National Guard and some may have died in Iraq. Hollywood honors them and will miss them.

They are working men and women. They are my former brothers and sisters in union. They are Americans. Applaud them.

Homecoming

They're coming. They're coming home from every point on the compass: Kabul, Berlin, Korea. They're coming from Los Angeles, Chicago, El Paso, Eagle Pass and Tampico. They're coming here, not just because it's home to many, it's not.

It's just that this is the best place in the world to spend Christmas, maybe the only place. Yes, it's snowing in North Dakota and Colorado, there will be wreaths on the doors in Montana and Kansas, lights in the frosted windows in Illinois. But Christmas in New England is iconic, it's mystical, magical. It's etched in glass and framed in the hearts of most Americans.

Just look at all the traditional Christmas cards. There they are, all bundled up in fur robes and stuffed into nineteenth century sleighs. The horses all festooned with bells and red leather straps are puffing smoke into the purple twilight. Artists from Childe Hassam to Grandma Moses saw Christmas as a special New England thing. See the Christmas commercials? That's not Laredo or San Juan Capistrano. That's New England. It's Massachusetts, Vermont, New Hampshire and Maine. Yes, Maine.

So there it is. They're coming home, sons and daughters, nieces and nephews, brothers and sisters from all spots on the map. They're leaving the movie studios in Hollywood, the art galleries and Wall Street offices in Manhattan and joyfully, battlefields afar. To those uniformed pilgrims, coming home is a musical score. It is the crystallization of fading dreams into sparkling tinseled reality.

Not for all. Sadly, tragically, not for all. On Christmas week in 1941, only a pocket full of days from December 7th, families all over America waited in snowy silence for the phone to ring, for a letter to arrive, and in cold horror, a telegram to be delivered, or a military car to pull up at the curb.

On December 12th, my mother, who was wrapping packages, froze in time and space as a Navy car stopped in front of the house. An officer, Captain Schwartz, a retired shipmate of my father, who had died only nine months earlier, came to the door. My mother handed me a ribbon and put one hand to her heart. Captain Schwartz tapped on the window and smiled. That smile melted the ice and warmed the room. He had word that my brother Matt who was at Pearl, was safe and at sea.

For many, just as today, the word didn't come with a smile. Then, as today, too many didn't get off the planes and trains, pulling their sea bags and duffels behind them. Then as now, they arrived in flag-draped boxes stowed in the cold luggage chambers of trains and aircraft. On too many Christmases, far too many fathers lowered their eyes and went into the yard to cry, as mothers put one hand to their hearts, and muffled that silent primal scream that only a mother can hear.

It's here now. After weeks of scraping together money for gifts, of wrapping and cooking, praying and waiting for trains and planes and busses to arrive, it's here. They're coming. They'll stand by the tree and sit at the tables in uniforms and jeans, tweeds and wool. They'll laugh with us and remember all the times before. The good ones won't seem as good as this one, the bad, not as bad as they thought.

But as we turn the tree lights on tonight and lift a glass, let's take a moment to remember those not coming, those whose faces we enshrine in our hearts. As we grow older, that list grows longer. It's part of the game of life.

The great Irish writer James Joyce helps me end it best:

"It had begun to snow again. He watched sleepily the flakes, silver and dark, falling obliquely against the lamplight. His soul swooned slowly as he heard the snow falling faintly through the universe and faintly falling, like the descent of their last end, upon all the living and the dead." Remember them. Merry Christmas.

Wanna Buy a House?

Want to buy a house? Make me a good offer, and it's yours. It was painted only a couple of years ago, and the roof has been redone. It's a cheery house, with lots of room if you're a Kennedy with 15 kids, which I am not. So I'm eager to sell, and the first buyer down the shoot with the cash could move right in. The only problem is our outside. I have more lawn than Baxter State Park, which means upkeep, and upkeep means money which unlike the Kennedys, I don't have either.

I don't know how I got into this house-owning business in the first place. There I was some 30 years ago, minding my own business. I was really cute. I had a really neat bachelor's life of moving from one great apartment to another, with no strings attached.

There were no lawns at 274 W. 86 Street North or in the Village or up in the Bronx. I had two clean plates and silverware for two. I had two wine glasses and two towels. Yes. I lived in hope.

So there I was, a handsome, young actor shopping in Bloomingdale's for a Hathaway shirt. Then I run into this redhead whose brother is a vice president for C.F. Hathaway Shirt Company. Is that luck or what?

So we have a glass of Chianti, and one thing leads to another; the next thing I know I wake up one day and I'm married. Not only am I married, but I'm out of New York and living in Hollywood, California. Not only that, but I've got two daughters and I'm a homeowner. I'm thinking I should give up Chianti.

It was a nice enough stucco house with a brick-colored Spanish tile roof, surrounded by bougainvillea and rich lawyers and doctors. These are guys who can afford to own big homes in that neighborhood, but we were the boat people of that neighborhood.

Still, I put up a good show and pulled it off. Nobody was the wiser. So I figure what the heck, carpe diem, Baby. Let's have a Scotch and some shrimp.

The next thing I know I wake up and I'm 3,000 miles away in Waterville, Maine. I figure by this time I really have to give up Scotch, so I do, but it's too late. I'm a homeowner again.

Sure, it's a nice, big Cape with green shutters, and it's right down the hill from Colby College. I'm thinking, okay, I can sit on my front porch with the rake and watch the girls from Colby run by. What's the problem?

But there's the leaf problem. Millions of them drop from the million weary trees. I raked them up, and this guy came with a big vacuum and sucked them up with a big Electrolux. They don't like to die, they hang on for dear life.

So they're out there now, trillions of oak, maple, birch and some varieties of leaves unknown on this planet, covering the dead grass. I'm told they'll be there in the spring waiting for me, then the grass, if you can call it that, will be ready to cut again.

To make matters worse, three winters more, and the house will need painting again. I miss stucco.

And then there's the problem of the furnace. They call it the boiler here. It was installed when Jefferson was dating Sally Hemmings, so it could go out any minute but it won't, it'll wait for the next ice storm brought on by La Niña.

In case you haven't heard, La Niña is the wicked cousin of El Niño. That was a sucker that put me in a motel for eight days in the ice storm last winter. They say this is going to be worse, that New England is in for tons of snow. That will weaken the roof over the den, and run up my snowplowing bills.

So there I was having a Jack Daniels, when I noticed the cement section on the front porch is falling apart. Well, I'm not giving up Jack Daniels, so let it rot. I've got the basement to deal with. Say, you sure you don't want to buy a house?

It's Hot. Post It.

It's eight a.m., and it's 80 degrees. She who is officially retired, is running around the house now as she does early each morning in this heat wave, dealing with the windows. This seems to be a thing she learned from her very French Maine mother early on. She shuts those against the sun and keeps open those where there is the faintest promise of a breeze left over from the night.

The sun still pours in, but she assures me that the heat of it is trapped on the other side. How does she know this? She knows so many things, little tricks on how to keep cool, when to do the laundry and when not to. Truth is she has many tricks that do not work, but I don't tell her that because if she gets mad, she has tricks that hurt.

When she was teaching, she was gone on late August and early September days. She left instructions written on little pastel post-it notes around the house: "Do this, don't do that. Close this, open that...feed Jack, uncover the bird, water the plants."

I've collected those little notes over the years, and I hoped to read them aloud at her wake if she went first. But since she's retired, she has more energy, she looks healthier, younger and cuter. She's getting looks on the avenue that I used to get. I should get her a burka.

So each morning as I look in the mirror, it seems more and more likely that I will be first to go. I once had a dream that she would go first, and that days later I would start finding these little post-it notes again, fresh, newly written ones. Should I send this idea to Stephen King?

It's eleven a.m., and it's getting hotter now. I guess the sun's heat is trapped out there, but it still pours in. We don't have drapes. I never liked them. They were important in the city where apartment windows faced one another and were often barred like cages in a zoo. You and the neighbor were like tigers staring at one another. I ignored them at first, but then a model moved in across the corridor, and suddenly we had drapes.

In New York, no matter how nice a building you live in, someone else has a nicer building and you have a nice view of it. Even in Beverly Hills, most of those trillion dollar homes are plopped down right next to one another. Did you know that Glenn Ford's kitchen once looked right into Rita Hayworth's? It's okay. They were devoted friends. True story.

Here, in Maine where we pay enormous amounts of property taxes for all of this greenery, I don't want drapes. I want to see it all, even the weeds. I own those weeds.

It's noon, and my L.L.Bean thermometer with the loons on it says it's 90. That's hot, but it's New England hot. It's where Franklin Delano Roosevelt came in the summer because New York had killer heat.

Emily Dickinson lived here in those big bulky, heavy dresses she wore. She probably had drapes though, and I'll bet she shut the right windows.

I've known hot. I grew up in St. Louis and Chicago, where summers are so hot the Mississippi would dry up, and the gangsters always went to fish in Seattle. I went to school briefly in Louisiana and trained in Texas, where it's 99 at three in the morning. That's Africa hot.

Last night, after she had me open all the right windows to let in the evening breeze, I thought I should write a column about all the terrible and wonderful things that happened to me on terrible hot days. It turned out that all of the wonderful things happened in the winter...except for one.

I learned to swim at age 50 on one the hottest Hollywood days on record, by accident. I dropped two olives from a martini in my neighbor's pool, and when I went to get them out, I fell in. True story. If you have never dog paddled in a seersucker suit, you've not lived.

Listen to this: I just went to the fridge to get a glass of water. There was a post-it note on the juice. "It's running low, can you get some today?"

For All of My Life

The Irish have a wonderful saying, "A son is your son, 'till he takes him a wife. Your daughter's your daughter for all of your life."

I was very lucky, as a young father, to have daughters. To a man who has been in love with women, the idea of them, the smell, the texture and lore of them for all of his life, daughters are a blessing.

Now the God of my Catholic childhood, a fearful deity of strange moods and erratic behavior, could have, given my many sins against the celestial administration, cursed me with two sons and made my life unbearable. I have no idea what I would have done with boys. They might have grown up exactly like their father, with all of the unmatched psychic luggage that comes with that. They would, perhaps, if I were blessed, have fabulous IQs, good taste in clothing, music and art. They would be startlingly handsome, stylish and semi-brilliant. They would come to love opera, especially "Tosca" and Chet Baker, Mahler and Miles Davis, twenty-five-year-old Scotch and good pinot noir, as my daughters do.

Perhaps they too would become actors or quirky writers like their dad.

On the other hand, they might have inherited the genes from my five brothers. They would have a passion for soccer and other sports, and I would have had to attend "the games." They would want to play catch and, eventually, have a beer. My brothers, fearing that I would grow up to be "different," bought me boxing gloves, soccer and basketballs, baseballs and a glove. That happened.

Of course it's wrong to stereotype. We live in a new age of blurred lines. And all of those things are healthy and good, all very American. Many of my friends have great sons who are loving and bright boys, courteous and caring. Well...some of them. And of course these days girls have almost pushed boys out of the sports world. Girls exceed in every sport. But my girls just missed the cut-off point and show no signs of their uncles' genes.

Yes, it is a blessing to sons who will take them a wife and carry on the family name. But I've planned ahead, knowing that in the late winter of my life, bereft of good vision and hearing, I will be tucked into a blanket near the fire, fending off the ravages of winter and age with hourly hot toddy injections. It will be then that these two beautiful women will drop in from time to time to trim my toe nails and clip my hair and eyebrows. They will refresh my toddies and pull my blanket up around my chest. They will sit and read me the election results from their Blackberries and the latest books from their Kindles. Sons, approaching dotage, aren't usually up to that sort of thing. They would sit and watch "the game," whilst I fell asleep with drool slipping from my lips while dreaming of better days.

And when I slip this veil of tears, I don't want strong brave sons with dry eyes standing o'er my ashes. I want my three women there, and perhaps fifty or sixty drawn from Craigslist. I want feminine wailing and gnashing of teeth and tears darkened by mascara staining my ashes.

Yes. A daughter's your daughter for all of your life...and beyond. Happy Father's Day.

Danger

We're all doomed you know, everyone in this room is doomed.
— Fred Astaire in "On the Beach"

A scenario: About three years ago, word went out from an alley in Baghdad to an apartment in Munich to a cafe in Paris and perhaps Thames side in London. Maybe it was just a whisper, a wish list to the great dark turbaned Santa of all al-Qaeda children. Eventually, and probably accidentally, a clerk in a CIA room somewhere, eating a tuna sandwich, picked up what they euphemistically call "chatter," as if it were sexual whispers between teenagers.

Quickly, he ran it down one of the green halls to a higher authority who probably just came back from a sushi lunch. He in turn got on his cell and relayed the notion that al-Qaeda had targeted four of our largest financial headquarters for destruction, and that Las Vegas was next. Las Vegas? And nobody thought to warn Wayne Newton or turn off the fountains at the Bellagio? Egads!

Three years later the hot item made it up through a fog of manicured bureaucratic fingers, to hundreds of offices and computers, by email and messenger, to the West Wing. Three years later.

Always on his toes for a promotion, another faceless agent acted with characteristic speed. Upon being handed the yellowing fragile document, he ran down the corridors and breathlessly handed it to someone who worked for someone who worked next door to someone who looked up words in the dictionary for speechwriters who worked for Karl Rove. Bingo.

The writers pooled their talents and came up with a line. Karl grabbed it and ran down the halls to the Oval Office, knocking aides and gofers aside. Tapping on the door and being asked, "Who is it?" Karl replied, "Karl."

Within seconds, Karl doctored it and gave George Bush a line to read and showed him the door to the Rose Garden. Then he ushered George to the door. George stood on his toes peering over the podium at the press and said, "We are a country in danger," and then waited 7 seconds to react.

Consider this: Nichols D. Kristof in the New York Times reports: "Graham Allison, a Harvard professor whose terrifying new book, "Nuclear Terrorism," offers the example cited above, notes that he did not pluck it from thin air. He writes that on Oct. 11, 2001, exactly a month after 9/11, aides told President Bush that a C.I.A. source code named Dragon-fire had reported that al-Qaeda had obtained a 10-kiloton nuclear weapon and smuggled it into New York City." All hands went into action, but nobody told New York. Not even Giuliani, to avoid panic. Luckily, Kristof reports, it didn't pan out.

That night, al-Qaeda-ians sitting in their caves watching the results, chuckled over their Moroccan beef stew and rice. Without losing one soldier or spending a dinar, they had thrown us into another billion dollar frenzy. Expensive SWAT teams, overtime-loaded street cops, and transit police hit the streets. THIS is how they manipulate our economy. Is this how Karl Rove manipulates the election results? That would be pretty difficult to do. Too many people involved. But it doesn't hurt to spin it, does it?

"We are a country in danger?" We always have been. Only this week, Mainers were told that 85 percent of the fish in their lakes is loaded with lead. The fish hauled from the ocean in nets filled with the debris of oil millionaire yachts are all poisoned. Hurricane Alex has just kicked the wind out of the lower East Coast and more are warming up. The climate is changing dramatically, deserts are growing, water tables dropping. Chicken Little is under her desk.

Even young beautiful wives, heavy with child, are being murdered in their sleep by over medicated hubbies.

Los Angeles, sweltering under the heat from the fires that are ravaging her hills, lives in "danger" of a massive 8.0 earthquake that could reduce Grauman's Chinese Theatre, MGM studios, Jack Nicholson's house and several Starbucks surrounding it, to rubble. They've lived under this "danger" since General Santa Ana took the last bus to Tijuana. Don't even bring up the increased lung damage from the fire soot or the fumes from star packed Hummers parked outside of De Niro's new Ago Restaurant.

In Washington D.C, where snipers roam the top of the Capitol, the murder rate is still the highest in the nation, gaining it once again the title, "Murder Capital of the U.S." In 2002, there were 262 people who were "in danger" and didn't know it until it was too late. The same goes for St. Louis which just became the "Most Dangerous City."

While we here in Maine spend the twilight hours waiting for Al Qaeda to acquire a ten megaton nuclear weapon, we sit in Canadian rockers and on lawn chairs on rain soaked grass, the Disneyland oasis of West Nile infected mosquitos. We swat and sweat and watch the horizon for the mushroom cloud that doomsayers say will eventually rise over Boston, the ultimate Bambino curse.

Summer is almost over. We sit on our decks, draining the last of the wine, munching the last of the strawberries while the "Moses" Kerry and "Aaron" Edwards rattle across the land promising to free us from Pharaoh Bush's clutches. Will we at last be free of the great Mr. Malaprop of West Crawford and his minions, or will Karl Rove achieve his promised and lusted for hegemony, drawing us deeper into the abyss?

Safe in Maine: I think not. We are in as much mortal danger here as anywhere. We are one of the fattest states. Our arteries are thick with gook. We race along slick wet badly paved streets and wrap our SUVs around poles. Yes. We are in danger, but we are also a state with one of the highest aging populations. So with such little time left for all us, why worry. One ten megaton firecracker will simply evaporate us from Jackman to Kennebec. It beats slipping away in an air conditioned nursing home to the sound of a nurse down the hall humming Manilow tunes. Smile, it's later than you think.

Singing in the Rain
I love the rain. It's my favorite weather.
—Mark Twain.

The local weather man says it's going to rain Monday. Why do I care? I'm not going anywhere on Monday. There is that tiny leak in the roof of the closet in the back of the house, but unless it's a torrential downpour, the kind we have every June in Manila and Singapore that causes mudslides that kill thousands of people in the Philippines and China, I can't worry. But like that one we had last week, which revealed the leak, that's a pain.

So then why do I and people like me get so obsessed with the weather? Define obsession. Here's what I watch:
Each evening I watch three weather reports, the early, mid evening and final at 11:15. Okay, that's probably a lot. Channel 6 starts first, then quickly I cut down to channel 5 that follows a few seconds later, and then channel 8 that is always behind. They basically give the same report, but one focuses on the south, the other floats around central Maine, and the latter kind of covers Bangor and the north.

Why do I care if it's going to rain in Bangor or Freeport? I think it's because I have what I now call OWWD. That's like obsessive compulsive disorder, which I also have, but this is Obsessive Weather Watching Disorder.

It's one thing to be concerned with the weather in California, because I have family there, but Minot, North Dakota? Cuba? the Lesser Antilles? I don't know anyone in the Lesser Antilles, do you? Where are the Greater Antilles anyway? Is that where the malls are? Is there a Starbucks in the Greater Antilles?

All the different stations have different weather people. This is very important. One station has a very cute spokesperson. I like her because when she first started, she was a little heavy.

Now, she's clearly lost about 15 pounds and is wearing less black and more flowered dresses and has even started wearing horizontal stripes.

I like this, because I'm on a new nutritional lifestyle, and I feel it's important to applaud the healthy-weight folks who come into my living room via my television. It's equally important because I have a very large screen which makes large folks appear even larger. I was thinking that I should send her a note, but she who keeps all the note paper and stamps in her desk drawer thought it might appear as though I am stalking her. One of the stations I watch has two men, an older personable fellow who laughs a lot and a younger spokesman who steps in when the older guy goes to play golf or bingo I guess. Young guy is very professional. He's losing weight as well, and I have to say I applaud that. I won't be sending him a note either.

But all of these weather people have a limited amount of time, and with the exception of the occasional mini tornado or damaging winds over Skowhegan and Pittsfield, nothing much happens.

If you are like me, OWWD, and really want action, the Weather Channel is where you want to be, and they have the real heavy hitters when it comes to on-scene announcing, and in addition, some really talented and handsome on-camera personalities.

I love watching them trying to stand up in 187 mile an hour winds, or standing knee deep in flood waters. It makes me feel all comfy in my jammies and slippers.

If you were glued to the screen following Katrina or Hurricane Sandy when it hit Jersey and New York, you are probably a fan of big Jim Cantore, on-camera meteorologist and storm tracker. Cantore is a big weight lifter guy with a terrific sense of style, and an encyclopedic knowledge of everything frightening and dangerous in weather. I sleep better knowing Jim is out there.

America's favorite, the Today show's Al Roker, is there, and the lovely Kait Parker and Maria LaRosa. That may be a tad sexist, but it softens the guilt to have someone beautiful to listen to when you're watching tornados take a house apart, or the Manhattan subway go under water.

Don't get me wrong. Local weather is important if you're planning a cookout or wedding, I can tell you, but when you've had enough about the temperature on Mt. Washington or tomorrow's heat at Mary Ellen's camp, there is nothing like switching to channel 33 and watching Kim Cunningham tell you if it's raining in Taiwan. A bit of guilt goes with that as well. What if they're having a "Taste of Taiwan" tonight? Wouldn't you feel really bad if the Taste of Taiwan got rained out, wouldn't you? Guilt comes with OWWD. It's a Catholic thing.

Jack on Top

By now Seamus, the Romney's Irish Setter, has found himself a place in political literature, and has almost replaced Lassie as the most famous dog in American history. All this because Mitt Romney, now the official Republican candidate for the presidency, shoved the big dog into a travel cage and lashed him to the top of the family car for a long ride to Canada.

Poor Seamus. He simply needed a snack before being loaded aboard, so he stole some turkey from the kitchen counter and gobbled (pun intended) it down. Seamus got the runs and disrespected the Romney's car.

Some pet owners have suggested that Mitt should have lashed one of his multiple sons to the top of the car and kept Seamus inside. This is a cruel and partisan jab. This could have happened to anyone, and there are some historic legends, perhaps a touch apocryphal, to back this up.

George Washington owned the first presidential dogs, Tipsy and Drunkard (true names) and may well have brought them along when he boated across the Delaware. Some have suggested that artists painted them out of the historic picture. I'm just saying.

Franklin Delano Roosevelt, of course, had his beloved Scottie, Fala. FDR never left the White House without him, and took him along on the presidential plane, ship and train trips. There is no foundation whatsoever to the Republican myth that Fala was strapped to the top of the plane or train, in a crate. Another cruel partisan jab.

This all came to mind this week when she, who loves to travel, expressed a desire to motor across America this summer to visit our daughters in Los Angeles. The big question arose as to what to do with Jack, our very large Old English Sheepdog. As Jack and I share a common mental illness, SAT (separation anxiety trauma) I refuse to leave him in a kennel. I've visited several of these kennels, and I start to tremble at the thought of putting him in one. I know they're clean and healthy, but Jack isn't just a pet.

Jack is possessed of the spirit of a deceased loved one. I believe it is that of my late father-in-law. I kid you not. Not only does he love crackers and cheese like the Judge, Jack is super protective of her. He always takes her side in contentious situations. If I should, on occasion, raise my voice to her, he moves between us and fixes me with a deadly stare, and I can see baring of teeth. Her father, a lawyer and judge, was never that fond of her marrying an actor, and never really warmed up to me. I can see that familiar look in Jack's eyes from time to time.

So what to do? We do have a very large crate left over from one of our deceased and unpossessed dogs that looks very comfortable. So in a test run, I put it on top of our Prius and gave Jack a look at it. Jack/Judge stared at it for a long moment.

"C'mon, Jack," I said. "Give it a try. Look how big it is. Look at the blanket inside. Feel how soft it is. Isn't that nice? We are going to go on a long ride across America. You'll get to see Kansas and Oklahoma, Arizona too. You may even get to see some movie stars' pets. Wouldn't that be nice?"

Jack/Judge stared at the crate, at the Prius and then at me. The growl was deep and forbidding. I could see some teeth. Then he walked slowly away to stand by her side. She pet him sweetly. I never get petted.

Today, the crate goes to Good Will, and the trip has been postponed, unless of course we can find a live-in sitter who likes crackers and cheese.

When Jesus was Jewish

I liked Jesus when he was Jewish, didn't you? He was so calm in those days, speaking Aramaic softly to small crowds.

I kind of liked Jesus when he was a statue in St. Mary and Joseph's church on Minnesota Avenue. He was so quiet standing there with the little red light from candles flickering on his face. Paddy Carr used to say it made him look like he was frowning at us. I thought he was smiling.

Of course most of us Catholic boys didn't know until college that Jesus was a Jew. The priest never mentioned it, and the nuns hushed it up.

I'm talking now about AARP Catholics, those of a certain age from pre cell phone days when churches were quiet contemplative places without guitars and tambourines.

But now Jesus is born again as a rock star on billboards and tee shirts and movies, and not just any old Christian, but a bigger than life marketing tool for the POF (People Of Faith).

To support my claim: In the New York Times, Tuesday, March 29th edition, the fashion section, there He is. The Fashion Section.

There on page A16 is movie star Ashton Kucher, occasional boy toy live-in to Demi Moore, wearing a tee shirt that shows "Jesus is my homeboy."

There's a fashion model wearing a Squared sweater with "Jesus Loves Me," embroidered on it.

Larry Bullock, manager of the gay club, The Civilian, a Fire Island night club, is modeling a tee shirt that has a picture of Jesus saying, "Put down the drugs and come get a hug." Was that in the Sermon on the Mount?

Someone named Trapper Blu models a sweater that says, "Last night a D.J. saved my life," featuring Jesus as a disc jockey. Cute.

A Manhattan shop, Urban Outfitters, sells a shirt printed with a rosary that spells out "Everybody loves a Catholic girl." Wow! I sure do.

Bowling bags, belt buckles and dog tags are on sale in major cities that read, "Inspired by Christ." It's marketing gone crazy. You can buy a wrist band that reads "Live for him," and "Death to sin, Alive to Christ." Sales for these items reached $85 million last year alone.

The craze is reaching out into the teen sports market as well. Cornerstone Christian Fellowship in Chandler, Arizona has formed the King of Kings Skateboard Ministries. Their message is "You can be a hard core skater and still have a heart for the Lord." That's so up to date. When I was a kid, you went to Hell for playing pool.

The group's celebrity here is Stephen Baldwin, Alec's less talented, born again, rocker brother who said, "I told God, I'll do whatever you want me to do, but it better be cool, it better be gnarly." Take that, Jesus.

His fellow evangelist said, "Jesus would be a skate boarder today. I know St. Paul would." Right on.

Many of you, reading this this morning, will be outraged and offended by my words. You will demand my banishment.

My question then is, why aren't you outraged by the blatant marketing of the man you consider to be the son of God?

Why aren't you offended by the crass commercialism of the Prince of Peace?

Yeah, I think I liked Jesus better when He was Jewish and quieter, when He spoke of peace and love and forgiveness, instead of "rad skating," and became a disc jockey and slogan peddler. Sister Imelda used to say, "If you sit quietly and listen carefully, God will speak to your heart." Radical idea, dude.

Paddy Carr

We had many adventures together, Paddy and I. We stole Pepsi Cola bottles off the back of the delivery truck when the driver was having a lunch time belt in Skeeter O'Neal's Saloon. We acted together in small plays in the basement of St Mary and Joseph's church. One such great moment was when he played a nameless saint, and I, Baby Jesus. Al Powers' big brother, Neal, played St. Christopher and carried me across a paper river painted blue in a great wash of watercolors. I ruined the tableau by waving to my big brother Jim who was sitting in the first row.

Some sleepover nights, when we were boys, Paddy and I bunked in his private bedroom which was in the basement of his father Dave's Michigan Avenue Cleaners which also served as the storage room for the cleaning. We would fall asleep under a rainforest of big plastic bags, a canopy of wool, gabardine, cotton and linen as we listened to his mother's record player upstairs ....Tommy Dorsey and his orchestra.

The last time I saw Dave Carr was when Paddy visited him at Jefferson Barracks down by the river in South St. Louis. He was all turned out in his brand new khaki uniform and garrison cap. It was a proud moment for Paddy and his brother Richard. I shared it with them. I wasn't there when he came home, but blessedly, come home he did. I moved away after that and I never saw Paddy again. I understand that he came to my brother's funeral and I was told that he limped, that he had permanent bad feet. I was sorry to hear that.

Members of my family have had no luck in tracking Paddy down over the years. I know that June 8th is his birthday. You never forget the birthday of your best friend.

Childhood friends grow up and other wars break out. I don't know that Paddy served, but one rainy night in a tent city outside of Tokyo, where I was in charge of keeping track of ingoing and departing troops, I saw a Richard Carr's name on a list. I had missed him. But there was another. Neal Powers, Alan's big brother who, as St. Christopher, had carried me across the paper river. I waded through the mud and pouring rain deep into the tent city to catch him before he departed for Korea. He showed me his St. Christopher medal and asked me if I remembered the story. Of course I did. I hope his medal and his Jesus carried him home safely. I never saw or heard from any of them since.

The Keys to My Life

No one can drive you crazy unless you give them the keys.
  –Douglas Horton

We lose things. We all lose things. I don't mean ball games, elections or friends, and we don't really know when we're losing our minds. We need other people to notice that and warn us. I mean little annoying things, pens, books and keys. Keys are the worst.

For some people, and I appear to be one of them, losing stuff is a psychological tic that never goes away. Most people grow out of things like that. The only thing I ever grew out of was my diaper, and that, an older friend reminds me, returns.

For example: Skate keys. The good thing about those old skate keys is that they all worked on everyone's skates, so when I lost mine, Margaret Reichenbacker, beautiful Helen's younger sister, loaned me her key. Margaret was even more beautiful than Helen, but she had a lazy eye, and boys made fun of her. Later in life I went to dancing school with Margaret, but she always picked a different partner. I knew it was about the skate key.

1956, New York City. I had a date with this sweet Japanese girl who designed bathing suits for the Jantzen company. She had a five floor walk up in Greenwich Village. The only drawback was her door buzzer didn't work.

You had to shout up, and she would drop the key. It was attached to a piece of wooden broomstick to make it hard to lose. It's a New York thing. You had to be there.

So I shouted. She tossed it down. I was never good at catching things. It hit me square on the nose and fell into some garbage. My nose bled like a gunshot wound. I just pressed any button, and someone rang me in. We had a quiet dinner, and she said she had to get up early. I understood. She smelled a key loser, and of course it's very difficult to make out with pieces of toilet paper sticking out of your nostrils.

I think it's about luck. Luck is funny. Good luck is fickle. One day you've got it, the next it's gone. Good luck never hangs around. Bad luck is like the crazy aunt who won't go home after Christmas, or like gum on running shoes. You can never get it off.

Example: Six months after I first met she, who never loses anything, she let me share her apartment on York Avenue in Manhattan. She wasn't supposed to be sharing the apartment, and so only had one key, which she loaned me. Okay, don't start with me. It was an accident. My jacket had a hole in it and I lost it in the snow. She was working in the theater, and I had to wait for her to get off of work, and then wake the superintendent at two in the morning. I could stay, they said, but they upped the rent. She made me kick that in, and pay for the new key.

You would think that a judge's daughter from Maine would have good sense like Margaret Reichenbacker, who had her eye fixed in the eighth grade, then dumped me and went to the prom with Walter Robinson whose father was in plumbing supplies.

No, this one hung on. She said she loved me. I always knew it was pity. A key loser smells of pity. But when you've got a good thing like her, you swallow your pride and hang on, hoping things get better.

Some guy once said, "The more things change, the more they stay the same." I don't know who it was, Mitt Romney maybe. But it's true of people who lose things? We never change.

For example: When Truman was president, and you lost the key to your car, you went and had one made. You can't do that with a Prius and most new cars. The Prius key is a small computer. You can't go to the local key guy and get one made. You have to order one from Toyota, and it costs $250 bucks. So when she went to Boston for an overnight, I demanded that she leave her Prius key with me in case I lost mine. I didn't lose mine. I lost hers. I'll say this for her, this woman is major forgiving, but at a steep price. I have to pay for the new key and wash all the windows. I look at it this way, love is like luck, when you're a key loser and you've still got it, flaunt it, baby.

You Can Leave Your Hat On

Holy Dollars! Are you even faintly aware that there are thousands, maybe millions, of people making a living in the "separation of church and state" industry?

On one side, Jay Sekulow, Pat Robertson's legal John the Baptist who runs the American Center for Law and Justice, makes millions for his group and himself. He's constantly on talk shows from CNN to MSNBC and has his own radio show.

Christian groups working to strengthen the bond between church and state number in the hundreds of thousands. These can't all be volunteers. Somebody's making money.

On the other side of the aisle, AU (Americans United for Separation of Church and State) is a huge bureaucracy.

Not only do they have a web site, publish newspapers and produce radio shows, their legal department alone must employ thousands of lawyers, clerks and fact checkers, not to mention the teams going around the country looking for crèches in courtrooms.

Now you know this separation problem is never going to be solved, nor does George Bush want it solved, because it would throw millions out of work and skewer his re-election figures.

I can see the headlines now: "JESUS BACK IN SCHOOLS...MILLIONS FILE FOR UNEMPLOYMENT BENEFITS. BREADLINES LENGTHEN."

I don't have a dog in this fight at the moment, but I think enough is enough. I'm all for keeping prayer in church, supermarkets, movie theaters, even sporting events, BUT out of the algebra class.

I think crèches are okay on government grounds as long as there is a lighted menorah, a handful of lighted joss sticks and a neon crescent moon hanging in the tree behind it. A couple of wickens doing a harvest dance would be fun.

But even in our craziest moments, we haven't yet gone as far as the French. Yes, those French, the ones in Europe. What have they done now?

A French presidential commission is pushing through a law that will forbid Muslim women from wearing the traditional Muslim head scarf, or hijab, in schools, places of business and public offices. This has created huge unrest.

France has been pushing this since the first law was enacted in 1905. It's gone largely ignored until now when the Muslim population of France has become the largest in Europe. Somebody is getting scared over there and here's why.

Islam is the second religion of France with 4 million, 200,000 adherents. Catholics come in second with 45 million. That's a lot of hijabs and an issue very scary to the French.

To cover up their fear and obvious prejudice, they're dumping on everybody. The law will prevent Catholic Jeannette Louise from wearing a "large" crucifix to her comparative religions class, and orthodox Jewish Pierre from wearing his yarmulke. What about the saffron robe of the Buddhist student? This is expected to work?

To make matters worse, and the French have a knack for that, some segments of the government are talking about banning the turban of the Sikhs. Now Sikhs make up a very small portion of the Gallic landscape, but as any New York cab patron can tell you, Sikhs are deadly serious about that turban. Sikh children in France will actually drop out of school should this silly law take root.

First of all, I like hats, especially religious hats. I remember fondly a little girl, whose name I think was Mary Lister, back in the fifth grade when I was an altar boy. She sat in the second or third row and had a big crush on me or so Moo Moo Hagany told me. I could see her reflected in the glass panels to one side of the altar. She wore this beautiful lace mantilla that her brother had sent from Spain. Many women of our parish wore them, or big fancy hats. It was a rule, like no meat on Friday and no impure thoughts.

But I guess that went the way of all Catholic rules. You can eat Big Macs on Friday now and women wear hardly anything to church. The jury is out on impure thoughts.

Yes, religious hats are fun. Look at those big furry numbers the Hasidic Jews wear in Brooklyn. They're called shtreimels and are very cool and warm. I like yarmulkes (skull caps) too. Catholics liked them so much Catholic cardinals started wearing them in red.

The Pope's yarmulke is always white, and according to canon lawyer Patricia Dugan, it's made by the Pope's personal tailor Gammarelli and is made of pigskin. "It has terrific suction and never blows off," Dugan tells us on her web site.

I doubt the Pope comes under French law, but is Chirac going to tell the Hasidim they have to give up their shtreimels? Open the Bastille.

I say the French should take a page from little George Bush and open a line of faith based hat shops and chill out. Vive la chapeau, or as Tom Jones sings, "You can leave your hat on."

Chocolate What?

Is the Easter Bunny a space alien trying to implant us with his eggs? Because I will so swear off chocolate right now.
— Thomas Quakenbush

I'm glad Sister Rosanna is dead. Don't misunderstand me, I'm not really glad, because Sister Rosanna was my very favorite nun. If fact, if she were alive today, I would bring her to Maine to see how well I've turned out. Well, maybe that's not such a good idea.

But I'm just glad she's not visiting me here in Maine and shopping with me tonight, because I couldn't handle seeing her expression when we walked down aisle ten in my favorite supermarket together, passing all that Easter candy. There it was, right there with all the Cadbury eggs, row after row of assorted candy eggs, jelly bean eggs, chocolate bunnies the size of a small child. A chocolate cross. WAIT! WHAT? A CHOCOLATE CROSS? Not just one, but six boxes of them, all in yellow boxes with cellophane windows like IPhones or plastic razors.

Now I'm a long way from being the little Catholic boy who wanted to be a priest when he grew up. (That ship sailed the summer day at the public pool when I laid eyes on Rosemary De Branco, she of the one piece royal purple swimsuit and white fudge hair.) But I have enough of the dogma drug still in me to be taken aback at such a sight.

I could have tried to avert Sister's gaze, but that would have been impossible. She had the legendary eyes in the back of her head. But this. OMG. A chocolate cross. It could have been worse. Thank God, it was just a cross, the plain kind Protestants have in their churches, empty, without the body of Jesus nailed to it.

I was born and raised directly across the street from the convent of the Sisters of Saint Joseph. Those Sisters were almost like real blood sisters to the Devines. We always rushed across to the gardens where they strolled, to show off our loot on Christmas day or birthdays, and especially on Easter.

My sisters were eager, after Mass, to rush over and show their favorite Sisters their new Easter dresses, shoes and bonnets. Of course they proudly took their Easter baskets full of colored eggs and big chocolate bunnies with them. Naturally, the Sisters, smiling and polite, complimented all the girls of the neighborhood, but there was always one, and usually that was Sister John Bosco, the mother superior, she with eyes like Crazy Joey Gallo, a powerful woman who never had to use a ruler or raise her voice. Just the sound of her waist beads clicking as she came down the hall was enough to freeze your saliva. At the gate on Easter, she would ask the inevitable question, "Can anyone here tell us the true meaning of Easter?"

There was usually a moment of silence as everyone looked at one another until Sister pointed to someone like Nina Karenbrock, the oldest girl in the bunch, who already had a bad tic and stutter.

"Nina?"

"It's about the dead Jesus getting up and walking out of the hole," Nina replied. Well, it was something like that, a broken, stuttering, terrified reply. Sister John Bosco simply took a deep breath and closed her eyes for a long moment. Now that I think of it, she always did that, exactly like that. I never gave much thought to it until I married She who used to do the same exact thing, when I tried to explain why I put some silverware away with food still on it.

Chocolate coating religious symbols isn't new. While in San Francisco in the '50s, my bunk mate Arthur Silverman, told me how horrified he was to spot a chocolate menorah in a kosher delicatessen window. A dreidel maybe, but a menorah?

I think it might be fun this Easter, to surprise my very Catholic, chocolate addicted wife on Easter Sunday morning by putting one of those chocolate crosses on her breakfast table. I kind of miss that deep breath and closed eye thing.

Leonard Rosenberg Died Today

Leonard Rosenberg died today. He was born in Tulsa, Oklahoma, on February 26, 1920. He majored in theatre at Northwestern University in Chicago and went on to become a major television, film and stage actor. He came into your theatre, your living room and your hearts for years. Those are the facts.

Here's a true story. One spring day, as a young actor making the rounds in my tweed overcoat and clutching my pictures, I grew tired. I used to walk home through Central Park, a good twenty blocks. But I was tired so I took the bus up 5th Avenue. As I was watching the crowds, Leonard Rosenberg got on the bus somewhere around 57th Street.

Leonard asked me politely if he could sit in the empty seat next to me. Nobody ever does that in New York. They sit, flop, push and squeeze in. They open a paper and cough or sneeze and ignore you. But they never ask permission.

I recognized Leonard at once because by now he had become Tony Randall, comedian, actor, writer and passionate devotee of opera. They didn't mention that in the obits today, but Tony knew more about opera than almost anyone, except Burt Lancaster who knew everything.

I was reluctant to tell him I was an actor. One doesn't walk up to Pavarotti and start singing. But I did. We chatted. Mostly about the cool spring weather. He was wearing only a dark suit, a white shirt and tie. We didn't talk about acting, his career or my short one. Just about the weather and the potholes on 5th Avenue.

A few blocks past the Plaza Hotel, he said goodbye and jumped into the hole where the door opens. When the bus stopped, he waved to the bus driver and smiled at me and leaped off the bus. I say leaped, that's what he did. He leaped. It made me laugh. He moved like a man who liked to dance. Watching him cross the street made me laugh. I had already seen him in a dozen things and he always made me laugh.

But this day, he literally danced across through the traffic to the other side with a smile on his face, as though he had just come from the doctor and been told that he was in perfect health and would live to be a hundred.

By now, you will have heard all the news obits, read all the blurbs and know all you need to know about Leonard Rosenberg who grew up to be Tony Randall, who grew up to work on Broadway with Ethel Barrymore, Katherine Cornell, Lilli Palmer and Cedric Hardwicke.

He grew up to go to Hollywood and steal scenes and whole movies from Rock Hudson and Doris Day, Joanne Woodward and Marilyn Monroe.

Most of you knew Leonard/Tony from television, from "Mr. Peepers," with the wonderful, heartbreaking Wally Cox, about two teachers in the inner city. When Tony took over the role of Felix Unger, from Neil Simon's "The Odd Couple," that Art Carney had created on Broadway and Jack Lemmon had etched on film, he became a household name.

Tony actually was the best Felix that ever was. Jack Lemmon was bigger, broader and more nervous in his interpretation, but Tony got closer to the edge, to the vulnerability of Felix. He was fussier, a master of the deep breath, the painful sighs that Felix kept locked inside.

Tony brought that part of Felix to the role of Sidney Shorr in a movie of the week about a gay man living alone in Manhattan. The networks were still nervous about gay people then and when it became a series, the "powers to be" pressured him to go easy on that side. It flopped.

We all cheered when Tony formed the National Actors' Theatre in New York. He persuaded friends to throw in money and talent to make it succeed. It never really blossomed. Tony knew what the great George Abbott told his students, "You can make a killing in the theatre, but you can't make a living."

Spring has come again to Manhattan. The tulips are blossoming on 5th Avenue, and the busses are still running up past the Plaza and Central Park. I'm sure some young actor, cold and tired, will take the bus the last ten blocks and then cut across Central Park to his tiny apartment on the West Side. I'm sure there will be an empty seat next to him. But Leonard Rosenberg won't get on and ask to sit beside him. Leonard Rosenberg, who grew up to be Tony Randall, died today at 84.

The lights will dim on Broadway tonight and actors everywhere, in the coffee shops, on the subway, in the cheap diners and fancy uptown cafes, and those watching the news on the big screen up above the statue of George M. Cohan will take a minute to remember the kid from Tulsa, Oklahoma. Goodnight Tony, wherever you are. I hope we get to share a bus ride again someday, somewhere.

Letter from the Gulag

It's garbage day and it's snowing. I have my nose pressed against the frozen glass, as I look down the long driveway to where my big, black garbage bags have to be laid. It's the longest driveway on the block, and I know there's ice under that snow.

I had a dream last night that I was ice skating in the Olympics, and fell and broke my leg. Do dreams come true? None of mine ever do. But what if I should fall and break a leg, and it has to be put in a cast?

That reminds me of Betty Birdsy in high school in Seattle. She fell and broke her leg while skiing on Mt. Rainier. She came to school with this enormous cast and had to lean on a ski pole. She was the class hero. Everyone rushed to sign her cast.

Who would be anyone's hero who broke his leg putting out garbage? I only have three friends here, not counting she who is my best, and none of them will brave this driveway. So I will limp around the house with a cast with only her signature on it. I notice as I lean my nose against the frozen window pane, that as I exhale, it produces a cloud that I can write my initials on. I am worried that such thoughts in a grown man's mind are symptoms of something much worse than a broken leg. I've noticed a drop in my cognitive skills, since this polar vortex dropped on us.

I write the words "polar vortex" in the cloud on the window. I'm not sure what that means. I will Google it later.

I walk to the far window with a view of the entire street, and where the L.L.Bean thermometer is hung. It says -8. I've seen that number before. In my youth, I worked a summer job that flowed into a winter job on the Elgin Joliet and Eastern Railroad in Waukegan, Illinois. The rail yards were right on the edge of Lake Michigan. One night as we were bumping cars down the tracks, the brakemen discovered one of the locks was frozen.

Four of them were jammed into the cab with myself, and the engineer, passing around a bottle of Wild Turkey. They knew they had to go out there and open that lock. Long story short, it wouldn't budge. So the engineer and the four brakemen went out and urinated on it and it thawed out. True Americana story.

I can see now that everyone down the street has their trash out. Jack the sheep dog stands beside me, with his paws up on the windowsill, studying the street where not a creature or car is moving. He refuses to go out. He just stares at the icy deck where he had slipped last week and hurt his leg. Dogs remember stuff like that.

I blow on the glass again and then write "K+J." I know it will go away before she comes home, but I'll tell her I did it.

She made it down the driveway this morning. Nothing short of another major ice storm could keep her from teaching her one Spanish class a day. I watched her drive down. She's pretty good at that driveway. She was born here and on a January day. I think that counts for something.

It's starting to snow again. This has been a horrible winter, worse than the railroad job winter. I shouldn't be here at my age. I should have followed my original dream when I retired from Hollywood. There was an ad in the Los Angeles Times from a man in the San Fernando Valley, where it's so hot they call it "Hell's Waiting Room," that wanted to sell his pony ride business. I would have loved that.

You get to buy all his ponies, and then name them. Kids love riding ponies. I looked into it, but it's more complicated than you might think. You have to keep the names he gave the ponies, and then make sure they get shots and licenses every year. The cost of hay and feed is expensive, and you wouldn't believe how much those tiny saddles cost. But you get to meet interesting people like those gorgeous LA soccer moms who bring their kids to ride the ponies.

I cut the ad out anyway, but she found it and threw it away. I wonder if they have pony rides in Maine? I'd better get that garbage down.

On Letting Go

When my daughters left for college many years ago, I could not bring myself to repaint their rooms. She, who doesn't paint or build, but knows how things should be done, hated the colors the girls chose and wanted them changed. But I couldn't do it. Those colors were theirs.

I couldn't throw out bundles of their old papers, crystals hanging on strings, marked up school books, and posters plastered to the walls. I couldn't let them go. So how is it that she expects me to take down the Christmas decorations?

It was a rare, icy, crazy, wonderful Christmas, and who knows if I, or anyone for that matter, will be here on the next one. I'm not being pessimistic or morose, just realistic. There is constant talk lately about meteorites coming ever closer to the earth, some just barely missing us. The other night there was a Nature Channel story on all the volcanos. Did you know that there are thousands of volcanos we thought were extinct but aren't? Old Faithful in Yosemite National Park, for example, is one. It could let loose at any time.

So it's only natural that I just can't let go of the fun things I have collected.

I hold onto the silliest things. In a closet upstairs I have two of my first ancient Apple computers, covered with dust. I can't let them go. I wrote great stuff on them once. Imagine if Hemingway had given his first typewriter to Good Will.

This, you'll think is crazy: I have a pair of socks I brought here from Los Angeles thirty years ago. I haven't worn them all this time of course, I just keep them in a drawer with my collection of ten watches. The socks are thin, California socks with palm trees on them I think they represent the LA I loved and miss.

Of course it's not the same place anymore, but I can't let go. When I think of the tacos and the warm wind I get fuzzy.

Those memories and the socks got me through the polar vortex. When I get sad, I just take them out and hold them against my face. I'm kind of like Linus Van Pelt in "Peanuts." I know it's an aberration, but I deal with it. It's not like I do it in public. I used to take them with me when we traveled but she made me stop. She has no aberrations.

The watches. I don't even wear watches anymore. Watches are an old person's fixation, and I'm trying desperately not to be an old person. So when someone asks me what time it is, I flash my big smart phone and hold it up. I feel so cool and young.

I have eight pairs of glasses, nine counting the pair I'm wearing and the ones on my head that I forgot about. Most of them are old prescriptions. They're in the drawer with the socks and the watches. Every once in a while, she will say things like, "What if something happens to you and I have to deal with all of this stuff you refuse to throw out? How will I know what to do with it?"

I tell her that everyone goes through that.

Once I suggested that if I "go first" she should arrange to go soon after. Then she can just leave all this stuff, except for the socks, for the girls to deal with. They're young, and they'll have more time and energy anyway. I hope they'll just throw it all out.

I did suggest that she give the watches and the glasses, but not my socks, to a charity. I'm sure even the very needy all have socks, but there are people who need a new watch. Sometimes I don't answer her. Sometimes I just stand there and sulk until she feels sorry for me. I've mastered that technique. In years of acting I've learned how to fill my eyes with tears. Then she hugs me and walks away, and I go back to dusting my watches. They say you can't teach an old dog new tricks, but if the old dog is smart, he keeps the old ones in his pocket...with the socks.

Lucy in the Sky

I was sitting in my car on Main Street in Waterville, sipping my coffee and reading my paper. My daughter in Los Angeles rang me up on my cell. She said, "What are you doing there?"

"What?"

"Step outside the car and wave. I'm watching you."

Astonished and amazed, I did. She told me what I was wearing. What the weather was like, the color of cars passing by. My daughter was watching me from three thousand miles away.

"Look up, "she said. "It must be there somewhere in front of you."

And there "it" was. There "it" is. Perched on the lower right hand side of the huge Waterville Centre sign that tells us what's inside the building, is a small, almost invisible camera. I call it "LUCY" now. Apparently, "Lucy" has been watching me for some time, months? Perhaps years? She's been watching me talk to you, to strangers, to beautiful women, to children. Lucy has been watching me read. She knows what paper I'm reading and how long I've been parked there.

If you sat and ate at "Taste of Waterville," she watched you eat, monitored your table habits. Did you use a napkin? Steal something from another plate? Argue with your husband? Lucy knows. I've not watched her at night yet. That might be another story.

I dragged some bystanders into the camera's eye: two tourists from Oklahoma, one from Indiana, a former mayor and several business owners on Main Street, none of whom knew Lucy was there.

"I think it's for traffic monitoring or crowd control," one suggested. Crowd control on Main Street in Waterville? Well, it does cover two banks and a jewelry store, so traffic in and out of them is convenient in case of robbery.

You can watch the passersby, the cars parking and driving away, citizens strolling down the block, jaywalking, schmoozing. You can only hope that your mate hasn't learned of Lucy, but I doubt infidelity is a sport often practiced on Main Street.

One can go on line and search and find all the Lucy cams in Los Angeles and New York. They're watching bridges and tunnels.

Now I'm super aware. When I drive up to my bank, a lovely woman smiles and calls me by name as she has for years. It's a family bank. A member of my family was once on the board. But as she fishes for my money, I look up and see a small camera smiling back at me, a bank "Lucy" scanning my face for recognizable features, cataloguing my glances. It doesn't care that the clerk knows me. It cares not about family. It cares about me. It's filing me in some gray box somewhere in case I decide to become a bank robber.

Okay, let's turn Lucy over to our side. Why not organize a "Surveillance Theater." We can form bands of players in wild costumes and set pieces. "Waiting for Godot" in front of CVS?

Let's write some "street camera theatre" pieces to perform. As there is no sound, this would be in the tradition of the old Mack Sennett/Charlie Chaplin silent one-reelers. As you watch, you can play some music to enhance it. I'll be directing. Who's up for it? Will Lucy be amused? Or will the black Humvee pay a visit?

Live Longer

You've lost your job. Your credit cards are maxed. The unemployment rate is at 10.2, and your daughter and her college educated English major who specialized in archaic poetry and is therefore unemployable, have moved into the basement play room. Factories are closing daily, the dollar is down, and though we may have just missed a repeat of the 1929 Crash, we're still embedded in a great recession, but I hope it's worse. I hope it's a Depression with a capital D. I'll tell you why. If this is true we are going to live longer. Let's hope this is true. Now I mean an economic depression, not the depression you're in because of your daughter and her husband or the economic depression. Does that make sense?

You and your spouse, who are the main breadwinners supporting the archaic poetry major, may not find another job until you're both ninety-nine. But you will be ninety-nine so just hang in there. That job is going to wait for you.

Of course you may have lost your house and your wife and kids may leave you because you're a failure, but take heart. You are going to live much, much longer thanks to this recession which has to turn into a major depression for all of this to happen.

You don't have to take my word for it. This news comes to us from Julia Whitty of *Mother Jones* magazine. Julia tells us in her fascinating new article "Death Declines During Depressions," that people live longer during depressions, and if you happen to live in areas like Detroit, New Orleans and almost anywhere in Maine, your neighborhood is about to turn into an old folks home. So whatever you do, don't throw out that Canadian rocker you have in your garage or those lawn chairs. If things get worse, you're going to be very, very old, and you'll need something comfy to sit in.

Yes, I know facts can be misleading, but overall health improved during four years of the Great Depression as well as in the recessions of 1921 and 1938. Those who died in the off years or when the economy got better, just had bad luck I guess.

Here are some of the reasons Ms. Whitty gives for this amazing fact. People working a lot eat more poorly, either richer, fattier foods, or fast junk foods. I can attest to that. I work very hard typing these columns and keeping the house up to Her code, and I eat a lot of Lucky Charms.

I remember visiting a friend near Wall Street a couple of years ago, and I watched what happens at lunch time. Fast, greasy, over-fried food trucks set up business nearby, and they were swamped. The lines in front of falafel stands and hot dog stands were mobbed. I can tell you that those falafels were delicious and worth dying for.

The bad news is that recessions like the one we're going through now apparently don't count. They have to be like the big one back in the Thirties. This news comes too late for my father who worked very hard in the Great Depression. He had retired from the active navy and became a civil engineer for the government. Had he just given up like his friends who outlived him, and gotten into one of those breadlines downtown, he might be with us yet. Of course he would be about 130 years old, and considering how cranky he was at 67, he would have been intolerable at 77, and my mother would probably have killed him at 87. Things seem to work themselves out, don't they?

So keep your fingers crossed and pray that the public option works out. We're going to need all the help we can get.

Love In a Cardboard Cup

It's the ubiquitous dark universal drug of choice. Okay, it's not officially a drug. Then what is coffee? You tell me.

Coffee. It's all about coffee, I drink one a day and I don't even like it. So why do I do it? Where did it start, this drinking something I only like when it's iced and it's 95 degrees?

Caffeine hits my brain like a car leaving the track at the Indy 500 head on. Too much at a dinner party, and I turn the room into a club and never shut up until people start drifting into the kitchen and staring back at me, as I stand there talking to empty couches. This embarrasses She, who only drinks fruit juice.

So when I do it, it's decaffeinated. Almost no one does that. People who drink decaf in America are like bare foot skiers in the Alps. Who does this? It's so rare that the baristas at the various coffee houses stare at me for a moment and then say, "It'll take a minute to brew some."

"Why?"

"Because you're the only one who asks for it."

"I can't be the only one."

"No, someone came in last week and asked for it."

So why do I drink it at all? Where did I learn this?

After my father's death, my mother started sleeping later and later. Then she started having migraines. She was after all, only 48 when her husband died. Menopause and death is a bad brew.

I was always up early and made my Wheaties. One day, she taught me how to make her coffee, so much water in the pot, so many scoops of Maxwell House. It was fun. I took the white enamel pot and ran the water as I was instructed for one minute, and then filled it up to the assigned mark, then put the coffee in the silver basket, sat down and ate my breakfast in the blue light of early winter morning while I watched the coffee perk. I saw the coffee bubble up in the glass top and then it was ready.

Percolated coffee. Who does that anymore? Only, I suppose, those who remember the day Lindbergh flew the pond.

One day after a long period of mourning, Mama came down in her robe and poured some of my coffee in my father's cup, sat across from me and stared out at the yard. Then she took a sip and held the cup out to me. I took a big sip and made a face. She laughed, the first time I saw her laugh in weeks. She put some of my sugary cereal milk in it. I liked it. After that she let me drink it when she did. It was a healing moment, a bonding between two humans who had lost the love of their lives. That's where it started for me. Life is funny, ain't it?

Coffee plays a strong part in all of our memories.

You got off the Greyhound on a cold rainy night in Louisiana, and there it was sitting alongside a piece of lemon meringue pie.

You were waiting in the chow line on an air base in Texas. You moved along and poured it from the big vat. Now you're grown up and drinking it black the way Mama did.

You're standing guard duty in a tower and somebody said if you fall asleep, they'll shoot you. You're scared, and somebody brings you up a white cup full of it, and the sun comes up.

It's about romance: Before you had money and lived uptown, coffee used to be the ideal opening line. You were standing next to the most beautiful dancer in the world.

"You wanna like...maybe, like...get a cup of coffee after rehearsal?"

She says yes, and it's snowing and at this little place there's the refill at no extra cost. It's bitter and you don't like it but something in her smile provides the sugar, and there's money to share a piece of pie and your fingers touch and suddenly it's love and it was all about coffee. And to think it all started at a kitchen table on a cold winter morning.

Life is funny, ain't it? Wanna get a cup of coffee?

Travel Plans

Do you have a minute? I've been thinking of going down to Manhattan for my birthday. What do you think? Manhattan is a fun town, "The city that never sleeps," and I haven't been there in years. I feel like I should do something risky except flying, that's too risky.

My real fear is that there are so many ghosts there, and old faces you think you know. There is that. Did you ever have that moment where you're in another town, and you're walking along and someone passes you and you stop and grab them by the sleeve. "Bernie Feldman?"

Of course it's not Bernie. Bernie worked with me at a bookstore in Hollywood. He was eight years older than me and had three kids. He would be in a nursing home now in Santa Rosa, not walking in the street in Manhattan.

So I come all the way down here to Manhattan and what happens? I scare the hell out of a stranger. The guy would call the cops and they would bust me and take me to Manhattan South where my old friend Jimmy Cartwright was a detective, only Jimmy has been dead for years and could obviously be of no help.

She, who didn't want to come anyway, would be back at the hotel correcting the kids' papers she always brings along on our trips, and because she never keeps her cell phone close by, would not hear it, and I would be sitting in a cell with "Rico," the drug pusher, telling him about the Franco American Festival going on in Waterville. No, this is not dementia. I play around with these scenarios in my mind to pass the time. Don't be alarmed.

Reality check: My old friends from Manhattan are all dead or have achieved trustee status with library privileges in prison. Who would I call? Who would have coffee with me, go to the theatre, meet me in a bar for a drink? It seems that while I was hiding out up here in Maine, things fell apart, and people started dying without notifying me. It happens to us all.

So I go on Google Earth Live and I'm looking at the corner of 42nd and 7th Avenue. There's a chicken waffle cafe. What the hell is that? There used to be a bar there with shamrocks painted on the windows and long rolls of flypaper hanging near the door. I'm not surprised, I mean, who hangs flypaper anymore?

Once upon a time when people were still humming songs from "My Fair Lady," and "Bells Are Ringing," I could walk in that bar and see friends. I could see booths full of people I knew. Jerry Orbach and Joe Bova would be sitting there, my classmates Geraldine Page, Zero Mostel, Annie Bancroft and all those 1950s blacklisted Hollywood actors and writers I drank with would be three deep at the bar.

Should I go, I would take a cab to the White Horse Tavern in Greenwich Village, the saloon where the poet Dylan Thomas imbibed 18 whiskeys and died shortly after. Bennie Gazzara would be lying on the floor next to a booth of friends because he had a bad back. True story.

But it's raining hard here as I sit in my den in Maine Googling Manhattan where it's raining harder. It looks like it's rush hour and it's been raining all day. I know that rain. It's a city rain, cold and unfriendly. It's not like rain in New England. When it rains in Manhattan, especially in late fall or early winter, it's an angry rain, a Katrina force, the kind of rain that fell on the dead at Anzio and stopped the battle at Fredericksburg.

Thanks for giving me a minute this morning but I guess I'll stick around Maine this year. Everything else is so far away and full of ghosts. I just found my old polka dot Speedo so I'm thinking maybe...Old Orchard Beach? What do you think?

Memorial Day

On an insufferably hot "Decoration Day," as it was known then in 1938, my father took me down to Jefferson Barracks Military Cemetery in St. Louis, to pay respect to one of his old comrades who was being laid to rest. He was the last of my father's company, who had fought in the Spanish American War in the Philippines. Pop, with reluctant blessings, had joined the Marines and was sent to the Philippines. There, with his now deceased buddy, he contracted "stomach poisoning" from some bad Philippine hootch and a case of malaria.

Even though the war was virtually over by the time he got there, Pop didn't like the "hootch," the mosquitos, or sleeping in sand, and when it was over, he drifted into the navy, and rose through the ranks to commander.

And it was on this day, as Commander of the 7th Naval Reserve Unit in St. Louis, he pressed his dress whites, polished his visor, whitened his shoes, and we all went downtown to watch him lead his group in the annual parade. After lunch at a riverside fish shack, he took his youngest on the Broadway street car to say goodbye to an old friend.

There were hundreds of mourners there that day, all floating around from grave to grave, planting flowers and flags. But at my father's friend's grave, there were only two or three. Pop said his friend had no kids so these were probably nephews or nieces. But after a while a handful of veterans drifted over to this lonely pile of fresh earth to salute one of their own, even though they didn't know him. They knew he was a Marine. There was a twenty- one gun salute and a sailor in whites wearing leggings, who played "Taps." Pop saluted with one hand and held mine tightly with the other. After that he dragged me along to visit veterans in the nearby "old folks" hospital. I followed behind him as he went down the aisle of wheelchairs and small beds. To this day I can smell the salves, the lotions, the medicines and body odors. Pop shook each hand as though they were his friends.

Pop was the son of Irish immigrants, but he was no "professional" Irishman. He was a proud American, an officer and patriot. He went on to serve in the "Great War," aboard the old *New Orleans*, and had he not died unexpectedly in March of 1941, he would have rushed to serve his country, a few months later on December 7th. Five of his sons went in his place. The oldest, Matt Jr, served on his father's old ship.

The next time I visited Jefferson Barracks Cemetery was for Pop's funeral. This time, there was a bigger crowd. There was the twenty-one gun salute and "Taps." I remember sitting next to my mother on a cold metal chair as they folded the flag and presented it to her. There were other children there this time, cousins mostly. But standing behind all, next to a wrought iron fence on a hillock that overlooked the river, there was an old man holding the hand of his small son. I didn't know them. They were not our family. I imagine now in my old years, that it was someone who knew my father and brought his boy to honor him.

Today, this scene will play out all over America. There will be fresh earth and flowers, flags, big and small. There will be grave sites with few and many on the grass. There will be old men with old memories holding the hands of small children who will hold their ears when the shots are fired. And when they are, the birds will smash up into the sky, the eternal sky. And the beat goes on.

The Mother's Day Box

Oh Lord. There she is, all of 40 or more years old, sitting in a swing on a porch somewhere with me on her lap. I think that was my Uncle Pat's house over in East St. Louis, across the river and back up into the trees. I'm sure it is.

There is a danger each spring, of cleaning out drawers and boxes of old snapshots. Memories are trapped there in black and white. They can be sweet and bring a laugh or be land mines that explode the heart.

She is smiling here. There are only a few memories I have of her where she was not smiling. She had a kind of smile that said, "It's not a good day, kid, but tomorrow will be."

She loved having her picture taken and no wonder. She was a beautiful woman and proud of her looks, of her hair and clothes. Looking at this picture, I can smell her perfume and that piece of Juicy Fruit gum she's holding still in her mouth. I can smell it even now.

All of my memories of her are connected to her scents, on her breath, in her hair. She kept sachets in all her drawers, with her slips and hankies. Even when the world we once had imploded, and we drifted, the two of us, lugging our suitcases, from apartment to furnished apartment, she carried her scents with her. Each bathroom smelled of Hinds Honey and Almond hand cream, various colognes and soaps wrapped in colored paper.

In each strange place, she'd take one of her doilies, and put it on the back of each furnished chair, calling each new place home.

She was the darling second daughter of Jim "The Dude" Conlon, an Irish immigrant riverboat builder and gambler who had come up the river from the South and built a good business. She and sister Mamie were spoiled creatures who shared a pony and the most expensive first communion dresses in their class. Those were the good days.

When my grandfather went bust, lost his money, his house, and died, she was seventeen and had to go to work as a clerk in the factory that had made his shirts. She never forgot that. It broke her heart and burned her soul. She was never the same again, but the smile never faded. The smile that said, "It's not a good day kid, but tomorrow will be."

In this picture we are very close. I am her beloved son, she my darling mother. It is a safe place. There is love here, there is trust.

But one day, when things went bad for us, she had to temporarily put me in a foster home run by a strict religious church lady she knew well. I carried my own bag this time and unpacked it alone. There were no sachets. The smell of her was gone and so was the safety and the trust.

I remember looking out the window as she left and got on the streetcar. She looked up at me in the window and waved goodbye. She had that look on her face that people have when they have to shoot a horse or put a dog to sleep. I was there only a year, but nothing after that was the same. The knot was untied, the rope cut. In this entire box of pictures, there is not another one of us together. Not one.

It's raining today as I put this picture away. It's not a good day, kid, but tomorrow will be.

Here's To You Mrs. Robinson

This morning the rain stopped and the sun came out. Everything was green and fresh, and you could see for miles. We tend to take all of this for granted, the clean air, the grass and sun, the peace. I came 3,000 miles for that, for the peace.

I was feeling good about all of this until my daughter called from Los Angeles to say that Anna Maria Louisa Italiano had died at 73.

So last night I saw her on an old "Charlie Rose" show. Anna Maria Louisa had that same smile that made you think maybe she was in love with you. She said to Rose, "Sometimes, you have to take a step back, and decide what you're looking for." Rose asked her what it was she had been looking for. She said, "Peace...just peace."

You knew her as Anne Bancroft, American actress, movie star. Actually you knew her as Mrs. Robinson in "The Graduate." She was brilliant in everything she did, but Mrs. Robinson stuck.

I knew her long ago as Annie with the crazy curly hair and the smile that made you think that maybe she was in love with you.

Annie was my classmate in an acting class up on the third floor of an old building in lower Manhattan in the very cold winter of the 50s. That was yesterday when we were both young, and we sat in class in overcoats and ate pastrami and drank coffee from a paper cup.

Annie always left early because she had to be at the theatre at 7 o'clock to act with Henry Fonda in "Two for the Seesaw." She didn't need a class, but work, the discipline, was ingrained in her.

Annie watched every scene I did. Then one day, she told me to meet her at a coffee shop on Broadway at 45th Street. She had arranged for me to audition to understudy a part in my first Broadway show.

She bought me a cup of coffee and took me backstage to the theatre and right out onstage and read with me for the part. This was Annie Bancroft whose name was in lights a block away. I was a twenty-something nobody. Who would do such a thing? Annie would.

We were not close friends. I won't be asked to her funeral. She was just a figure in my personal landscape, a memory in blurred amber. We were just classmates. One day she won a Tony and got too busy to come down to 14th Street.

I spent the next 30 years driving through neon nights and dirty yellow air days, running from one job to another trying to glue together a "career," one drink to the next. I made lots of money. I had everything I wanted, except for peace.

One day, I took the step back, way back to this morning laying in the new mown grass in a garden in Maine, picking grass from my dog's hair.

There are no sirens in the night, no constant hovering helicopters or roaring traffic. Peace.

I only share this with you this morning, because you'll read about "Anne Bancroft," movie and Broadway star, the celebrity and you'll say, "What did I see her in?" I just thought you might want to know Annie was more than a movie star. She was the former Anna Italiano, who took the hand many years ago, of a young nobody and gave him his first break. Isn't it ironic that the movie that made her famous wrote her epitaph:

"Here's to you Mrs. Robinson. Jesus loves you more than you will know.

God Bless you, Mrs. Robinson. Heaven holds a place for those who pray."

    –Simon and Garfunkle

What's In a Name?

Q. When is a birth certificate not a birth certificate?
A. When it is a certificate of live birth.

Yes, I know it's stupid, but that is a document offered by the State of Hawaii as proof of birth, and if you want anything else you'll have to go to Hawaii and ask. And while you're there, check out the blue fin tuna sashimi at Alan Wong's in Honolulu. Fabulous.

I had no intention of jumping into this "birther," thing but it's become personal and now I'm concerned that I won't be able to use my legal rights should I decide to run for President of the United States.

Yes I can. I'm approximately the same age as John McCain, and he ran for President. I have the same aches and pains and memory problems as Senator McCain, and I would probably have picked Sarah Palin as my running mate as well, based purely on the fact that she is a hot lady. She dresses well and has a great snappy walk. McCain and I are both Irish and we both have great taste in picking women. Look at his wife. Look at my wife.

But now, because of this Obama birth certificate flap, I can't even run against Waterville Mayor Paul LePage, let alone President without my multiple names coming under scrutiny. I'm not going to put myself through that. And what about that Baptist girl in Texarkana, the one I told I was Ernest Hemingway? They'll dig her up.

Here's my birth story so you can see what I'm up against. I was born at home on September 9th. The year is not relevant for this story. A doctor and midwife were present, as was my father and a man I can only remember as Barney. Barney, it seems, was having a late afternoon pick up with my father at the bar in Skeeter O'Neal's Saloon a block away celebrating the impending birth of a new son. That would be me. Barney and my father were sent to the kitchen to wait out my birth. That is neither here nor there, but I have to fill this column with something.

Ten days later, the midwife, one Rosie Chambers who my father sponsored over from Ireland, was sent down to City Hall to register my birth. This was the exchange between Rosie and the city clerk, as Rosie told it, over and over for almost fifty years.

"What is the child's name?"

"Jerry," she replied.

"That would be Gerald I suppose?"

"Whatever," Rosie answered.

Upon hearing this, my mother went into postpartum catatonic shock. This was not the name she intended to give me. So when I was baptized at the font at St. Mary and Joseph's church up the street, I was given the name my mother intended. Jeremiah Padraic Devine.

However, Gerald was forever emblazoned on the official city hall birth certificate, or, if I had been born to Don Ho, a "Certificate of Live Birth."

So for all of my life and in the service of my country, I was called G.J. The Irish love initials. Not until I got married, and sent for my church birth certificate, did I know I was Jeremiah Padraic, so named after my mother's first boyfriend.

It gets worse. When I joined Actor's Equity, the theater union, I gave my name as Jerry. Then in Hollywood when I joined Screen Actors Union, there already was a "Jerry Devine," so I took my confirmation name of James. When I was hired as a freelancer for the *Los Angeles Times*, I used J.P. See what I'm up against?

Can you imagine what Rush Limbaugh and Michael Steele would do with all of that? I have the solution. I'm going to run under the name, Ernest Hemingway. It worked in Texarkana, didn't it?

My Life with Guns

When I was 22 years old, I killed a cop. I was serving in the Air Force in San Francisco, and I stood no more than six feet away from him, and I shot him four times and he fell, but not before my ears started ringing and kept ringing for 3 hours.

Now that I have your attention, I can tell you that I was an actor on stage in a San Francisco theater, and the pistol held blanks. In the first professional job of my career, I was playing a young, psychotic gunman in Sydney Kingsley's "Detective Story." Afterwards, my hand shook for hours. I loved the applause. I hated the gun.

It got worse: In Air Force boot camp, we all had to qualify for the carbine. On the firing range, the wooden top flew off of mine and hit me in the face causing a flow of blood. I did not qualify for a Purple Heart, because I was not shooting at a Korean. For years I told girls at parties that the scar was a war wound. I really did. Women love men with scars. This is why the Prussian officers often self-inflicted them. It didn't work on she who has grown skeptical of my ploys. She claims it's probably an acne scar from childhood.

After the wound healed, I was advised by my instructor not to apply for military police. I wound up as a master typist in the AF intelligence office at a base in California. Mostly I filed classified stuff that they wouldn't let me actually read.

At five o'clock after office hours, I, and two gun toting military policemen wheeled the day's paperwork down to a burner and incinerated it. I was compelled to wear a .45 pistol on that short journey. Because I was so skinny, no ass or hips, the gun belt kept slipping down.

This frightened the two MPs, and they relieved me of the obligation. True story.

In the beginning as kids on the block, playing cowboys and Indians was all the rage, my friend Neil had a cool Red Ryder bee bee gun. I had a Gene Autry gun and holster set which never stayed up either. I later traded it to Alfred Weber for 25 comic books and a Captain Midnight de-coder badge that I never learned how to use. I think it was broken.

With World War II, every boy in America had a collection of warrior equipment: copies of rifles, helmets, ammo belts and rubber bayonets. We even had realistic canteens, which we quickly learned to fill with Kool Aid. Kool Aid played a part in my life later in the middle of the Pacific Ocean. It's a great true story, but I'm saving it for my memoirs.

One wartime Christmas, my sister and her friend, Margaret Eichelberger, got nurse sets, complete with Red Cross aprons and caps. The sets came with bandages, stethoscopes, and vials of "real" blood of a gooey nature that if spilled, did not come out of upholstery or aprons.

I don't know how this will reflect on my sexual identity, but I really wanted to be a nurse for a few hours and use that stethoscope. Maybe it was just all about Margaret Eichelberger. You can see that my life with guns never really got going, but now the NRA's propaganda has me concerned. They keep saying things like "what if someone bursts through your door looking for drugs?"

Well, all I have are two pills for cholesterol and baby aspirin. However, if things get worse, and I'm forced to keep a gun in the house, it will be for her. So I'm thinking a pearl-handled Derringer that she can tuck up inside her skirt like Bonnie Parker did. I understand that Clyde Barrow liked that. It's all immaterial. If they do a background check on me and ask my old Air Force instructor and those two MPs, I'll never get a permit anyway.

Now that's Italian

> *The trouble with Italian food is that five or six days later, you're hungry again.*
> —George Miller

We're in trouble. Hurricane Gonzalo is heading towards us and ISIS is gaining in territory. The Ebola thing is getting scarier, what with suspected patients taking weekend flights to Cleveland, Ohio. Having Ebola is bad enough, but why make it worse by going to Cleveland? If I found out that I had Ebola, Cleveland would not pop into mind.

All of these things are keeping me awake, and now to make matters worse, word reaches me that Olive Garden is in trouble. I can't stand it. When my latest copy of the San Jose Mercury News came in the mail today featuring an article by Candice Choi, I learned that once loyal customers and greedy stockholders are upset with the chain. People are complaining that the prices are going up, and to make matters worse, they're cutting back on the breadsticks, and the ones they are getting are cold.

I haven't seen any shortage in the breadstick baskets, and the ones served to she, who is the only one in my house who eats them, were very warm. I don't eat anything white including bread sticks, which by the way, used to come to Italian tables looking like real skinny sticks. Now they look like hot dog rolls. Back in 1995, as you read in these pages, the chain, to keep loyal customers happy, began a promotional tack called "The Never Ending Pasta Bowl," which was very successful. It immediately caught on with the general population. Last month, O.G. sold the pass card for 100 bucks and guaranteed "never ending" pasta, including breadsticks, salad and soup, my personal favorite, for 49 days. According to their press release, they sold out in an hour and now the cards can be found on eBay for hundreds of bucks more. I love this country.

As I say, I don't eat pasta these days, which would account for my new sleek streamlined body. But I do have a weakness for Italian soup, and Olive Garden delivers terrific pasta fagioli and minestrone, and you can get seconds. So I tweeted Darden Restaurants, the parent company of Olive Garden, encouraging them to promote "The Never Ending Bowl of Soup." I have yet to hear back from them.

The problem doesn't end there for Olive Garden. Now many regular customers are complaining that the food isn't as good as it used to be. I don't know who these folks are, because when I visit OG, the lobby and tables are full, and there is always a long waiting line on weekends. This is why she, who is always on top of these things, learned that we can call in when we're on our way, thus insuring a quick seating. I promise you that this works.

Still the complaints from some snobs keep coming. "The noodles are too soft, the sauce not hot enough." This reminds me of Bernie Goldman's father's joke: "The food at this place is terrible, and they serve such small portions."

This is not a promotional piece for Olive Garden, I wouldn't be allowed to do that, especially by my nephew Mateo, a genuine Italian chef with two restaurants in Brooklyn where he cooks real Italian. But in an honest effort to promote the general American economy, I think Olive Garden is getting an unfair hit.

I don't know anyone at Darden Restaurants, but I do know several of the servers at the Olive Garden in Augusta and as in most American eateries, they are hardworking American men and women dependent on meager tips. Many of the younger ones are working their way through college, putting the "Never Ending Pasta" on your tables.

I should say that I have one complaint. They only put two olives in their salads. In fairness, when I mentioned that the establishment is called OLIVE Garden, not SALAD Garden, the chef sent out a small bowl of ten olives. Now, that's Italian.

No Country for Old Men

Each Christmas or birthday, Father's Day, Rosh Hashanah and spring, my daughter renews these subscriptions to *Esquire*, *GQ* and other fashion magazines for me. It's so annoying. She means well and I don't want to tell her, but I can't find me in there. Who are these guys? I know I used to look like them back in my magazine modeling days, but that was a long time ago, so long ago I was smoking in some of them and wearing white on white shirts with collar clips. Not even gangsters wear white on white shirts with collar pins anymore. I think John Gotti was the last.

I think she's scared that I'm starting to slip into that long goodnight, the big dirt nap. I think it was the new beard that scared her. It's all white. It doesn't come in black like it used to. Nothing comes in black like it used to except the ear hairs. That's a mystery for another time. It's the magazines that concern me now. I also get L.L.Bean and Land's End for men. L.L.Bean's clothes are so drab it's a wonder these guys can stay awake when they're hunting or fishing in those big rubber waders. Land's End isn't much snappier.

I'm thinking that *GQ* and *Esquire* are subscribed to only by high school kids or early college. I don't see myself in there. The only two magazines that have guys who look like me are *AARP* and *Arthritis Today* and even they don't dress like me. They dress like really old guys. You know the ones, those guys who ride around in golf carts and pose with grown grandchildren.

Television ads aren't much different. You must have noticed that at exactly 6:00 p.m. the TV ads all switch to appeals to dying, ailing fellas who keep jumping out of cars and running into gas station men's rooms. Or those ads for Cialis. Even the men in those ads look younger than me. I'm looking at one right now on my office set. This guy looks to be about 47 years old.

He and his wife are smiling at one another like they just met on Facebook. "For when the time is right," the voiceover says.

My daughter is an agent. She casts television commercials. She says if I want to come back, I'm the right age for this market. I can play grandpas and judges, she says. I can be that guy riding around in the golf cart or the old guy staring into the sunset, and his grandson has to come get him because he doesn't know where he is. That's sad. I'm gonna be there soon enough, why should I want to play one this early? Money is the answer of course. There's big money in playing senile old incontinent men with bad feet who are waiting for that moment when the "time is right."

Old Men, New Fire

They sat at what most consider the best winter table, the big Formica topped booth in the sunlight at a coffee shop outside of Portland. There were five in all. These were old guys, older than I am, and I fit perfectly into my mother's favorite description of "no spring chicken."

They had the skin and hands of men who had worked hard in their lives, probably in the factories, roofing and construction in Maine's summer heat and winter's numbing cold. They were clearly old friends and felt comfortable with one another. Of course they did. I have always felt as comfortable in the company of old men. As a boy, I spent many a night at the feet of a posse of survivors, my father, uncles, and their friends who shared that twilight hour after supper with one another, with the aroma of pork chops or fried chicken still floating in the air. They were old friends and cousins sitting on the back porch with the last beer of the day, swatting mosquitos, munching toothpicks and sucking on the occasional cigar my mother would not allow in the house.

These were warriors who had survived the Spanish American War, the "Great War," and the Great Depression. They had been shot, wounded, gassed and hobbled by frostbite and horse kicks. They told great stories, these old men. They were my radio, my television and movies. They bought me bottles of Orange Crush, and let me sit among them and listen. I have often told my children that I have memories that don't belong to me. They are the memories of others now long gone.

So I was, of course, intrigued by the camaraderie of this booth of old guys laughing and chatting. It brought back sharp and sweet memories. Hundreds of miles and many states and years apart, they were the same men. I moved into the booth behind them, opened my paper and eavesdropped.

They gossiped about politics of course, taxes, their grandchildren and the "sissies" who were still down in Florida. They spoke of cataracts, hip replacements, colonoscopies, funerals and weather, the chatter of the old. Coffee cups were re-filled, pastries shared, napkins crumpled, and some gossip whispered followed by bursts of unanimous laughter. One of them, I noticed, kept rubbing his knee. I know that feeling.

The man in the middle took out an envelope of snapshots. They were of his great-grandchildren in Texas, he said. They all took turns looking at them.

Then it changed. A latecomer arrived, a thick-bellied man with a slight limp. They all shouted at him, and he pulled up a chair and joined them. He had a surprise, he said. He placed a cloth-covered tablet on the table, and opened it up to reveal a new Apple iPad. His daughter had bought it for him for his birthday, he said, and said how it took him two weeks to learn how to use it. A man at the next table, and his wife, came over to look at the new toy. They had smartphones with pictures of their grandkids as well, and showed them off. But Mr. Late Comer clearly had the edge. Proudly he passed it around the table to great amazement. They all gathered around as he displayed his children, his grandchildren, and the picture of a large dog.

Driving home, it occurred to me that what I had seen was an evolutionary snapshot. I remembered those old grade school pictures of early man amazing his clan with a flaming torch that lit up the caves and killed the darkness. He had discovered fire. His cave mates gathered around the flames as these coffee shop buddies did here, and these boys of radio and leather-covered family albums, sat there in the sunlight of the 21st Century looking at the new fire. And the beat goes on.

Adios, Peppermint Patty

"I'm glad Milton Hershey is dead and not here to see what's been done in his name. Milton was a good guy, a good American, alas, probably a Republican like Walt Disney and VERY patriotic, but a good guy.

What's happening in American Candy World today in his name would fade the colors on his lapel flag. We Americans were raised on candy bars, and Hershey was always at the top.

The Hershey name is as Coca Cola, right up there with Mom's Apple Pie, Thanksgiving and the Saturday garage sale. That's why it saddens me to learn that the current traders on that name have sold out their country.

Friday, in Reading, Pennsylvania, the flag is coming down. (Taps play here.) Word has come to me that Hershey is pulling the curtain, shutting the door, turning out the last light on the small factory that has, for years, made the great York Peppermint Patty. That's right. The York Peppermint Patty. You didn't know that, did you?

That smooth chocolate, the crisp, snappy cool taste of peppermint, it was like a cool breeze filling your mouth. There was an art to eating a York Peppermint Patty. You had to buy one along with fresh popcorn as you settled into the movie. First, you took a bite and then a chunk of popcorn. The combination ranked right up there with Roquefort and pinot noir, Stella and pastrami.

To be fair, the York Peppermint Patty didn't start with Hershey, it started with the York Co. founded in the 1920s. The York Cone Company manufactured ice cream cones and waffles, plus selected confectionery items in York, Pennsylvania.

In 1940, York peppermint patties were introduced and sold only locally. Shortly thereafter, demand became so great that all other product lines were discontinued.

The York Peppermint Patty first came to Maine, and then to Ohio, Indiana and Florida, then broke out across this great country. In 1988, Hershey Foods Corporation, now a giant conglomerate far from Milton's tiny kitchen with the two big pots, swallowed up York peppermint patties. Now, after 23 years, Hershey's Chocolate is closing the plant Friday and moving production to a new factory it has built in Monterey, Mexico. MEXICO! That's fine and dandy for our unemployed amigos to the south. With all due respect for my Latino brothers and sisters, I'm sure they'll do their best, and we probably won't even know the difference unless they get creative and add some jalapenos or cumin to the mix. But that's not the point.

This is just another slap in the American laborer's face. It's about more than chocolate and peppermint. In doing this, Hershey, once a proud job creator, is pulling the plug and taking 300 jobs in the southeastern Pennsylvania city, Pennsylvania mind you, a state, along with Ohio and Michigan that has been hit hard by this broken economy, and sending them to Mexico. It gets worse. We're informed that this is part of a bigger move to eliminate 1,500 jobs and one third of its production lines. You know what? I'll bet the Hershey people never really liked the Peppermint Patty anyway.

President Obama, in his Tuesday night speech, repeated his promise to take punitive action against companies that sent our jobs away by eliminating tax breaks for them. You hear that, Hershey? No soup for you.

I know it's a common thing now. Nothing in my house is made in Pennsylvania or Ohio. And I can live with talking to "Dave" Jindara in New Delhi about my computer or cellphone, but this is a knife to my heart.

I'll miss my Peppermint Patty. I'll miss taking that silver disc from the fridge and snapping it in two. Popcorn in the movies won't taste the same without it. Even movies won't be the same. But each time I took a bite, I'd be reminded of those 1,800 jobs floating over the border. I hope you join me in this boycott. I hope Susan and Olympia will as well. Adios, Peppermint Patty. Vaya Con Dios.

Go Reboot Yourself

Maybe it was the 104 degree cabin fever. She thinks it was the overdose of Pepsi Cola, Ben and Jerry's Karamel Sutra ice cream and Farmer's Market Fudge, I'll never know. But in the middle of a snow storm, my computer suddenly reached the end of the known universe, and I was unable to control events as the screen went Google nuts, exploding with Obama's health care bill, underwear bombers, one Tiger Woods girl after another, unemployment numbers and Haitian bodies all bursting out of this giant electronic piñata, melting together in a great confluence of flashing lights and screaming voices.

My 22-inch screen detonated in a kaleidoscopic rainbow of maddened, unemployed Tea Baggers, roaming the streets with signs of badly misspelled slogans and lynching ropes, chanting made up songs like 1917 Bolsheviks hunting for the Czar's golden toilet, or like those crazy rummed up throngs that filled the streets under Eva Peron's balcony while she belted out Andrew Lloyd Webber's hit song.

Then the system shuddered and went directly from the Huffington Post to iTunes Store and started playing the Bee Gee's "How Do You Mend a Broken Heart?" I called Apple Care in a panic.

Twenty minutes later, a young man with the smooth voice of the late Merv Griffin calmly asked, "Have you rebooted?" Rebooted? It always sounded frightening, like a surgical procedure.

"Simply go to the Apple logo," he whispered, "slide down and touch restart." So that's what it means. I took a deep breath and touched the button. The screen went blank and then came back on with that familiar Apple theme. Afterwards, in a state of tranquility I realized that not only had I rebooted the computer, but somewhere deep in my soul, I had rebooted... me. Somehow I had reached Apple Nirvana, that perfect state of mind that is free from craving, with certain exceptions, and anger, well, sort of.

I was at peace with the internet with compassion for all (some) and ready to give up obsessions (most) and fixations. (Define fixation.)

Rebooting is the answer to everything, isn't it? Everyone is doing it. NBC, booting Conan O'Brien out the door, thus reestablishing the network's late night hot chair, is rebooting. Senator Chris Dodd and Lou Dobbs have rebooted, and Sarah Palin changed her hairstyle, which is simply a fashion rebooting.

Now, as the snow falls softly across the city on the living and on the dead, I have a mirror so positioned that I can see the screen from my tub where I sit with a frozen banana daiquiri. If I move the tiny umbrella in the glass slightly to the left, I can see Senator Harry Reid. His lips are moving but I have it on mute.

I see Elizabeth Edwards snarling at John, and Mika Brzezinski bobbing her head to Morning Joe's rhythm. There's Sen. Bernie Sanders of Vermont. He has nice teeth. I think they're false. I can see Speaker Nancy Pelosi waving furiously, her eyes popping like big olives in her tapioca-colored frozen face.

The daiquiri is taking over. I'm calm, banana medicated. Without my glasses I can't read the crawl on CNN and MSNBC. Those were so annoying anyway. I always caught the last three words..."died of cancer" or "will soon explode." Then you had to wait through a long Cialis commercial to find out what it meant. So I rebooted. Shut the set off and turned it back on. Voila! It's Jeopardy. The question is big enough to read, "What sea did Moses part?" No one gets it?

After my bath I received an email from David Plouffe asking me to "Regroup, refocus, and re-engage." He forgot to include reboot. I deleted him. It's almost as much fun as rebooting. I love this stuff.

Remembering Robin

> "Show me a hero, I'll write you a tragedy."
> –F. Scott Fitzgerald

On a hot August night back in the mid '70s, a group of struggling stand-up comics, myself included, was standing in the parking lot of the old Comedy Store on Sunset Boulevard, waiting for our five or ten minutes on stage.

The Comedy Store and Bud Friedman's Improv club on Melrose Avenue were the places to go each night for struggling young stand-up comics.

They were drop-in places for agents and producers looking for new talent, who would come by after dinner to catch the fresh acts. In those early days, David Letterman, Andy Kaufman, Richard Pryor, Jay Leno, and yes, the late and sadly missed Robin Williams, all of them not yet stars, almost barely recognizable, would come by to try out new material.

A new unknown comic would get on the long list with the stage manager, and then go and hang out with the other waiting comics in the parking lot.

We would all stand around smoking various things and chatting, sharing stories and looking at our watches, hoping we'd get five minutes on stage before a star showed up and hogged the stage, and that happened often.

Occasionally, someone would bring a pizza or a six pack, and everyone would sit on some stranger's expensive car and share the joys and pains of trying to make a name.

On this night, stamped forever in my memory, five of us, including two close friends, the late Steve Landesberg and Ron Carey, both who later became stars of television's "Barney Miller," were laughing when we heard a loud thud in the street next door. Another comic crossed the lot to tell us a young guy in a James Dean red jacket had just jumped off the top of the next door hotel. "Oh my God," Landesberg said. "I saw him. He was standing here a few minutes ago."

He was, but nobody really knew his name. He was just another comic who was waiting to do his five minutes, gave up, and then walked away, went to the top of the hotel and fell 23 floors to the bottom of the obit page in the *Los Angeles Times*.

I'm thinking about my friends, all gone now, and that jumper, as we all mourn comedian Robin Williams, who once stood in that parking lot waiting for his five minutes.

Not long after that, Freddie Prinze, the gifted stand-up comic and star of "Chico and the Man," shot himself in his room at the Beverly Hills Hotel. Few remember Freddie anymore, but he, like Robin and the great John Belushi, who were both friends, all suffered the torments of drugs and the monsters.

A stand-up comic, more than any other performer, knows what it's like to come off stage after "killing" the audience. Laughter is a drug in itself, and when it comes in unstoppable waves, when people pound the tables and stomp their feet, it produces a stratospheric high. To be pumped up with that wonderful adrenalin, and then step off stage and be hit with silence is a punch in the gut. Laughter is wonderful, but when the laughter stops, the drop is breathtaking.

Comics have a high suicide rate. But you don't read about them unless they're like Robin. The graveyards are full of young talents who didn't have the luck or the great magic of Robin, and even after shots on Johnny Carson or Letterman, find a way into the darkness rather than going home to Nebraska.

They are the invisible kids who simply kept moving farther and farther back in the line, standing aside in the parking lots and lobbies until losing got too painful. Some do go home, others walk into the darkness. That darkness has a texture. I've felt it. It has a taste. I've tasted it.

I never really wanted to do stand-up comedy, I just wanted to learn how to write it. I think I have, and with all my comic friends gone, I'm grateful to be here. Goodnight Robin, where ever you are. To all the new comics standing outside in the parking lot, you were a hero.

Requiem for 2 Strangers

"Though lovers be lost love shall not; and death shall have no dominion."
—Dylan Thomas

Nobody will ever know who they were. They probably worked in the same office, sharing coffee and bagels each morning. Maybe they were married, both working for the same firm, coming to work each day on the subway or the commuter train, holding hands.

Maybe they were just dating. He brought coffee to her desk each day. At night, they might have gone to the movies, or out for sushi in the Village and then dancing, holding hands.

Maybe they were only friends, a single girl and a gay man who gossiped at the water cooler, ate burgers and sipped Diet Cokes on one of the benches in the nearby park.

But I like to think they were lovers.

There is a picture of them now that a lot of people saw. A man and a woman holding hands and stepping off into space, 110 floors up in the blue sky.

Who were they, I wonder, this couple who stepped out into the sky together, hands clutched, eyes closed, both mumbling prayers?

What could they have said at the last moment, as they stood looking north over Manhattan's skyline to John Lennon's Strawberry Fields in Central Park? You can see a long way from the 110th floor.

Where were they from? She might have been from the green fields of Iowa, a cheerleader, class president, prom queen.

He might have been from St. Louis, Missouri, or Portland, Maine, a football hero in high school or leader of the debate team.

They both came to Manhattan, the city of neon dreams and got their first jobs with this wonderful firm with offices high up in the city's sky, where they could see forever.

Now on this bright, beautiful September day, surrounded by strange thunder, flame and smoke, the exits blocked, the world gone mad, they came to the end of it, the end of it all. What they said to each other at that last moment will never be heard. I would like to think it was "I love you."

When it was clear that there was no other way to go, they stepped off into eternity and fell like snowflakes, like birds, like the rain. I would like to think that they never, for a falling moment, let go of one another.

I first saw Manhattan at age 25, stepping into Times Square on a rainy night, when the lights of the city floated in the rivers of rain like magic. She was like the most beautiful woman in the world at a crowded party. I fell in love. I love her still.

I'll bet they felt the same way.

I met a red-haired actress there on an escalator in Bloomingdale's Department Store at Christmas, and fell in love. People always fall in love in Manhattan. It's required.

They said that New York isn't America. They were dead wrong. It is America, and it's Oz, El Dorado on the Hudson and Xanadu.

Now part of Oz is gone, covered with blood and smoke and burning flesh. Someone came and tried to kill my beautiful city, the most beautiful woman in a crowded world. But they can't. She's too tough.

Manhattan will come back to life, dancers and actors will fill her rehearsal halls, musicians will play again on her corners, and dreamers will come up out of her subways into rainy Times Square again.

There will be new shows on Broadway, and somewhere on an escalator in Bloomingdale's or Macy's, a couple of young actors will bump into each other and touch hands and fall in love and live happily ever after.

Nobody knows who they were. They now belong to all American mothers who want to think he was their son, to fathers who are sure she was their daughter, and who may be comforted that at least they did not die alone.

Those towers may have fallen, others may have fallen, but those two holding hands? I like to think they flew.

The Last Roundup

The first one, ten years after we walked the stage, was held in the old gymnasium that still smells of sweat and old sneakers. There was crepe paper, and napkins in the school colors. Dixie cups and the glass punch bowl were supplied by Mrs. Conlon, the Latin teacher. Almost no one misses the first one. After that interest diminishes. With each passing year it gets harder and harder to mask the inevitable: the wrinkles, the loss of hair, cellulite. The first is about the great new job, the second, about the promotions, or lack of, and then it's all divorces, adultery, OUIs and foreclosures.

There was one, I'm told that was held at a Radisson ballroom in the early sixties. Whoever booked it bounced the check. Six divorces and four births were announced. The next one was at someone's camp. It rained, and there was a fist fight.

Word comes to me now of the 60th. 60th? Is that possible? Is there really such a thing as a 60th high school reunion? The mind that once grew numb with calculus and biochemistry, now boggles at the thought.

As I am the only survivor who became a writer it falls on me to envision it. Who will be there? Who is dead? Who is alive? There is only one scenario possible. It will likely be held in the visitors' lounge at the Rosebud Assisted Living Home. The staff will handle the decorations this time I imagine. I don't want to think about that. No chicken wings or tapas this time. Loud sport coats and too long dresses will be replaced by nylon leisure suits and robes. Men's hair will be silver or non-existent, women's will be in various shades of orange. There will be tiny tuna sandwiches and iced tea in plastic glasses. The paper napkins will be borrowed from the Burger King just down the street. Bowls of Beano will be supplied. Valet parking for walkers, I'm sure.

Memories will be shared, that's the good and bad part. There will be talk of Leonard who died in Korea and left his collection of Perry Como records to his senior class love, Laura Wharton, who broke his heart by running away with Alan Towers, who became a Kroger's Market night manager.

Music will be supplied, I imagine, by Billy Seeger, should he still be alive. Billy played the accordion and was fond of Polish polkas. The mandatory group photo shot should be fun. In 1967, I'm told, there were problems getting everyone back into the ballroom for the shot, and there was the marijuana incident in the parking lot.

It's always arranged by height. Louise Barker was the shortest, 5'1," as I remember, and had established a permanent spot in front, and Kevin Mueller, the tallest at 6'7," was always at the back.

It will be easier this time, I predict. After all that hip and knee business, most will want to sit down, even Kevin, who is now a wealthy dentist in Southern Illinois. If she is still alive, and I hope she is, Rosemary De Branco, she of the one thousand and one pastel-colored angora sweaters, will be seated center next to Barbara Johnson, both of whom always wore "White Shoulders" cologne and confused us all.

With the great possibility of major dentures, "Best Smile" will be eliminated. There will be a prize, I'm sure, for he or she who came from the greatest distance. I heard from Ron Cincena, now deceased, some years ago that the prize went to Phil (last name omitted) who came all the way up from Arkansas State Prison, where he was paroled after serving time for check bouncing. Phil, I'm told, passed away after a short career as a night bagger at Alan Tower's Kroger Store.

As usual, I won't be attending this year.

The Second Mrs. Jones

"In the coldest February, as in every other month in every other year, the best thing to hold onto in this world is each other."
–Linda Ellerbee, cancer survivor

Hers was a familiar face to me. I had passed her over the years in the markets, on the streets, the coffee houses. We had never mingled socially, she knew me from the picture atop this column. We smiled and nodded and occasionally exchanged the clichés about the weather. Never more.

She was one of those many faces that pass me in the walk through the day. Like them, I never knew her name, nor do I now. If I did, I would have forgotten it. My memory is a scary clown who stands just outside my reach, teasing me. To me, for this moment, she is "Mrs. Jones," one of the pleasant figures in my daily landscape.

Like many of these figures, she disappears and then reappears weeks, sometimes months, even years later. I'm sure neither of us ever gives the other a thought in this time.

But I always liked running into her. She is an attractive woman, pleasant, with a great smile. Mrs. Jones had soft shoulder-length hair, a shade of color that makes me think of early autumn. She was always in a hurry, it seemed. I don't even know how she passed her days, behind a desk? A counter, a classroom? No idea.

A month ago, on a hot day chopped up with rain and sun, I ran into her in the vegetable stalls at the market. The first thing I noticed was that she was wearing her hair in a new style and color. It was short and curly and a darker shade, the same Mrs. Jones. A new Mrs. Jones.

"I love your new hair," I said. As always, she was in a rush, but this time she paused, only for maybe twenty seconds, long enough to say this.

"Well, it's the way it grew back." There was a long pause as she looked down the aisle and then back at me as if she was considering how important it was to tell me the truth. "It was the chemo," she said. "It took the hair away, and then it grew back like this." There was a brief smile.

I felt the way we feel when we break an heirloom in someone's house.

"I'm sorry," I said, "that you had to go through that. I really am."

She smiled and shrugged.

And then the "new" Mrs. Jones was gone. I watched her walk away and wished I had kept my mouth shut. I'm sure she has worked her way past the worst part, but I'm just as sure that the specter never leaves her side, and that no amount of sunshine can completely part the clouds that hang around.

Since that day, I've had the painful occasion to meet three other "Mrs. Jones." Three other figures in my landscape, each with a new hairstyle. These were women I knew slightly better and hadn't seen in many months.

With the first of these, I chatted about weather and politics, about her kids that my teacher had taught. Something hung between us, like a thin ground fog. I knew what it was. She was a new Mrs. Jones, and she seemed to want to say more than hello, goodbye. "I'm better," she said, as if I had asked. It was clearly a practiced statement. I just looked at her and smiled. Then she said, "You know I had breast cancer."

I had the same reply on the tip of my tongue. "I'm so sorry you had to go through that." This time I hugged her. She hugged me very tightly. I'll bet she does that a lot now. Hugging is a rope we mortals use, hoping it won't break. More and more, we use it a lot.

Today at lunch in a cafe, I ran into a friend from my early days here. She was happy to see me. Her name was out of reach for me, but she knew it and offered it. Then it all came back. I reminded her of the first time we had met at a party, and I was sitting on a red velvet couch, and she came over to tell me how much she loved what I wrote. She was a bundle of energy then. A good deal of that remains.

Now, years later, looking even younger, thinner, tan and fit but with a brand new hairstyle, grey and wavy, she took my hand and squeezed it. It was the hug, the rope. There it was.

The numbers are cold and ubiquitous. 12 million people are diagnosed with the disease every year, and 7.6 die of it. It's not a headline, a "breaking news" story. It's just there and it won't go away.

A somewhat brighter view comes in a report from the American Cancer Society that claims that, as a result of early detection and better treatment, cancer rates have been going down. As of now, there are more than 2 1/2 million breast cancer survivors in the United States.

For me it has gone beyond the market place. It has come to my own door. I lost a dear sister and sister-in-law to its cold touch. There are three precious women now close to me. I touch their beautiful hair and hug their bodies to me as much as I can. It's all I can do. It's all any of us can do.

I go to my market every evening to shop. I try to focus, get it done and go home. I don't want to see another face, another new hair style, yet another "Mrs. Jones."

Each day, each morning, each evening, between bites of dinner, sips of wine, passing through the rooms, I touch the woman who has saved my life more times than I can count and hug her even more than I ever did. It's the same hairdo she has always had. It's that color that makes me think of early autumn.

Sometimes I Wave

All of us, as the year ends, have a story about people, those here and those gone. You have yours, this is my story.

On a cold snowy New Year's Eve, you take out the albums, run the home movies. There are the old black and white snapshots of lovers and friends: he in his sailor suit, she in her high school formal, huddling at a party. All now have become shadows on the lawn, the long dead we so loved, frozen in silver frames.

Dead is a hard word, I know. We soften it, we say, "They passed," or "They're with Jesus now." We hope there is a Heaven so that we can see them all again, well, maybe not all. But they're gone. There is no hiding it. They are gone, and when we see them paraded before us in home movies and shared photos, doors open we thought were closed.

You can put the albums away, stick them in a drawer and turn the framed photos to the wall when it gets too hard. It's not so simple for me. I come from the business of "Show," where once the camera looks at you, there you are, big or small, forever, here and all over the world. There you are. Forever.

On New Year's Eve and year's end programs, they run the obituaries of famous people, celebrities who have "passed." Some of those were friends, dear friends, close friends.

Some became big stars, some already were. Do a scene with Dennis Weaver, for example. Fame doesn't play a part. You're both actors, and then you do another and then you're friends. Forever.

Over the years as I hide out here in the forest, I put all of that behind me, all of those friends who "passed," or went to whomever they believed in. I close doors.

But every night when I turn on the television, watch Turner Classic Movies or re-runs of shows, there they are, old friends that I worked with, ate and drank with, old comrades, old lovers, who got sick and died much too young and left me here alone. Of course I'm not alone now, one of them stayed with me. She knows what I mean. She knew them too.

One minute we were young and fun, acting and dancing, singing in saloons, sharing dressing rooms and bar stools and beds. I was at their weddings. I babysat their children.

In the mid-fifties, New York was home and we were all poor but happy. We were working at our professions and not making much money. You won't remember the great Geraldine Page. Gerry and I shared corned beef sandwiches and beer at an Irish saloon across from our acting classes on 14th Street. Sometimes Zero Mostel and Annie Bancroft, Bob Culp, and Dom DeLuise sat with us in those old booths. The laughter never stopped. Mary Martin's son Larry Hagman, before he was "J.R." in "Dallas," and I spent a year acting together in a play at the Actor's Playhouse, where he introduced me to Natalie Wood. Gone. Both gone. Next door, sharing the same dressing room next to ours, Peter Falk and Jason Robards were working in Eugene O'Neil's "Iceman Cometh." We all ate dinner at Mother Hubbard's hamburger kitchen and stole fries from each other's plates. The laughter never stopped. And then it did.

Jerry Orbach, my old Waukegan High School buddy, made history in "The Fantasticks," and long after he was a big Broadway star in "Chicago," and "42nd Street," made "Dirty Dancing." Jerry became "Detective Lennie Briscoe" in "Law and Order." Once we danced with the red-haired girl with long legs in a dance hall in Gray's Lake, Illinois. He's gone now. Much too young.

As the years went by, some moved up to rarified air, and some of us became other voices in other rooms: writers, directors, teachers.

Of course this won't mean much to you. You have your own memories, your own names. And mine? They don't need me to keep their names alive. They're on your screens tonight. I write to keep that time and their faces alive in my heart. That's what a survivor does. Isn't it funny? It seems that when I think of them on the streets of Manhattan in the '50s, we were so young and we were always saying goodbye, shoving onto a subway, jumping on a bus or catching a cab, and it was always snowing as we waved goodbye. It's snowing now as I watch them on the screen tonight. Sometimes I wave.

Send in This Clown

OMG. I've finally found the answer, not only to my future and search for a new career, but an end to winter madness.

For many years, I've resisted the pleas of older friends to spend the winters in Florida, to be labeled a "Snowbird." I have had no desire to be called a sissy and relocate to a trailer park, one of those tiny hamlets six feet from a crocodile farm deep in the Everglades.

I get snapshots from retired Mainers spending Christmas in one of those tiny cottages adjacent to a miniature golf course and a coffee shop restaurant that caters to the elderly, and features a salt-free menu with "early bird" specials.

Despite the fortune I've spent on stylish winter clothes over the years, and flu shots, skin balm and L.L.Bean boots, I've stayed the course, slippery as it is, and hunkered down in the snow. But this winter has soaked my Southern California soul with Kafkian ennui.

Yet despite searching for some reason to relocate, I could not bear to don white shoes and belt, plaid pants and jaunty golf cap, and sip Metamucil with the elderly.

Then one day there it was, the perfect solution. In an *AARP* magazine an elderly person had left, in one of those electric carts in the supermarket, a story about the Ringling Brothers and Barnum and Bailey Circus Clown College in Sarasota, Florida. As you all know, my childhood dream was to be a clown in a circus. But one just doesn't apply to a circus and fill out a form. A clown, to follow in the footsteps of the great Emmett Kelly, Bill Irwin and Glen "Frosty" Little, has to have a degree, a diploma, training. I needed to go back to school.

There are other things I could do in a circus I suppose. I won't do a high wire act. I like swings, but I'm afraid of heights. No, it's a clown or nothing.

So I looked up the R and B&B Clown College in Sarasota, Florida. Imagine my heartbreak when I found out that the original school had closed. But joy to the world, there are others, and one of the best is in Lake Placid, Florida. Lake Placid boasts "the largest clown population in America." It's the home of Toby's Clown School. I'm going to make my application as soon as I finish this column.

Oh joy! A dream come true. To don the baggy pants and oversized shoes, the fantastic makeup and tiny bowler hat and get to pile out of one of those tiny cars along with my clown buddies. My brother Jug who first inspired me by slapping me on the back of my head at Christmas Eve Mass and whispering, "Stop clowning around," would be proud of me today.

At Clown College, you even get to pick out a clown name. I want one that begins with a D so as I age as a clown, I won't forget my real name. Some offered are "Dr. Pockets," "Doodle," "Dudley," "Dingbat" and "Doctor Delightful." I'm going for Doctor Delightful if it's not already taken.

Some of the curriculum looks exciting: acrobatics, stilt walking, make-up and pantomime. I would skip juggling. She keeps reminding me of the Christmas Eve I broke some rare dishes while entertaining the girls. They loved it.

I want to start as soon as possible, because the future of circuses, real circuses, not those traveling carnivals with merry-go-rounds and fried dough, is looking dim. People don't seem to flock to the thrills of circuses like they did when we were kids. I mean how exciting is it for a kid to watch a middle aged man with a paunch get shot out of a big cardboard cannon, when they've seen astronauts get shot out into space? And after Siegfried and Roy had that terrible accident in Las Vegas ten years ago, I would avoid a chair and a whip.

I've been looking at the weather for February and March, and it doesn't look good. She, who holds her hands over her face every time I bring it up, refuses to consider joining me. But it's only for the winter, and she's mastered the use of the remote and the garage door opener, so she'll be okay. I tell you, I can't wait. Hello, Toby? Send in this clown.

Home Alone

She, who is always here somewhere, isn't. She isn't upstairs ironing, not in any of the three bathrooms, not on the deck or in the living room reading. She's just not here. What makes "not here" so bad is that she is always here. It's like a step off the patio. You get used to it. You can do it in the dark. Take it away and you break an ankle. She took my emotional step away, and for twenty-four hours my ankle has hurt.

She's only been away from me once, in July 2000, when she took a much needed week vacation to go to L.A. to visit the girls. I didn't go, because I don't fly. My favorite destination is Freeport.

That week almost broke me down. I kept myself distracted by ripping the wallpaper off of two rooms and the foyer, and then painting them. I have discovered the trick to avoiding terminal loneliness is exhaustion. That week I got a year's worth of projects completed and spent a lot of our money doing it. So much money, in fact, that she hasn't gone away since, except for today.

Number One daughter, the once and forever bride, is in Boston for business, so she wanted her mother to come down for the night, just overnight, mind you, and then she promised to come home. What could I say? No, you can't go? Why? Because I'm emotionally nine years old and needy. Maybe I should have joined that monastery in Kentucky, where they make jelly and bourbon, and you have the camaraderie of older guys in cool brown robes, fellow monks who are ALWAYS THERE!

She and I have spent fifty-three years together building this structure called a perfect marriage, and now she wants to go away again?

"It's just for one night," she whines. But I explain that a night away from her isn't like a regular night, you can't just say,

"It's just for one night." That kind of night is like one night in a guard post in Siberia. It's like a year.

And then there is Jack. For him, it's even longer. One night in dog years is several months longer than ours. If she and I were dogs, I would kill myself.

Jack is a spoiled ten-year-old English sheep dog. He is emotionally and spiritually attached to her. He sleeps by her side of the bed each night, never mine, always her side. When she gets up to go to the bathroom, he follows her right into the bathroom until she's finished. When I get up, I seem to hit some sort of doggie trip wire. He just growls softly, sees that it's only me, and goes back to sleep.

When she is gone, he stays by the front glass doors where he is right now, and stares down the street looking for the red car. The red car is in the garage. I showed him. He isn't buying it. He keeps jumping up and looking in the windows as if I have her duct taped in the trunk.

I understand him. I miss her too, but I can't lay by the glass doors looking down the street. In my drinking days maybe.

Thank God. Finally, it's 4:00. The best part of the day is gone. The worst part looms ahead, dinner. I have been cooking every night for 40 years. I don't want to cook without her. A meal prepared for one person is a waste of time. I don't know who said that, J.D. Salinger, I think.

So I'll heat up a healthy Amy's organic frozen dinner and pour two glasses of wine. I can't watch anything on television, because we always watch the same shows together. When I put her on the bus, the last thing she said was, "Promise me you won't watch any of the good shows without me."

You know what? I think I'll just have another glass of wine and lay by the glass doors with Jack.

Sit Down Comedy

"I got a lovely check today from being a writer that I earned by sitting at home. That's rewarding."
—Harvey Fierstein

It's always a bad idea in the morning to have the television on across the room when you're trying to read the paper and eat breakfast at the same time. Of course it violates a core mindfulness rule of not engaging in social media while eating, but even the Dalai Lama has to take a potty break. My breakfast consists of keeping one eye on the paper, the other on the television and a third eye on my Buddhist inner calm. Sometimes this is stressful. In the words of lyricist Frank Loesser, "a person could develop a cold."

I keep my screen on MSNBC in the early hours, and they have this bottom of the screen crawl thing going where they cover Top Stories, International, Politics, Economy and Health.

The annoying thing about the crawl is that just when you glance over at the screen, something interesting, suspicious, and often terrifying is just ending. An example: ".......found dead near the Vice President's home."

Then it moves on, and you have to keep watching through some boring news stories, interviews, and endless commercials until that subject comes on again. When I finally catch it, it usually reads something like "A squirrel was found dead..in a driveway near the Vice President's home."

What was I talking about? Something I saw on..oh, yeah..on the Health Today button, that could be of great interest to most Mainers and Americans in the whole. It's about sitting. Just when I had standing, walking, lunges and crouches worked out, they bring in something new.

A recent study claims "prolonged sitting can cause health problems like cancer and cardiovascular heart disease." Oh boy! This is of great concern to me because I am a writer. Writers, and others who have to sit to perform their tasks on their butts, are in danger of contracting one or more of these terrible conditions. Of course Ernest Hemingway liked writing standing up, and he did avoid cardiovascular disease and cancer, but he shot himself. Not what I had in mind.

I guess I could write standing up, but one of my jobs is reviewing movies. Standing up while watching a movie comes with its own problems, mostly from the people sitting behind you.

But most sitters can't perform their duties standing up. Example: people who drive taxis, buses, train engines and garbage trucks. The guys who ride on the back, who actually work very hard picking up the trash, apparently will live longer, healthier lives than the guy driving.

Airline pilots fall into the difficult column. Astronauts who pilot space ships get off easily, they tend to float around a lot. Cops sit a lot, and I'm concerned about their cardio health. Of course cops have a lot more to worry about in the course of a shift than about how their heart is doing. As recent events have shown, sitting in one spot can be dangerous. They have to keep moving, but, always sitting, rarely getting out of the car. (I was going to write "except to go into the doughnut shop," but I'm reminded that cops often read this column.)

In my youth, only detectives rode in cars. Beat cops had to walk their beats. In freezing winter, roasting summer, night and day, they walked. That's where the derogatory term "flatfoot" came from. I used to work for a police department and got to know a lot of very old retired cops, but not so many detectives. Comedians seem to live longer than serious actors. That's why they call it "stand-up comedy." I see the point.

In the interest of science and my health, I spent today gauging exactly how much time I spend sitting down: thirty minutes writing a column, two hours correcting the punctuation, another half hour rewriting, an hour eating lunch at a cafe, an hour at dinner, then four hours watching three political shows and maybe another hour watching an old movie I had taped. That's about ten hours. That's a lot of sitting. I don't count sitting while driving, as everything in my little city that I need, coffee, groceries, wine, the gym, is only eight minutes away.

    I've been sitting here for an hour and I'm having a funny pain in my left arm. It could be from lifting that purple bag full of garbage. I'm going to finish this standing up.

Hold the Remote

Last night you taped your favorite shows. You had other things to watch before bed.

You taped "Glee" and "Modern Family," "Hawaii" and a movie, and you've settled in to watch them. In the middle of the story, up pops that annoying commercial. So you pick up that new remote and zip forward. Whooosh! We all do that. We're busy people for whom instant gratification isn't fast enough.

Most commercials are a bore, especially after you've seen them seventy thousand times. You're sick of watching the handsome couple in the twin tubs who have apparently just shared a "magic moment." You can't understand why they don't just get one tub like the one you and your sweetie had on the cruise last winter.

You dread those spots that try to sell you those drugs with the side effects that are worse than the illnesses they're designed to help.

I don't blame you. I hate them too, even though I used to make them. I wrote a few, acted in hundreds and cast and directed some. It was my life once.

Once upon a time in the golden days of television, actors would turn up their noses at selling toothpaste. They wanted to play all the leads on the soap operas and prime time shows. They wanted to do serious acting and get a permanent series. All actors want that.

But acting in theater, film and television is a tough, competitive game. As the competition grows tougher, the good jobs come slowly.

So when their agents suggested sending them out for a job selling toilet tissue, Kleenex, soap and cars, soft drinks and aspirin, shaving cream and diapers, they winced. But when they saw the money come in, the wince turned to a smile.

On your screen every night, hundreds of commercials roll by. You probably don't see them anymore. You press the button and move on. They matter little to you.

But to the thousands of actors, mostly unknown to you, pretty and plain, fat and thin, tall and short, selling you all the stuff you use every day, they matter a lot.

Many are kids, just starting their careers, getting their faces out in public. Kids of all ages make up the largest number of commercial actors. Many of these kids are salting away college money. Some of them are actually helping support their families. Ask the now famous Jody Foster about that.

Don't be fooled by those gorgeous young "party kids." They're mostly actors trying to make enough money to keep their Screen Actor's health insurance. They have to make $15,000 in four quarters just to maintain the minimum coverage.

That sun-splashed romp on the beach may be the only time they ever get to the surf in their busy lives. And that older actor pushing the car or the beer probably has a family to support, kids to put through college, a parent in a nursing home, a mortgage to salvage. Sound familiar?

They are all American union workers paying dues to three or four unions. They get up every day without a guarantee of a job. They have to go out and find one, make one. Between jobs, they wait tables, sell books and clothing. They juggle their job time so they can go stand in line in "cattle calls," and smile and look pretty, even if their stomachs are growling and they're down to their last five bucks.

I'm not asking you to feel sorry for people who live in the golden sunlight and don't appear to work as hard as you do. They chose their lives, and you never hear them grumble. They weren't born to the golden sand and permanent sunlight. They come from people like you, from small towns like ours, from Waterville and Sidney, China and Oakland. They're chasing a dream. So before you click away on the commercial tonight, take a good look at that handsome young face. It might be your kid or the kid down the street. Wave.

Man and Dog Wait for Snow

"You call this snow?" he shouts down from the top of his truck. I can tell he's an old timer who at age six found the snow high over his head. No. I didn't call it snow. I still haven't. Perhaps by the time you open this paper there will be. I doubt it. There may be a teaser, a patina of something that passes for snow. It will be white and coat my driveway from Hell. But it won't be snow.

"Something wicked this way comes," Shakespeare's witch intoned. It's called "earth warming." By now we should be at least up to our knees in something resembling snow. David, the snowplow man, is standing looking out his window, his hands in his empty pockets just as I am, and wondering where it is.

January is ugly without snow. At least with snow up to the windows we could all stand and hum carols and pretend Christmas is going to start over again.

Turning around to face the room is depressing. I took all the Christmas stuff down yesterday and swept up the glitter and cleaned the house. I've done two laundries and washed everything that looked dirty just to keep busy. It's all done now, which means I'm forced to sit down at the computer and ply my trade.

I don't want to work on my memoirs because I'm at a part that makes me cry. Actually most of it makes me cry. I had a rather exciting and adventurous but horrid early childhood that put on paper makes for good reading. I'm not going to write about that today, because you only paid a buck fifty for this paper, and I'll need you to pay much more for the book so that I can pay the snowplow man...if he has to come.

When the snow does come, many will be thrilled thinking they can finally indulge themselves in those pernicious games of winter the rich love so much. Looking out at the fluffy white stuff blowing by, they'll get the skis unpacked, the good brandy uncorked, and snowshoes readied for long cold treks into the woods. Of course they'll be disappointed because it will stop too soon and melt. This winter so far is like a magician's trick. Now you see it, now you don't.

I'm no fan of snow, but Jack the dog likes the snow. He likes to get out there and jam his nose in it and run around like he's a real sheepdog. I feel sorry for him as he watches the sky. I can imagine that in the primal corridors of his mind he's back in time looking for sheep to herd, to get them into the pen before dark and the drifts pile up. I've told him over and over since he was a puppy that he should give it up, that he's not a real sheep dog. He's an Old English Sheepdog. He was bred to be the stuff of calendars and stuffed toys, to be featured in movies where they need a big cuddly dog for everyone to hug and love, not run around and do serious farm work. He sulks when I tell him that.

He replies by telling me that I'm not a real writer but simply a cheerful hack trying to write himself into two rooms with a hot plate in Key West. A few flakes flutter past the window, and he whines in anticipation. So I let him out and watch him from the warm comfort of my kitchen, where I am making "ochanamizu." That's Japanese for tea water. See? You learned something entirely new today by reading this. Isn't that worth a buck and half? And he called me a hack.

Take One Squirrel

Nostradamus was right. AIG and CITIBANK are going down. It is the apocalypse, the end of days. Spiritus Mundi is in tatters.

50,000 jobs lost in November alone and more to come. 1.9 million since January. The auto industry is collapsing. The growling, porcine Rush Limbaugh is taking over the Republican Party. Bobby Jindal is slouching towards Bethlehem. Soon, they say, it will be nuclear winter. Rioting in the streets is certain. Bread lines will soon appear, wealthy children will be thrown from penthouse windows to spare them the indignity of having to go to public schools and grow up poor. Urbanites are fleeing to the woods, but we're already in the woods. What is the plan?

A hard rain is falling, my children, we have lost sight of the big rock candy mountain. The spectre of looted supermarkets looms large. Soon we will be faced with empty shelves and shuttered banks. Our children will bang their spoons on empty bowls. It is time my brothers and sisters to reconsider......the squirrel.

We cried to the heavens, "What's for dinner?" and the Lord saith, "Behold before you. I give you...the squirrel."

Yes, the common squirrel, or sciurus carolinensis or sciurus vulgaris, that cute, scampering creature that scuttles, hops and dances across the snow. Look out your window. There they are perched on the fence, clinging to the icy tree branches. In your heart of hearts you know I'm right. Our ancestors hunted squirrels and cooked them on open fires. American Indians enjoyed squirrel meat after the white honkies decimated the buffalo herds.

During the depression, folks went out to the Missouri woods, hunting squirrels to put on the family table. Hobos roasted them on the rails of the Chesapeake and Ohio. They tell me that they were quite tasty. "Taste just like chicken," they said.

We need to pick up some survival skills in the growing darkness of the economy. So I have mined the internet and old cookbooks to provide for you a couple of tasty recipes....for squirrel. Here then is my grandma's recipe.

Take one squirrel, cut up. C'mon, you can do this...don't forget to shave the hair and tail off first. Don't discard it. It's wonderful for packing that sleeping bag for the road. Add some flour, salt and pepper, 2 1/2 tablespoons butter, 7 cups of boiling water, some thyme to taste, 1 cup of corn, 3 potatoes, cubed, some cayenne, 3 medium onions, sliced and 2 cups of canned tomatoes...with juice. Mmmmmm yum. Ring that dinner bell.

I'm told that if you've lost your home and are out on the side of Brunswick somewhere with another band of homeless, you have to add about 70 squirrels and some butter beans and cabbage. It's called Brunswick stew. Yes, I'm sure there is an Albion stew.

I've learned that down around Arkansas, "Cajun" squirrel or "Gumbo" squirrel is a big hit. Just add some ketchup or Tabasco sauce, some red wine and a little garlic. Not even Diamond Jim Brady at his best beheld such a feast.

And what's a squirrel feast without an accompanying salad? With the ATMs closed and stores shuttered, you might want to try my father's old favorite—dandelion greens. Like squirrels, billions of dandelion greens are free out there on your lawn, the long disrespected, humble and spat-upon dandelion. They tell me that they are elegant in a salad or soup. I'm told that they also "support digestion, reduce swelling and inflammation, and treat viruses, jaundice, edema, gout, eczema and acne." Does it get any better?

You see. You were worried about how you were going to feed your family out there on the road come Great Depression Redux. Well, now you know. God's abundance is all about us.

You only have to keep your eyes open. And the Lord saith, "Now, my children, let's talk about candied crickets."

Taking Down the Tree

She was just ahead of us by the door leading out to the buses. We were all there saying our goodbyes. It was the end of Christmas, the end of the joy, the end of it all. It was that terrible time when, if your children have come from across the country and you only see them once a year, they have to leave.

We stood and laughed and told stories in a feeble attempt to make the pain of it go away, and all I could think of was I had to go home and take down the tree. That's the worst part of the end of Christmas, when everyone leaves and the house is full of a silence so powerful that you're startled to hear the fridge go on. And that's when I saw her.

We were very close to her and the young man and woman and small child who was tugging at her coat. I could hear their conversation, and I knew that the young woman was her daughter and the young man the husband and daddy of the little girl.

They were playing the same melody we were, that slightly discordant family carol of parting, working very hard to keep the notes in a major key. They spoke of the father in such a way that I knew he was gone. This was the mother of the young woman. That was easy. They had each other's eyes and gestures and even the same laugh. They talked, as we did, of summer when it was possible they might be able to come again. It was about his job and the difficulty of planning that far ahead.

I floated from them to my own family, trying to break free from a feeling of sadness. Then the announcement broke over the intercom, and we all hugged and kissed and did it again and they left together, my daughters and the older woman's family.

We all went out to the dock and waved once more as the bus pulled out. The windows of the bus were darkened, and none of us could really see them but we knew they saw us, and we loyally stood our ground and waved until the bus pulled out of the yard.

She left first, turning towards us and heading out. She smiled as she passed by; I could see the clouding of her eyes, the beginning of tears. I remembered how tightly she had hugged her granddaughter. She held her so close like someone holding onto a friend in a stormy sea, holding onto another life as it was slipping away.

When we got into our car she was parked in front of us, and I could see her holding a tissue to her eyes. She who will not help me take down the tree for obvious reasons, was wiping her eyes as well. The bus was gone and we left in its wake, tossing and tumbling around in a shared wave of sadness.

I'm writing this on a yellow legal pad I keep in the car, as I sit in the driveway of my house. I don't want to forget how that older woman looked, her eyes, the way she waved goodbye. I feel sure that she went home to take down her tree as well, and it will be harder for her I think. I have no grandchildren like the little woman. It will be harder for her.

Maybe she will keep the tree up for another few days, but I think not. I think she will want it down as I do. A Christmas tree seems to need the presence of children, and when they go, its magic goes with them. She will clean up the wrappings and wash some dishes as it grows dark. But it will be harder for her because she may find a toy the child left behind, or a forgotten sock or mitten to remind her of what was there in her home for a few precious hours. That will be hard.

It's getting darker now, and I can't see the words as clearly. I know I will have to go in and start the ending of things. I'm sure she's home by now, taking down the tree.

Is There an App for That?

> "You talking to me?"
> –Robert De Niro in "Taxi."

Old Barney had two really crippled feet, but he ignored them. Barney cleaned and waxed the floors in the church on Saturday mornings like he was Fred Astaire. I noticed when I went to altar boy practice, that while working, he talked to himself. Chatting away, he would shuffle back and forth with his broom.

Sometimes he would pause and wave his hands about like he was arguing with someone. I asked my brothers, they just said, "That's what he does." Frankie DeNoyer said it was because Barney was crazy. But he wasn't. He was just happy with himself.

One day at school, I asked Sister Rosanna why Barney talked to himself. Without looking up from correcting her papers, she said, "He's talking to God." I remember thinking, of course, he was in the church all day, of course he was talking to God.

What is prayer, after all, but talking to yourself? I talk to God all the time. It's not praying. It's conversation. You think God only speaks Latin? You talk to God in Hebrew, God answers in Hebrew. Talk in rap? God answers in rap. Are you really surprised that God is multi lingual?

Of course, my God is probably not your God. I made my God up, and she never fails to agree with me. So prayer then is essentially talking to myself. If God were listening to my prayers, it would never rain and I would have that lottery money in the bank by now.

On one hand, it scares me a bit. I'm scared because I've never seen other folks talking to themselves, except the occasional drunk or homeless person on the street in Portland. Are they crazy? No. It's what they do. Still, I am concerned.

She, who is the sanest person I know, says she doesn't talk to herself, but I know she does. I hear her upstairs in her office, and I call up, "What did you say?"

"I'm on the phone," she replies. I don't buy that for a minute. If I'm really suspicious I run up the steps, and there she is with her phone by her side.

"I thought you were on the phone."

"Wrong number."

"You were talking to a wrong number? Who talks to a wrong number? What did you talk about to this wrong number?"

She doesn't look up. "I'm busy correcting my papers." OMG. I think I married Sister Rosanna.

Is it a sign of age? Maybe, but I've been talking to myself since I was a child.

I've written ad nauseam about how I was very much a loner as a kid, because I was lousy at sports in a sports crazy neighborhood. So what was I supposed to do? Keep all those crazy stories and ideas in my head? Who does that? Nobody can do that.

So when I would walk home summer nights or afternoons after sitting alone through two movies, a newsreel and cartoon, I'd walk along practicing what I had seen and imitating all the actors' voices and gestures, walks and mannerisms. What was that but talking to myself?

What would Frankie DeNoyer say? He would say "Devine is nuts." My brothers would say, "It's what he does."

I forget to make grocery lists, so I walk through the aisles of the supermarket mumbling the list aloud to myself. "Cereal...wine...avocados" etc.

Women pass and smile. Do they go home and tell their husbands that J.P. talks to himself? Their husbands probably reply, "I know him. He's kind of nuts."

If they told she, who KNOWS I'm nuts, she would kindly reply, "It's what he does. He's a writer. He says that writing is talking to one's self, the rest is typing." That would be right.

But I don't want to have people come to my wake and whisper, "He was such a handsome fellow, but he talked to himself, you know."

"Really?"

"I used to see him in the frozen food section, running his fingers along the selections and mumbling to himself."

"No!"

"Yes, and sometimes he would giggle and gesture like there was someone in the case."

So to avoid this and any further embarrassment, I'm going to wear ear plugs wired to my phone. People will think I'm talking on the phone. I can giggle and gesture, even laugh aloud, and no one will know that I am nuts. Isn't that a great idea? I wonder if there's an app for that?

Loretta on My Chest

Breaking news: In October, 1991, a five-thousand-year-old tattooed man made the headlines of newspapers all over the world, when his frozen body was discovered on a mountain between Austria and Italy. You can Google it. I did.

The word tattoo comes, I've learned, from the Tahitian word "Tattau. Do you think? In ancient Egypt Nubian slaves were tattooed. In the l800s, because sailors saw them on the bodies of Polynesian girls, they became a big thing with sailors. Now you're nobody unless you have a tattoo somewhere on your body, especially if your bunkmate at Thomaston has one and you don't.

Once, at a carnival in Cairo, Illinois, my father introduced me to an old friend who had a belly dancer tattooed on the muscle of his left arm. He could make it dance. I thought that was wonderful. I think it started my life-long interest in show business.

My Uncle Pete, a sailor in the Great War, had a large rose tattoo on his chest with "Arnetta" underneath. Aunt Mamie could never find out who Arnetta was. Pete would often, under the influence of Wild Turkey, display it at family picnics, weddings and sometimes, to Aunt Mamie's horror, at funerals. A true story.

In my mother's day, well-bred ladies would never be seen with a tattoo or even a suntan. My mother said only gypsies and prostitutes had them. She made an exception for Mrs. Roache, the Irish gypsy lady who came to her card parties. Mrs. Roache had a shamrock on her arm. Erin Go Bragh.

Okay. Why, you wonder, am I spending so much time on tattoos on Mother's Day, especially when I've written about them before? Because I had long ago run out of ideas on what to give she, who has everything, and this, I think, will make her sit up and pay attention. I'm considering a tattoo. Not on her, on me.

I've looked at several tattoo catalogs online, and I've made a list of options. Skulls are very popular, especially with "Harleys Forever" written underneath. I hate motorcycles.

Angels are popular, especially with huge wings that span your back, but she never looks at my back unless I ask her to, as in, "Is this a melanoma, do you think?" Having not found a melanoma after a zillion tries, she now just shouts from the other room: "No."

Climbing flowers, fairies with tiny wings, alluring women's faces and etchings of famous faces are very popular. I'm a liberal, so it would have to be either Hillary or Nancy Pelosi. That would get old.

I dropped in at a local tattoo parlor and watched one being given. There is a lot more screaming there than you might think. Guys just clench their teeth, women do scream some, I'm told. I'm not into doing anything to my body that produces screaming, so I've come up with an idea.

I'm going to have an artist friend draw something on my chest with colored pencils, so I can wash it off afterwards.

I'm thinking a big rose like Uncle Pete's with a name like "Loretta." I like Loretta.

I tried to avoid all of this a week ago by claiming that I don't really have to give her anything. Only the girls should have to gift her. "I'm not your child," I said.

"Really?" she replied. I hate when she raises her eyebrows like that. Wait until she asks who Loretta is.

Television Sets Then and Now

Rosemary DeBranco had the biggest. Laura Karenbrach had one almost as big but wouldn't show it to us; her family didn't like us hanging around.

It was 1950 and television sets were popping up like acne at a summer camp. That first debut year of the Great American Television they were only talked about, rather like UFOs. Most had heard of them, some had seen one up close, but the only real place to see one was in an upscale appliance store window like Katz and Sons on Grand and Meremac, the corner where they turned the Bellefontaine Avenue street car around.

There were three sets, different sizes. The sound wasn't piped outside yet, so one could only watch and pretend like watching a silent movie without the organ. Through blistering heat or windswept snow people came and stared.

Then the flood gates opened and sets became more affordable and more people had them. Your more fully employed relatives had one, and they used them as status symbols inviting the hoi polloi of the family over on Tuesday nights to see "Uncle Miltie." My brother-in-law Ricky had one first.

Ricky's set was a beautiful piece of furniture, well-crafted and polished with a ceramic black panther "TV light" on top. Sadly, the screen was a tiny gray oval in the center. You had to really want to see what was on; when it flickered, we all gasped. My mother stood with one foot out the door. She was convinced it would blow up and wanted to be the first one in the car.

Then one day color came in and the whole world changed. The DeBrancos got one–the biggest of course–and the Sottos. They got a huge set in at the YMCA and that stopped the dancing for a while; but soon the novelty wore off and everyone went back to leaving early and parking up on Art Hill.

Today, in the world of DVD, MTV, and digital sex, all of that seems like it happened on another planet, in another life or a solar system far, far away. Today we have systems that promise 500 channels and something called HDVD is on the horizon. We have portables and palm-sized sets; they pop out on airliners and buses. They're everywhere.

One night this past week, I drove slowly through the Elm City, cruising the streets and peering into windows. From the appliance store on Meremac to Burleigh Street in Waterville in a few short decades, we have accomplished the entertainment version of walking on the moon. If medicine had evolved as fast as the average television sit-com, we would be disease free by Friday morning.

From Ricky's tiny porthole to the 21-inch set in my living room, things have moved so fast, I sometimes think I was there when Lindbergh landed at Orly Field. Now, black and white is the television version of the Packard. A friend of mine was watching the old black and white movie "From Here To Eternity" one night when his son walked in and asked what was wrong with the set; tempus fugit.

How Ricky and Rosemary would have laughed, had they heard my friend Renee exclaim only last week about the evening's fare: "Jeez ... nothing's on."

"Nothing's on." Yet we have 55 channels, all in brilliant color and surround-sound. We have dozens of sit-coms, sports shows, soap operas, twenty-four hour news, weather and talking head shows. You can watch sex channels or books being discussed until three in the morning. And when the night's schedule is full of re-runs, along comes a war.

You can always count on a war when things get boring; just hit the remote for a full list: war in Bosnia, Chechnya, the Sudan, Cambodia, all live from the spot right there on CNN and MSNBC. Dan and Tom will anchor the slaughter and Larry King will bring you the survivors live and in color.

Once upon a time, we chuckled as Jack Paar made pale jokes with Zsa Zsa Gabor. The words "virgin" and "intercourse" were not allowed. Now we watch live-action simulated lovemaking and listen to Dr. Ruth discuss masturbation with movie stars.

Once we watched Dr. Kildare take six weeks to make a date with a nurse for coffee; now we munch popcorn with our kids while we watch two young singles on "Seinfeld" discuss how great sex was on their first date. Tempus big-time fugit.

A few nights ago, I remote-punched from Kosovo to the Sudan, from a train wreck in Illinois to a torture scene in Truth Or Consequences, New Mexico, a cop shoot-out in New York, two screaming guests on Geraldo Rivera, six talking mouths on Larry King to a hockey game in French. I decided there was nothing on.

I shut the set off and sat in the darkness remembering the corner appliance store where the Bellefontaine Avenue street car turned around on a cold night before Christmas when the whole world was in black and white. We all stood there in the falling snow watching black and white people laughing soundlessly from behind tinted glass. Too bad we couldn't have done the same with the entire impeachment process.

She'll know

If I turn my head slightly to the left, I can see it from here. I went there once and saw what appeared to be the end of the universe. Now I avoid it. It's too risky. I might be careless and move something. She'd know. She'd say nothing, but she'd know. It's only five, maybe six feet away from my desk. It's a sunny spot that gives a warm misleading glow that must not be trusted, for this is a magic place in the darkest sense. It's her desk, her domain, her place in the sun.

This is a big room we share. It's called "the office." I work at one end, the cluttered end. Hers appears to be cluttered. Trust me. It's an illusion. There she sits in her zone, pencil in hand, correcting students' work, making notations in the corners of mysterious papers. Sometimes she mumbles softly, incantations? Ancient formulas or spells, maybe curses? I'm curious but cautious. I don't ask because her answers are complicated, soaked in mysterious "teacher talk" that makes me sleepy.

Once, long ago, curiosity got the better of me. I was looking for candy. I knew she often hid some there deep in the folds of mysterious things kept in the three drawers. As I searched, I was drawn to the myriad piles of papers stacked side by side in neat rows. These I knew, were our bills, the ones she paid each month as she huddled over them like Bob Cratchit at his workplace. I knew when they were favorable by the tone of her mumblings, the soft sighs and as she folded them into envelopes and said, "There." That was good to hear. I knew there would be trouble when she hissed out things like "OMG!"

Candy was my mission, but my attention was diverted by the envelope of the month's bills. This was something new, an adventure. Despite all the chatter about being a "partner" in this life, basically, I'm an errand boy. Okay, my bad. I designed it that way so as to avoid too much troubling responsibility. So then I made a few mistakes. So I lost the checkbook...twice. Did the world end? Eventually I was reduced to a benign aide de camp, sort of like Joe Biden.

My eyes fell on the numbers. There they were, tiny mysterious figures, hieroglyphics of commerce, rows of them with dates beside them. I was filled with admiration. It was like looking at the keys to some mysterious kingdom, a mosaic of magic symbols all arranged in formation.

Somewhere, I knew, there was stored the last of the Halloween candy. I know it's March, but candy corn never seems to go stale or grow mold. Candy corn, like love, is forever. I could smell it. I knew it was in there somewhere.

I picked through her collection of colored paper clips, a tube of Burt's Bees lip cream, Scotch tape, notes, receipts, she loves receipts, a tiny silver whistle. A silver whistle? There were buttons of all sizes, her father's desk set of brass scissors and letter opener. She is inordinately fond of the letter opener. It makes clean, neat incisions that leave no jagged edges. She loathes jagged edges even on envelopes that will be discarded. Once on a summer's day, I brought her a bill I had opened in my usual careless, impatient way. The corners were torn, some pieces missing. She stared at it without touching, as though it were Martian excrement. I knew I had erred.

She looked at me and sighed; I know that sigh.

I'd better find the candy corn before she comes home. Did I leave everything as it was? Was that blue paper clip on top of the yellow one? If not...she'll know I was here. She'll know.

Behold the Griller Guy

The artist-writer has long been considered effeminate, a wastrel drunk who dresses in linens, soft silk pocket hankies and slip-on espadrilles, whilst lolling around friends' pools or sipping wine in Parisian or Manhattan boîtes.

This is the stuff of myths, a pack of lies made up by the tragically uninformed, and must be dispelled. When I came home after acting in a play in New York many years ago, my hair, done for the part, had been curled. My five brothers sat across the table at a barbecue and eyed me suspiciously. One asked, "You don't play in a band or anything, do you?" That was Irish cop code for gay, or as it was spoken then, "queer."

At one time or another, my brothers, when they thought of me at all, endeavored to "guy" me up, make a man out of me. In my late teen years, they introduced me to Budweiser. When I asked for a glass, they wept. They taught me the navy way to light a cigarette in the wind. The smoke and ashes blew back into my face and made me cough. They wept.

I twisted an ankle attempting soccer, broke a finger at baseball and suffered a nose bleed when struck with a football. They wept. Then they gave up.

Over the years, I've studied the way of the macho warrior, the "guy" who kicks sand in the face of the wimp at the beach, who always catches the tossed ball, hits a nail right on the head, knows how to spit, never splits the wood when sawing, doesn't drip paint on his espadrilles and can barbecue on a grill. Not one of those little black and red bowls that take charcoal and hours to heat up, but a big grill, a "guy" grill. I envied my "guy" friends who could slap on that frightening jug of propane, light up the flame and prepare an outdoor meal for five or six, or ten.

I watched my best friend do classic burgers, roast veggies and corn on the cob, all the while sipping a martini, or a beer...from the bottle of course. When the women around him watched, they sighed and applauded, hugged him and praised his skill. I wanted that. I craved it. I wanted to be a guy. I've never played in a band, not that there is anything wrong with that, but deep in my heart, in my Irish genes, I know I harbor the seeds of a "Guydom."

So this week, when my oldest daughter came visiting from her home in Los Angeles, she brought her love, Rick, a television art director and chief set constructionist. He's a big guy, a genuine "guy-guy," an Iraqi war veteran who can build anything in ten minutes and tear it down in five. Nevertheless, he is a sensitive man, a perfect blend of both worlds.

I offered him a beer, no glass.

He talked of his state-of-the-art barbecue grill back in L.A., on which he can grill a coyote if one should wander into his organic garden. As a gift, he brought me a brand new power drill. I knew then that I may have found a mentor, a true griller who can hammer a nail and drink from the bottle without spilling it on my espadrilles.

As a family, we went up to Home Depot to buy a grill, no little bucket thing, but a genuine "guy" grill. So there it sits on my ancient creaky deck. Rick bought me all the necessary tools and cover, about a hundred bucks worth, as an added gift, and we ran several runs to test my new "guyness."

It's getting dark now. It sits there like Darth Vader's personal pod, waiting for my solo flight. She, who paid for it, watches from the kitchen window. I lift the heavy metal hatch. It drops and bangs my finger. She turns away and weeps.

Osama in My Phone

I think I know where Osama Bin Laden is. I know you're laughing now and thinking what a fool I am, and that this is just another of my crazy stories, and that I'm just treading pond water until they put me in the nursing home, but you're wrong. I know where Osama is, well not exactly me, my new cell phone does. I can't prove it, but when I studied the manual and watched the CD that comes with it, I got the tingly feeling that this thing has so many features that it absolutely must know where Osama is, and maybe even President Obama's birth certificate.

Not only that, but it's possible that with this ultra state-of-the-art technology I'm tapping into, that it's possible to see Sara Palin's house from here. Not Russia mind you, but her house. The Google Search feature on this phone came up with a house that looks like it might be hers. There's a big moose head over the door.

My daughter, she who makes more money than I do, or even the other She who makes more money than I do, bought me this new cell for Christmas, and I am so psyched. It's called an android. How cool is that? I can tell you I am absolutely mesmerized with anything called an android because I love science fiction, and an android is a robot that looks like a human. So your suspicion about your husband may be right?

In my search for the perfect phone, I discovered that cell phone companies feature a panoply of phones with colorful, fun names like "Mesmerize," "Chocolate Touch," the "Jest," "Karma," and "Mythic." I imagine that those are hard sells to guys who shoot deer and crush beer cans on their buddies' heads. Car companies do that better for them with really butch names like Tacoma, Ram, Cougar, Tiger, etc. I think a phone called "Chocolate Touch," is for men who can get in touch with their feminine side like House Speaker-to-be John Boehner.

This is cool. When it rings, a picture of the caller appears on the screen, and you'll be envious to know that I have a full AMOLED display. I can't tell you what that means because 1. I don't know, and 2. I think this thing is listening to me. Perhaps I'm being a tad paranoid, but when I asked a lot of questions of the clerks at the store, they all looked at one another suspiciously, and my daughter said she thought she heard this strange buzz that passed between them. Then they all went to the back room together and peered around the corner at me. I don't think there is anything to worry about here, but I am concerned that so many of the clerks have the same blonde hair and blue eyes, except for one with hair the shade of black not found in our solar system.

This reminds me of an old friend of mine in Hollywood who thinks that cell phones are a plot devised by space aliens who walk among us. He says that one day we will all get the same call that will program our minds and turn us into androids. He thinks that Facebook is part of the same plot, so he refuses to join. It's ringing. There's the picture. It's her with the strange black hair. I have to change my password.

Visits from Mickey

You've seen the scene many times in the movies, travel magazines, post cards: Tall beautiful Washington palms etched sharply against a gorgeous early evening orange sky over Los Angeles. You want to go. Fuggidaboudit!

Here's the dirty little secret all City of Angels citizens know, but you don't because you don't live there, and if you're visiting, the Chamber of Commerce keeps all of us from telling you. There are rats in those palm trees, way up at the top, big rats, rats the size of dachshunds. True story.

At dusk, in some neighborhoods, wealthy and poor, you can see the occasional rat scurry down, run along telephone wires and drop down. At night, when the hot Santa Ana winds raise the temperature, they come down and drink from the swimming pools in Beverly Hills and Brentwood and Hollywood. Rats drinking from the swimming pools. Snap!

Los Angeles can be a very dry place most of the year, and some water conservationists like to cover their front lawns with wide swaths of drought-resistant ivy. The rats love those too. I suppose those are rats with fear of height issues who disdain the palms. True story. Rodent elimination is a billion dollar business in L.A. Bigger than recreational drugs.

Those memories come to me today, because of my own problems with rodents. I don't have rats, I just thought you would like a different kind of Hollywood story instead of the same old piece about Amanda Bynes and Justin Bieber.

So I started with that story to get your attention focused on a less exciting story about mice, tiny creatures that Walt Disney made a fortune on, by giving them cute ears and buttoned pants. We all love Mickey and Minnie. But not actively living in our Cheerios.

Last year as my technician Brent at Toyota went looking for a problem in my Prius, he found that some mice, looking for warmth in my engine bed, also had chewed up some wiring. A mouse chewed into my Prius.

It gets worse. That spring, my relatively new big black two-doored Frigidaire started leaking slowly near the bottom. When Todd, the technician from the store where I bought it, investigated ,it turned out that a mouse, perhaps the same one not fully sated on my Prius cables, had chewed through a water line. Todd replaced it.

Clearly I had a Mickey problem. Apparently with the help of many Minnies, Mickey had started a tiny family behind the push-in stove in my kitchen. Mickey had, with the help of his clan, found and enlarged a hole there and set up a condo. My carpenter, Skip, informed me that this is what they do, move in and in a mousey way, lean forward.

It turned out that the little black droppings I found here and there weren't really part of the bird seed I had spilled in the kitchen. They were Mickey's and Minnie's droplets.

Reluctantly, I furnished my house with myriad tiny boxes of mouse poison. I know. I don't like poison either, and I don't care much for finding little corpses of Mickey and Minnies in the basement, laying there, like a crime scene from "The Killing," all fuzzy grey and white, mouths agape, having passed on unexpectedly to the great mouse hole in the sky.

At first I thought it was damn nice of them to end their lives out of sight in the basement, instead of letting us find them spread out lifeless on the kitchen floor as we were sitting down to dinner. Then I was told that this poison drove them insane with thirst, so that they went looking for water which they drank until they died. I don't have a swimming pool, and they probably don't want to drink from the toilet, as I use those big pills that turn the toilet water blue. Who wants to drink blue stuff unless it's a Blue Hawaiian served in a martini glass.

So they go to the basement where, after having lived with me for a long time, know that when it rains, I have a water problem down there.

I feel bad about the whole thing. To die in a damp cellar is no way to go, even for a mini-rodent. Would it be macabre I wonder, to set out a small dish of water for them? OMG. Waiter? A double Blue Hawaiian, skip the lei.

The New Goodbye: the Long Goodbye

She stands at the gate watching her son board the bus. She talks to him on her cell phone. She is in her late 70s, maybe a well-kept fit 80. He is seated now and she can't see him, but he's there on her cell where they keep up the conversation they started at breakfast.

They continued in the car probably, going over the little things.

She makes sure he has his "smartphone," his books and briefcase. Even as the bus door closes, they keep up the patter. Standing beside her, it occurs to me that I could be doing the same thing. My daughters, on the same bus, are way ahead of me. They ring up and we talk, continuing the conversation we started in the car. One has an iPhone, the other a Blackberry. It's the long goodbye. It's the new goodbye.

Of course, the new technology has changed so many of our lives making them softer to the touch, for evaporating time and space.

Christmas Day night we sat around after dinner and played with the new "toys" with all of their apps and flashes and sparkles, their sounds and images. And when we packed ourselves into the car for the long drive to the long goodbye, each of their phones rang with different sounds, jingles and words. Those who were waiting for them back on the other coast where the sun was still up and warm, called to affirm arrivals, to collect data and confirm dates.

It wasn't always so. Those of us who remember the long ago, that space and time beyond the sunsets and risings, past the wars and depressions, past the years that belong only to us, we remember it wasn't always so.

In 1952 I stood with my mother in the billowing gray white steam of the 2:20 Ann Rutledge Special out of St. Louis Union Station bound for Chicago. I stood in the cold with Mother, she with her new Christmas coat and bag, I in my uniform and blue overcoat, duffel bag at my knee. We chatted about Christmas then and Christmas past, about little things, simple things. Did I have enough money, toothbrush, clean underwear and passport? Did I remember that big tan Manila envelope that I had hugged so close all week, the envelope that held my special orders? Yes. I did. It was under my arm. I wagged it under her nose. She laughed. It was the last time she laughed.

We hugged and hugged again, and when the train pulled out, I sat quickly and waved. She could see me and waved back, standing there in the gray white steam. The windows were dirty, railroad dirty, not the Concord Line's blue-tinted, and then I was gone. It was a short goodbye. A very quick, short wave and I was crossing the river. I looked back, and then it was all gone.

I called her as often as I could, from Texas and Louisiana, San Francisco and Seattle. I would drop quarters into pay phones in Waco, Dallas and Los Angeles, and speak briefly with her. On those lines, we sounded exactly as far away as we were. Tokyo and Korea were too far away and impossible to reach.

Now, in this new age, soldiers call daily from as far away as Iraq, Afghanistan, Germany and France. They converse on mutual screens with their parents, their young wives, and wave at their children as though they are down the street or in the next town. Magic.

On the way home from the bus station, the girls texted us with dozens of tiny messages, reminders, hints. It was as if they were in the back seat. The new goodbye–the long goodbye.
In Memoriam: To Steve Jobs who made most of the magic happen.

The Piano

It sits in the far back of the house in one of the big empty rooms where we stuff everything that we can't fit into the main house. I dust it once a month if I remember, otherwise it just sits there with things on top of it, magazines I don't want to throw out, old albums and a Teddy bear that says, "I have a friend at New York Law." It's a piano, and it's older than me, older than her or this house, maybe older than city hall downtown.

She, who doesn't play the piano at all, bought it for me in Los Angeles as an anniversary gift. I think it was maybe the tenth. Those were the days when I really played the piano.

Someone brought it down from San Francisco where, the dealer told her, it came from a brothel that burned down in the great earthquake and fire. It has a third pedal that when you press it down something happens that gives it a harpsichord brothel sound, like the old pianos the guy with the striped shirt and arm garter played in those cowboy movies.

It's a beautiful piece of work, but it's way out of tune now and the genuine ivory keys are all stuck because nobody plays it anymore. I stopped playing the piano years ago when I heard Errol Garner play at the Blue Note in Manhattan, and I knew I wasn't ever going to be that good.

So there it sits, this piano, back in the cold room with the stuff on it and the keys all stuck together. There's no room for it in the main house and I can't sell it because my oldest daughter, who lives in Hollywood, adores it. She says she and her sister remember me playing it when they were small, and how the night my mother died I played my mom's favorite song which was "La Paloma." I didn't play it as well as Mom but to my daughter it was as good as Errol Garner.

The empty nest, you see, is never really empty. Long after they go away to war, to commerce, to orange blossoms and far away homes, we all get stuck with the debris of childhood, the albums, yearbooks, mementoes and pianos.

When we threaten to sell it she gets very angry, not angry like when someone cuts her off on the freeway but the kind of angry that rattles the windows, frightens the horses and makes strong men tremble.

I said I'd ship it to her, but she lives in a one bedroom condo with a balcony that faces the sun when it comes up over the palm trees, and awakens the Mexican parrots, and there is no room there for a piano that size.

So there it sits, this piano, back in the cold room. I put her picture atop it now so that it knows whom it belongs to. But I imagine that in the night when we're all asleep it dreams of San Francisco, fog horns, cigar smoke and champagne back in the 1800s, when powerful men in white tie and tails left their wives at home and took a carriage to the Barbary Coast to sip wine with ladies of the night, and listen to a black piano player in a striped shirt with a garter on his arm play a rag. Play "La Paloma" for me, Sam. Play it.

The Sun and Mary O'Hara

True story: I rubbed sun tan oil on Mary O'Hara's back, just before she went into the convent. It was on a beach in Connecticut in the summer of 1957, a month before she entered the order. I'm concerned now that it was just baby oil, designed to burn and hopefully turn one's skin into a swell tan, and it certainly wasn't a sun block. It was hardly my fault. No one thought of blocking the sun in those days. We wanted sun. We worshiped sun. Sun was God. It made plants grow. It made us tan. Cloudy days were yucky. Our happiness was based on a sunny day, and to be perfectly happy, blissfully happy, we had to be TAN!

Why Mary, who was very Irish with red hair, pale skin and blue eyes, wanted a tan when she was about to go into the convent of a cloistered order, and forever be clothed from head to toe in "the habit," confused me, but I didn't question it. I thought I was in love, even though we had only kissed twice that summer, and both pecks were short and simple.

So just letting me rub her back was a big deal for me. It was just her upper back, you understand, the backs of her legs were out of bounds. I knew even as an altar boy of ten, that to rub the backs of a sister's legs, even a novice, even a pre-novice who was still conflicted about being a novice at all, would send a boy plummeting to Hell.

I put on a lot of the baby oil she gave me, and kept rubbing even when she fell asleep. On the train back to the city, her burn was so bad she had to sit up straight the whole way.

I think about Mary today in light of the flood of bad news about what we once thought was cool and sexy. To be tan today is still desirable, but cloaked with anxiety.

Any dermatologist will tell you that a tan means you've actually ruined your skin. You may look pretty, handsome, alluring, desirable and sexy, but you've RUINED your skin.

Of course, as one of comedian Billy Crystal's characters is fond of saying, "It's better to look good, than feel good." Amen to that.

My heroes all had tans. It came with being young and sexy. Steve McQueen had a great tan.

Jack Kennedy, even though he was constantly ill with myriad health problems and living on various pills and injections, always had a gorgeous tan. The great singer Al Jolson had the best tan in Hollywood the day he died of cancer. Even the car wash guys had tans. I remember that Fidel Castro almost never had a tan. Who wanted to look like Castro?

At the Catholic boys' school I attended for a spell, we were all pasty and pale, even our Jesuit teachers were pasty and pale. At my public high school, everyone came back in September with a tan except for Warren. Warren was the smartest guy in my junior class. He spent the entire summer in the Michigan Avenue library. Very smart. Summer in St. Louis is Benghazi hot, and that library had big stand-up black fans in every room. There was this very cool guy, the Tuesday night ping-pong champ at the Loughborough Ave. YMCA, who was always tan. But he was Mexican, and even at Christmas he looked great.

Those days are gone. The sun, celebrated in thousands of songs like "Walk on the Sunny Side," and "I Got the Sun in the Morning" is now the enemy. It's happy making when it comes up each day, but by eleven o'clock it turns into Godzilla, ready to give us terrible skin cancers.

I write this in memory of the sweet Mary O'Hara, who became Sister-someone and broke my heart. That was her real name, and I use it here because it was such a beautiful Irish name, and her sweet mother and father are now long dead. I doubt that the cloistered convent has wifi or a subscription to this paper, but Mary wouldn't mind anyway. She thought I was a wonderful writer, and she'd be happy to know that I finally made it into print. I'm sorry about that burn, Mary, and you'll be happy to know that each time I think about rubbing your back, I say ten Hail Marys and six Our Fathers.

Third Man from the Left

I saw Bobby Ratner on television last night. He was the third man from the left, just behind the star who was dining in a posh restaurant in Beverly Hills. Bobby is not his real name. Not even his real name is his "real name." It's Hollywood, Jake.

I'm still a member of the Screen Actors Guild, and I've always known that of the more than 125,000 members of that guild, almost 98 percent are, at any moment, unemployed. 98 percent. Bobby is almost always one of them. From time to time, Bobby is employed, not like a roofer or a plumber, or an accountant with a bank book and a summer camp. Bobby is employed by the day, or if he's lucky, by the week. Bobby is, I discovered last night, an extra, or as I think they call it now, "background," or "color." Bobby and I started out together in New York on the stage. We had some good parts, but we wanted to be movie stars, so we went to Hollywood. We didn't become movie stars, but we worked a lot. We were employed. We did small parts with maybe one or two lines, then as people got to know us, they got bigger but not that big. Still, you can make an awful lot of money being "not so big."

So we made lots of money. We bought nice cars and a big house. We sent our kids to private schools, and we drank 25-year-old Scotch.

But still, every couple of days or weeks, we were back on the unemployment line. "Between jobs."

In those days before the internet, you picked up your cash, and promised the lady with fluorescent skin and dead eyes at the window that you would continue to look for work. A few days later you got another job. And the band played on.

And that was the script, and for many, it still is. One day you're standing next to a star, sipping Scotch out of cut glass. The next day you're standing in an unemployment line, sipping coffee from a cardboard cup. I once stood there next to Edward

G. Robinson. Yeah, that one. Eddie came in a Rolls Royce and picked up his cash.

Last night I saw Bobby again. He used to be the good looking guy who got to kiss the leading lady on the neck. Then one day Bobby woke up and he was 65. The acting parts disappeared. So Bobby became "color."

Lots of good people make a great living doing that. It's clean and honorable work and beats waiting tables or selling movie star maps.

But when you came to town to be a star, that's where the sidewalk ends.

And then something happened to me that changed my life. I went to the movies one night, and saw a big time Warner Bros. movie star from the forties, selling popcorn and candy behind the counter. He had the shakes, and I knew it was from years of too much 25-year-old Scotch. I went outside and cried. I knew that could be me selling candy bars at 75, or worse, for me, being the third guy from the left.

The last I heard of Bobby, he was divorced and living in a hotel room on Hollywood Boulevard. You have to be an actor to really know what that means.

Tonight when you're watching television, look past the star, past the glitter and the glass. Bobby, or someone just like him will be there. He's the third man from the right.

Changing of the Apron

"This story shall the good man teach his son: and spring shall ne'er go by but we shall be remembered–we few, we happy few, we band of brothers, for he today that sprays his orange clean Pledge with me, and dusts the tables, vacuums the rugs with me, shall be my brother...and gentlemen in Maine now-a-bed shall think themselves accursed that they were not here."

Thank you, Willie Shakespeare, for letting me gently paraphrase your sacred words as I go about my daily chores, that which my mother called "woman's work."

Since time began, it did fall upon the women to keep the dust of farmers' boots from the floors of the caves and cabins.

The male of the species grabbed dinosaur bones to slay the dinner, went hunting for work and gathered the bacon to bring home for the "little woman" to fry. And if you think that's a tale of yesteryear, you're mistaken.

I did a survey in the marketplace, of married couples of all ages, two same-sex married couples as well, (believe me, we're all the same) and despite both mates hustling in the agora, the "little woman" still comes home from bagging, selling, tending to the sick, chasing felons, and teaching, to fry the bacon, do the laundry, and sweep the cave.

I came to this place where a "woman's" work became mine, because of guilt and a rise in self awareness.

I soon discovered that the lot of the teacher, poorly paid and abused, worked as hard as a ditch digger. The teacher, after a fifteen minute lunch break, comes home weary of the day's work, eats and spends an hour or two or three to complete that day's work.

Further research shows that most go right to the market, shop and then home to cook and do dishes. Occasionally, the male species, if not occupied with an obsession with "scores" will "dry." There are exceptions I'm sure, but too few to mention.

Early on in our union, guilt gobsmacked me in the heart. If I were to pretty up each day and strut about the stage of show business, and still have hours left untouched, while she strained her eyes trying to decode the scribblings of her wards, I had to step up, grab an oar and help paddle our ship of life to the future. In the immortal words of Facebook's Sheryl Sandberg I "leaned in."

I was surprised. I took to it like a merganser to fresh water. I cooked, cleaned, guided the day of two daughters, and still made auditions. There is, I believe, a picture of me in the early "Home Daddy" hall of fame.

Now, many years later, with the girls gone, and she, who is about to retire, I stand in the golden glory of my home-daddy career, still crazy after all these years.

This July, she will regain her title as queen of the mansion and resume her duties, whilst I put aside my oar, retire to the local Starbucks to tell old Hollywood stories, and regale all with my adventures in maintaining the family ship. It was a long and exciting adventure.

Not so fast. Already, impediments in the transference of powers are popping up.

It seems that we have different cleaning and cooking habits. Mine are time tested. Hers drive me crazy. I'm an improviser, she's been breaking out her mother's cookbooks two at a time. I knew where all of the cleaning and cooking tools were kept. She's taken to putting them back in different places. As a cook, she favors meticulous measuring procedures. This week, she bought a new set of measuring spoons. Great chefs don't use measuring spoons...do they?

With dust cloth, vacuum and broom in hand, I tend to flit from room to room, staying within a tight time frame. She, on the other hand, will spend an hour in one room, sometimes on one table or mirror, picking, wiping, re-picking, re-wiping until she's satisfied with the result. It's almost painful to watch, like watching paint dry.

Laundry: She folds everything and then smoothes them. They're tee shirts, who knows they're wrinkled? Who cares if they're wrinkled?

I'm sure things will work out in the end. I have to move the computer now. She wants to do this table again. I polished it this morning. Would one more year of teaching kill her?

Wanna Buy Some Rabbit Ears?

I'm glad my mother is dead. I loved Mom, and in many ways I miss her, but I'm sure glad she's not here now so that I would have to explain this analog/digital conversion thing. I know enough to know I don't need it, but if Mom were here, she'd be calling all of us who are left to ask if she has to get a new television set for her room at the Rosebud Nursing Home and Retirement Village. I'm sure someone there could explain it all, but she wouldn't be happy until she bugged us.

Once upon a time, the entire world was covered with roof top antennas, or those little rabbit ear things you could put on top of the set. When Arthur Godfrey went blurry, or started weaving in and out, all you had to do was fiddle with the rabbit ears.

Mom had this little black and white Zenith, but the picture kept rolling up and down and made hissing sounds. She complained about that so much my brothers, who were living then, had to buy her a new color set. I think it was a Motorola, and I remember her calling me and worrying that she wouldn't be able to get the old black and white movies.

But Mom is gone now. She's probably in some great nursing home in the sky with Arthur Godfrey, Julius LaRosa and Dorothy Kilgallen. Let them explain analog/digital to her.

Last week, an older gentleman stopped me in the aisle of the supermarket, and asked if I understood what the blazes this was all about, and why didn't I write explaining it.

I said as how I didn't understand it either and that I would look it up and get back to him.

So I went online and asked. This is what I got from someone who was clearly the sixth member of his family to graduate from MIT.

"As a technology," the site explained, "analog is the process of taking an audio or video signal (in most cases, the human voice) and translating it into electronic pulses. Digital, on the other hand, is breaking the signal into a binary format where the audio or video data is represented by a series of "1"s and "0"s. Simple enough? I'm glad I can't remember the name of the man who asked me because I didn't write any of that down. I'm a writer, and I can't even remember which remote to use to go from digital television to the digital DVD player. There are three altogether. But in case I ran into this guy again and he asked me, I went looking for a simpler answer. I found one on Yahoo.com from a concerned high school graduate.

"Digital is cheaper than analog," he explains. "You can cram more into the signal and put more signals out there with digital TV. It's like the difference between records and CDs. (OMG why didn't they say that earlier.) CDs are cheaper (and much easier) to produce, smaller, and allow you to put on more (and clearer) information." Huh?

The site goes on to say that, "The analog channels will be reused for government broadcasts but not public stuff. "Does that mean, do you think, that things like the voting for Obama's stimulus plan or the Illinois senate impeachment of Governor Blagojevich will be on analog and we won't have to watch it? Mom would be happy to know that. Goodnight Mom, wherever you are. Say hello to Arthur Godfrey.

Tick Party–Bring your own Tweezers

I've been invited to the first wedding of the season, to be held in a gorgeous open field overlooking the ocean. A flock of New Yorker friends of the couple will be there. These are sophisticated people who are looking forward to a summer wedding in Maine, and meeting some genuine Mainers. I've been waiting all winter to wear my new seersucker suit and white bucks. A question: Do I really want to be the only guy there with his pants tucked into his socks? They're great socks, to be sure, lavender and gray argyles. But my pants tucked into them? Really?

Does the happy couple really have to add to the invitation "Be sure to wear light-colored clothing so it will be easier to see the ticks before they bite you?"

I can just see the reception on the dock with the out-of-towners all checking their ankles, as the groomsmen hand out individual pairs of tweezers and pamphlets instructing one how to extract the tick. This Lyme disease thing is no longer funny. They are, apparently, everywhere.

My yard, front and back, still looks like areas of hurricane Sandy overlap, full of sticks, clusters of mildewed leaves and here and there clumps of tall grass waiting to be mowed. My gardener, who has been ill, won't be around for a few weeks, and I can tell you that I'M not going out there.

Recently this paper printed some news we can all use, and it's frightening. It describes the symptoms of Lyme disease: fever, headache and fatigue. Sounds suspiciously like a hangover. Don't be fooled. Just to be sure, don't do any serious yard work after a night of partying, and forget about those cute gardening shorts for women you see in J.C. Penney ads. An entire bare leg is a smorgasbord for hungry ticks.

PREVENTING TICK-BORNE DISEASE:
Wear light-colored clothing so that you can see them (ticks.) (Reading glasses for the aged come in handy).

This is good news for me as I am way into summer white linens. Be very aware. If it moves, it's not pepper or coffee grounds.

Also, it's very restrictive. What about seersuckers? I have three pair in various colors, blue stripe, green stripe and red stripe. Is it possible for these ticks, tinier than the tea leaves in my Starbuck's Calm tea, to hide in the colored stripes?

And what about the guys in the wedding out in that field, who are wearing tuxedos? Black tuxedos? That's a virtual breeding ground for the little monsters.

APPLY REPELLENTS TO DISCOURAGE THEM:
Be serious. I bought a couple of tubes of such repellent, and none of them smell remotely like Chanel Pour Homme or Jo Malone of London or even that old drug store favorite Old Spice; they smell like repellent or the stuff you put on your toes to keep from getting that dreadful toenail fungus.

Full disclosure: I had an early attack of said toe fungus, and used a topical ointment to contain it. Everyone around me on the deck at the lake spent the evening sniffing the air. "What is that?"

CONDUCT BODY SEARCH after returning from the outdoors:
Okay, that can be fun, especially at an evening beach party after substantial amounts of sangria. And it's a great opening line. No longer does the young man have to ask, "What's your sign?" or "Didn't we meet in the infirmary on the Carnival cruise?"

Now, it's simply, "We walked down here through some heavy foliage. I think the prudent thing to do would be to conduct mutual body searches."

IF A TICK IS FOUND remove using tweezers. This, of course, is a money maker for small business. Now, before we go camping we must add tweezers to suntan oil, swim trunks, beach towels and umbrellas, not to mention paperback copies of Fifty Shades of Grey.

AFTER REMOVING tick, disinfect the bite site and wash with soap and water. You can add Irish Spring and Neosporin to that store list.
My advice? It turns out that Carnival cruises may be safer than your garden.

Anniversary Song

This year marks my 30th year at writing stories for a newspaper, 25 of them for this company. It had a different name when I started. I can't remember what it was, and it's changed hands a number of times since. I've had more editors than I can remember. Editors seem to come and go and still I'm here. Where do they go I wonder? I've asked the ones still around, and they don't seem to know. They just went to other papers I suppose. I can't remember their names, and I'm sure they can't remember me. They passed by me like smoke every day I was there. The one I've got now wasn't born when I started writing, but he seems to like me and is good at correcting my errors without wagging his finger at me.

Probably most of the others really wanted to be writers and became disenchanted and took up other lines of work. They might have gone to medical school and have become brain surgeons. Twenty five years is a long time. You can become a pretty good brain surgeon in that time. It's possible.

It's important for a writer to have had many jobs in life. Zane Grey, who was probably the greatest western writer of all time, was once a dentist. He sold his first book at the age of 40 and was able to give up drilling teeth.

The great Langston Hughes worked as a bus boy in a hotel, Jack London was an oyster pirate, whatever that is, and Harper Lee, who wrote "To Kill a Mockingbird," was an airline ticket agent. Kurt Vonnegut sold cars, and J.K. Rowling taught English as a foreign language before Harry appeared to her.

I guess that bodes well for my future, limited as it is. Because I loved clothes and had no money, I had more after school jobs than anyone in my family, and I had no experience to bring to any of them. I dressed windows and display centers, setting up furniture displays in department stores.

My favorite brother, a cop, got me a job as a police clerk on the St. Louis Police Department, where I watched the human comedy and tragedy of life unfold. There, one night, I checked in a high school friend who had just had his throat cut. He lived. I watched cops try to save the life of a small boy who swallowed a lollipop. They failed. Cops tell great stories. I can't remember their names, but I remember those stories.

I had a paper box and route when I was eleven, and had a lot of fun as a copy boy for the St. Louis Post Dispatch, in a news room full of smoke from cigarettes, pipes and cigars and the familiar smell of whiskey. I free lanced for the Los Angeles Times where a guard checked you for weapons before entering the building. After high school when my future was a blank piece of paper, I made plastic feet in a shoe factory, where I had lunch each day out of a brown paper bag on a loading dock with old men who told me hundreds of stories about the Great Depression and "The Great War." I can't remember their faces, but I remember the stories.

My other brother got me a job as a fireman on a diesel engine. That's the easiest job in the world. You simply sit looking out the window and try to keep people from walking into the train. The engineer was a happy drunk who knew all the words to just once song, "Don't Get Around Much Anymore," and finished an entire bottle on the run from Waukegan, Illinois, to Gary, Indiana, at full throttle.

I've been a reservation clerk at the Waldorf Astoria in New York and a date for debutantes who couldn't get one for the ball. Now, near the end of my sidewalk, I'm a cook and live-in housekeeper for a famous teacher, and about to publish 30 years of this stuff into one book. It's almost easier than keeping people from walking into trains.

The Twinkie. I'm Just Saying....

One day at recess in the school yard at St. Mary and Joseph's Catholic School, I fell down and seriously skinned my knee. Everyone laughed and ran off, except for Mary Lister. Mary came over and pulled her luncheon desert from a brown paper bag and handed me my first ever Twinkie. This is a true story. I fell in love that day, with Mary and with Twinkies. Thank you, Mary.

Twinkies, in those days, were filled with banana cream. They were criminally delicious and probably still are. Children today, and nutritionally challenged adults who think they love Twinkies, have no idea what they missed with the original banana cream filling. OMG.

Today we're informed that the Twinkie mother ship, Hostess, is sliding into bankruptcy. They say they will re-group and come bouncing back. This is, I'm sure, for many, good news. Of course, no serious minded healthy eater as yours truly, would put a Twinkie in the shopping basket. I'm just saying.

Twinkies, it seems, were invented in Schiller Park, Illinois, in 1930 by James Alexander Dewar, a baker for the Continental Baking Company. He took the name from a billboard in my home town of St. Louis for "Twinkle Toe Shoes." I remember those shoes. They were sold in Koelen's Shoe Store, along with Buster Browns. Upon tasting the first Twinkie, it is reported that Mr. Dewar quoted the Bhagavad Gita and said, "Now, I am become Death, the destroyer of worlds." Of course it was J. Robert Oppenheimer who said that upon viewing the first atomic bomb. I just think mine is funnier, and most nutritionists would agree.

Don't deny it. You and I grew up eating the worst junk food on the planet. Twinkies and its sister treat, Hostess Cup Cakes, those delicious chocolate cakes with the squiggly white lines on top, were part of that menu. Like most Depression babies, I was fed a good diet of veggies and fruits at home. But in the streets, where we all lived out our true lives, chili dogs, French fries with catsup, Pepsi Cola and the ubiquitous Twinkie, were the true survival foods.

An interesting note: Twinkies have played an important role in the romantic chapters of my life. Mary Lister, who gave me my first Twinkie, went on to hold my heart in her Twinkie smeared hands up to the sixth grade. Mary also gave me my first Valentine. I still have it in an aging scrapbook.

There's more. I first met and fell in love with my high school sweetheart, Rosemary DeBranco, she of the one thousand and one Angora sweaters and simple strand of pearls, in Cleveland High School's cafeteria. Rosemary, who was the prototype for all future white fudge, glitter sprinkled blonde bombshells, reached across the table and handed me her one Twinkie. Rosemary and I were also famous for inventing the "Twinkie Kiss" which involved sharing a Twinkie in the moonlight. You had to be there.

I'm sure that upon reading this, most of you, even the young, will have your own wonderful Twinkie stories. Of course we all know that not one of us would ever think of eating a Twinkie this late in our years. One only has to read the ingredients on the label to go into convulsions.

The Twinkie, despite those weird, and some suspect, extraterrestrial fillings, has a romantic primal fire about it. Some say that the Twinkie ranks right up there with our first kiss, first beer and first spiritual experience. Some say that it rivals the cigarette. Imagine having the first Twinkie of the day over a hot cup of coffee at a cafe in Paris, or after making love. Think about it. I'm just saying.

VJ Day 2009 - the War is Over

This week we celebrated VJ Day, August 15th, 1945. The war in the Pacific was over. Now, all these years later, most have forgotten it. I have not.

For me, it had special meaning because five of my brothers, all naval combat veterans, were coming home safely. The war for the Devines was over.

And then in August 1951, only six years later after that day, I found myself standing on a dock in Yokohama, the son and brother of warriors. Of victors.

There I was at 18, a young airman, standing face to face with Japanese dock workers, still wearing scraps of their old uniforms.

Even then, seven years after a bloody war, when we "Gaijin" came down the gangplank, the workers smiled, doffed their caps and bowed. Some of them were my age, but most were older. These may well have been those who had tried to kill my brothers, and my brothers in turn returned their fire.

All of us growing up in WW II had heard the tales of horror, the Bataan Death March, the prison camps, the torture and murders. We had heard of the Kamikaze planes that had killed our love ones. Stories were told of the bayonet charges, the ruthlessness, cruelty and inhumanity of the Japanese. The racist invectives became part of my childhood language, and now here I stood in uniform facing that "enemy."

In my almost two years in Japan, I was lucky to be able to live off base in the small village of Fuchu near my air base. All the ugliness I had learned as a child fell from my heart like cherry blossoms in the rains of April. When I got off the rickety train in the evening, to a village that seemed almost unchanged from the 14th century, I stood on the platform and watched peasants working in the rice fields, using century old tools. It was eerie. Mystic.

Down my narrow graveled street in the evening, I could hear someone playing the Shakuhachi flute. I could smell the foods being cooked on traditional hibachis, fire bowls that had been used since the beginning of time.

When I picked up the language, I befriended my landlord and his family, the local grocer, the man who delivered my ice, the farmers in the fields. And the flute player? An ex-Japanese admiral who now delivered newspapers.

When my family sent me dozens of American colored tee shirts, I gave most of them to the local kids who were thrilled. At night, I joined my neighbors in the tiny movie theater in the village that showed mostly Russian films and the occasional Laurel and Hardy comedy at which we all howled. Comedy, the music of peace.

I saw no evidence of what my brothers had seen in war. Japan had returned to peace time. I was not viewed as a conqueror, nor did I behave like one. I learned the language, ate at my landlord's hibachi, drank his saki. His name was Mr. Watanabe, and he had been an officer in the army. Now, a devout student of the Buddha, Watanabe's war was over.

On winter mornings, as the sun rose on Mt. Fuji turning the snowy cap pink, I sat in the local police station with the cops, our legs warmed by a hibachi.

Only once did I come face to face with the vicious past. A legless veteran on a train, perched on metal limbs, came at me swinging his crutches, his face a mask of hatred. But he was subdued by students who apologized to me.

When it came time for me to go home, the base sent a Jeep to take me to the Haneda Airport. As we drove down the graveled street, my neighbors, and all the children wearing my American tee shirts lined the block, waving goodbye to me. These were children whose fathers had fought my brothers, and many had died at their hands. But now we were friends, neighbors. VJ Day, 2009. The war for the Devines and the Watanabis is over.

We'll See Won't We?

Long ago on a rainy, romantic, candlelit night in New York City, I asked a girl a question. She twirled the little paper umbrella in her Mai Tai and replied, "We'll see."

"We'll see?"

I began hallucinating. She reminded me of my mother. Suddenly there was Mother, sitting there in a housecoat and hair curlers, sipping the Mai Tai.

"Whatever you're trying to get this poor girl to do, you can bet it's a sin."

"Will I go to Hell?"

"We'll see." Yep, that was my mother.

"We'll see" is the most chilling tool in the women's trick box. Men never say that. They never use that. It's wimpy. It's a woman thing, most of all it's a mother thing.

"We'll see" is the retort of choice of mothers from the caves to today, from Berlin (wir sehen) to Rome (vedremo) to Madrid (veremos) to Paris (nous verrons). It's the universal stall.

Religion has used it against us for centuries. We're told that if our prayers weren't answered not to despair. It's simply God saying, "Well, we'll see." That's the New Testament God of course. The Old Testament God was easier to deal with. You knew where you stood with him. He dealt in sores, pestilence, floods and raining toads. None of that wussy "We'll see" for him.

Doctors use it in the most frightening manner. "Does it look bad?"

"We'll see."

"Am I going to die?"

"We'll see."

With women, it means one of two things: They really, really don't want to comply, but don't want to risk losing you. Or, they DO want to comply, but feel they can parlay it into getting a better deal.

Then I got to thinking. Every politician has been put through this parental wringer. Why didn't they use it at the debates?

"Do you have a plan to get us out of Iraq?"

The candidate can pause and then say, "We'll see."

"Do you have a solution to the outsourcing of our jobs?" "We'll see."

Eastern liberal elitists wouldn't put up with that dodge for a second. We're all in analysis, but Bush red staters don't care what he says as long as he drops the "ing" on the end, promises a tax cut on their double wides and two hound dogs in every outhouse.

Sometimes it doesn't work. Edwards to Cheney. "How is your lesbian daughter Mary? "

"What lesbian daughter?" No plan is perfect. You can't trap Dick Cheney. We don't even know where Dick Cheney is.

There are other questions that fit, but for which only a flat no will do.

Will the "insurgents" surrender?

No.

Will Iyad Awalli turn Iraq into Omaha?

No.

Will there be amendments to the Constitution allowing Bill Clinton to run again, or Arnold? Will we ever know what was on George Bush's back in the debates?

No.

Okay. You can probably tell by now that I'm avoiding the inevitable question. Am I upset? Am I suicidal? Have the results of this disaster sent me into an alcoholic coma? We'll see.

But, I am resilient by nature. If it took the Sox eighty-five years to regain the title, we can do the same. And it will probably take that long.

Liberals have wandered into the wilderness. There is no Moses in sight to lead us out. Hillary? Gimme a break. Obama?

You have 20 years? Will I live to see an elitist, metrosexual, gay loving, gun hating Democrat in the Oval Office? We'll see.

And She Chuckled

We were sitting across from one another at Riverside Market in Oakland recently, having a nice salad, iced tea and corn bread and trying to decide which one of us should die first. This is not as macabre as it sounds. It's a practical and sound conversation. Our actual planning is still inchoate, and nowhere near a final decision. You can't rush stuff like that. We're both in very good health, but it's like the paint job I did in the dining room. You don't want to look too closely.

I suspect that more and more couples our age are having this conversation.

We've discussed it over the years in lighter more comedic forms, but now it's coming up more often and with less comedic tones.

It goes like this. She pays all the bills, does the taxes and carries all the credit cards. Since I lost our checkbook twice in the past three years, I am no longer allowed to actually carry one. I am required to ask for a check if I need to pay something. It's kind of like those convicts on chain gangs in the old movies. When a prisoner had to go to the bushes to relieve himself, he was required to raise his hand and then the "Walking Boss" would give him permission. I am the chain ganger and she is the "Walking Boss." Yeah. Like that. When I promised that I would never lose the book again, she chuckled.

Recently I was forced to confront the fact that I actually don't do anything of real value around the house that she couldn't, if pressed, do. As she is busy actually working at a job, I shop daily, cook the meals and clean up. I also do the housework each week. She could do all of this if necessary. I could not do anything, not one blessed thing she does. Not if I were water boarded could I balance the checkbook. I am bad at math and quite possibly I am ADD. This is where the discussion comes in.

If, God forbid, she were to pass first, I would be forced to deal with her desk. If you could see her desk, you can understand why I want to go first. Whenever I feel guilty and ask her if I can help her with the taxes, she chuckles. It's so demeaning.

Her only problem, should I join that great saloon in the sky first, would be handling Jack. Jack is our sheep dog. He is big and lovable but has severe separation anxiety issues. He is strong and likes to run and jump and play with the girls, much as I did at his age. But he would be difficult for her to handle.

She has always been troubled with opening jars and small bottles. But then she bought this gadget that does that for her. You can see where this is going.

My ace card is that she has not yet mastered the Time Warner remote in all of its complexities. She says she doesn't need it anyway. She has only been to the basement twice in 25 years. Once to see what it was like, and the second time to see the new boiler. She says she can hire a guy to do that.

For all other matters I'm forced to admit that I'm virtually dispensable.

But just as this luncheon conversation started to look like she was ordering my urn, I brought up the matter of the head and foot rubs, dragging the black garbage bags to the curb, handling the complex clasps on her collection of beads. And who would leap from the warm bed in the dead of a winter's night to check out the strange sound downstairs? She agreed that I had some validity. So as I finished my salad, I cheerfully asked her if I could drive the car home. She chuckled.

Who's at the Door?

"Don't stop thinking about tomorrow."
—Fleetwood Mac

It's just a rumor, but the Tweet is that two women went to the homes of Texas Senator Tom Cruz and Kentucky's Mitch McConnell on Halloween, dressed as Hillary Clinton and Kathleen Sebelius. I understand their Jack O'Lanterns were smashed, and McConnell's trees were Tee-peed. Both senators were unavailable for comment.

Antics aside, the noise you hear is the rustling of skirts and stomping of smart boots. Hip people in Washington are reading the tea leaves. The old white guys in the glass towers and the cleated shoe golfers of both parties know change is coming, but they have no idea how bad it's going to be.

Imagine hurricane Sandy in pant suits, Vesuvius in Jimmy Choo shoes. It isn't going to be pretty. It's going to be a category five.

I'm going out on a limb now and make my fantasy prediction, even though I probably won't be around to see the full change of things to come. Although it would be fun to live to see the first woman baseball commissioner.

By 2025, the political gender-scape of America and possibly the universe, will be unrecognizable. As we speak, women are beginning to kick down the doors, rip out the glass ceiling and are taking over.

The male political front runners now jockeying for position are about to hit a brick wall, and its name is woman.

President? Some mentioned include Maine's popular Susan Collins, others are chanting for Elizabeth Warren of Massachusetts, and the Tea Party is scouring the bushes of the Deep South to find a replacement for Michele Bachmann. But Vegas is cleaning up on Hillary Clinton, and this week, a coffee klatch of Democratic women senators sent a letter to Hillary, entreating her to run. Look out the window boys, suits and loafers are fading away. Pastels are the new black.

Futurist planners are envisioning a day when women will control the House, the Senate and the Oval Office. Both sides, of course, are hoping it's their crowd. Even the Tea Party will have a candidate.

Red or blue, the new gang will sit down at breakfasts and teas. Between board and strategy meetings, they will shop together and stage cookouts. After budget agreements, they'll rush to baby showers. Problems will be solved before end of business day. With no male egos smelling up the halls, there will be no petulant shut downs or cliff hangers.

Women don't like cliff hangers and Hollywood knows it. They like stuff all wrapped up and tied with a ribbon. They like comity with joy, smiles and weddings, and by 2018 it won't matter if it's Tom and Dick or Suzie and Jane. Fathers may fret over a gay son. Mothers just hug them and go about planning the wedding.

The corridors of power and the yellow halls of the west wing will hum with the buzz of straights and gays, Hispanic, Asian, Black and (God help us) Irish women. It will be good for business as well. Pant suits will be all the rage, and Ralph Lauren and Talbot's will expand their Asian factories.

The old white haired, white shoe and Haggar slacks crowd? One by cantankerous one, they will be sent home to play golf, drink their bourbon, snap their suspenders and watch the games of their choice.

Eventually, in this golden utopian women dominated America, perhaps planet, men, if they don't learn to behave, will be subjugated to the roles they have traditionally been best at: throwing and catching balls of all kinds, killing foreign enemies and growing facial hair.

There will always be the Chris Matthews, Bill O'Reillys and Rush Limbaughs loudly positing opinions, but they will not be allowed to interrupt the women they're interviewing when they're making their points, and may even, if some Catholic nuns get elected to higher office, be forced to raise their hands before asking condescending questions.

Finally, courtesy, manners and humor will, after decades of absence, be back and will change the face of Congress, Wall Street, city halls and state houses country wide.

Yes, there will always be a crazy or two and squabbles will pop up. Women who can't agree on the color of a new car certainly don't qualify as a monolithic voting bloc.

It's Halloween in America, old boys, who is that at the door?

Vive la Femme

Many years ago, Arthur Marx, son of Groucho, was denied access to a Beverly Hills country club pool because, it was stated, he was Jewish. Groucho protested. "My son is only half-Jewish, so can he go in up to his knees?" In the 60s when I worked in Beverly Hills, Groucho and I occasionally shared morning walks. I asked him if that was a true story. "You have my word of honor," he said, "...for what that's worth." True story.

Anti-Semitism and restrictions for Black Americans in these big private clubs is mostly a thing of the past, but for women, of any color, religious order, or political persuasion, the chains on many of the big doors are still there. Is there anyone else here old enough to remember when taverns had "Ladies Entrance" doors at the back of the bar?

The New York Racquet and Tennis Club is one of the last to hold onto this antediluvian silliness. I was invited to have a drink there one afternoon with an old actor friend, a Yale grad who, like his father, belonged to the famous club on Park Avenue. After a very large martini, my friend took me on a tour of the establishment. I learned that there was a spacious swimming pool, and that sometimes, in late afternoon, men could splash about in the nude if they liked. "What about the women?" I asked. "Oh dear fellow, women aren't allowed to join the club." I believe that rule still holds fast.

This week the gender flap threw a cloud over the brilliant sun at the famed Augusta National Golf Club. I wasn't aware the issue existed there, and I couldn't care less about golf but for the great colorful clothes, green lawns and sunshine. But no women? I lose my breath at the thought of any kind of sporting event that doesn't include women, that's why I'm no big fan of baseball or football. I do enjoy watching, those volleyball games on the beach in Florida. I'm just saying.

For myself, I can't imagine belonging to a club or society that doesn't admit women. Women, like wine, add poetry and color to life. What would be the point of dressing up, showering and brushing one's teeth and hair?

My own personal experience with male chauvinism came when I was only ten. I can remember the sting of it even today. Sonny Erb, Junior Reed, Billy Hagany and myself formed a club and built our own ramshackle clubhouse, just above the railroad tracks on the bank of the Mississippi. We called it "Gang Busters" after the popular radio show of the time.

As fate would have it, this was the summer that May Rose arrived like a summer shower, from a small town in Arkansas, to visit her grandma who baked cakes for the Altar and Rosary Society. May Rose was a stunning red haired girl, tall for her age, and blessed with two startlingly white and slightly protruding front teeth. It was love at first sight. I was thrilled when May Rose wanted to be a "Gang Buster." But the boys said, "No girls."

In protest, I withdrew my membership in the club. Luckily, later that same week, May Rose and friends decided to stage a family play in the basement of her grandma's house. She asked me to play the father. Chocolate milk and Oreos were served. And that's how I became an actor and future ardent supporter of women's rights. Vive la femme.

Namaste No More

A review of William Broad's new book, "The Science of Yoga: The Risks and the Rewards," recently appeared in these pages. It seems to lean heavily on the risks part. Mr. Broad speaks of shoulder and head stands that have caused injuries, lower back, knee and neck problems, and in rare cases, strokes in young healthy people. It's important to note that Broad, the chief science writer for the New York Times, hasn't changed his mind about the practice and remains devoted to it. Good for him. He knows there is a growing conversation in the agora on this matter, and it's an opportunity for him to sell a book.

I rise here this morning to make my own stand on yoga, and to add my own list of cautions. I have dabbled in the practice off and on for about four years without completely falling in love with it. I tried. Buddha knows I tried. No deal.

This past winter, after an unpleasant and brief conversation with my heart, I went looking for a program to reduce stress. I started up again at the School Street Yoga Center in Waterville under the guidance and patience of the gentle teacher, Jeri Wilson. It was, at first, pleasurable and relaxing. After eight sessions however, I dropped out. Yoga, it seems, isn't going to be my raison d'etre in my later years, but it has nothing to do with injuries. I suffered none, nor do I know of anyone who has, including my own daughter, a habitual student.

My problems with yoga are very personal and deal with the ego of an aging actor, bon vivant and fading raconteur. When one has spent one's youth in the world of entertainment, being constantly photographed, measured and scrutinized, it's painful, even in retirement, to grow old and lose that youthful glow of beauty and charm. The body fades, the ego goes from here to eternity.

This winter, I bought a yoga mat and the requisite loose fitting clothing and, floating over ice, bundled up against the wind, I went to my first class. Of course I was the oldest. There was one older gentleman, a doctor in his late fifties. But after a few classes, he vanished, leaving me alone with twenty or thirty women who fell into four categories: slim and young, attractive, gorgeous and fit. In the privacy of my home I can convince myself that I am still flexible, lithe and dashing. I can squint in the mirror and see Cary Grant. But surrounded by incredibly fit young women, I felt more like Ernie Borgnine.

Then there was the matter of my feet. It is required in yoga classes to be barefoot. Putting on my reading glasses, I studied my Borgnine toenails. I could feel the others averting their eyes. I tried to walk around with them curled under like a 14th Century Chinese bride. It just made me appear aging and hobbled. Toenails do not age gracefully. They require careful, constant attention, professional attention. Mat, clothing, toenails, tuition. It adds up.

It gets worse. One night, just before my last class, I watched a comedy show in which a middle aged firefighter attended a yoga class, surrounded by beautiful young women. In his effort to complete a perfect "down dog," the poor man suffered an attack of flatulence that rocked the stillness. I tried to imagine his heart breaking, soul shaking embarrassment. What, I shuddered, if that happened to me?

I managed to get through that class without such a disaster, but the very thought of it happening was too horrible to contemplate. It's bad enough to be Ernie Borgnine, but Ernie Borgnine with gas? No chance.

Ultimately, it's really a matter of discipline. I've never had much. She who could not live without it, has enough for both of us. I hate getting up early and having to be someplace, to sit up, even in a contorted lotus position, and pay attention. I will miss the garden of pulchritude, the chanting of Namaste, and Ms. Wilson. Wake me in June.

How Much for the Teddy Bear?

"The bustle in a house the morning after death/ is solemnest of industries enacted upon earth/The sweeping up the heart/and putting love away/ we shall not want to use again until eternity." From a poem by Emily Dickinson.

My very good friend Kyle has a dilemma, one not uncommon of a survivor. Kyle has a big house in Maine a few yards from a beautiful lake facing the moonrise. The house is full of antiques and nice dishes, paintings and rugs and pottery and an expensive old Teddy bear. All that's missing to make a perfect picture is his wife Denise who died of cancer at too young an age.

It took a long time to get over that, but he's a smart and resilient man. He has enough money now that he's retired, to get through the rest of his life comfortably, and he has begun to think of selling this house full of memories, and move somewhere to the South to play golf and walk on some beach and watch the moonrise over the ocean.

So now Kyle is thinking of packing it in here in Maine. He and his love had no children, and her brother and sisters are older and have no room or use for all of his stuff. So he's faced with the painful task of "sweeping up."

One day a few weeks ago, he and I talked of this job. He would, he said, at some point, hold an "estate" sale. That's a garage sale where everyone gets to prowl through the house touching things, sniffing at price tags and bargaining for his memories.

It's not a pleasant thing, we both agree. But the plan now is that he would sell the china, silverware, old clothes, chairs and tables, kitchen utensils and pots and pans, the dog dishes that belonged to Jack, their beloved Wheaten terrier who died earlier.

Everything that doesn't sell, he will throw into a large rented dumpster, and watch as it's towed away down the road to some distant landfill, where grass and flowers will grow over them, maybe, hopefully, with a view of the moonrise.

Except for the Teddy bear. It was a gift for Denise that Kyle found in a magazine, one of those famous Teddy bears. It was an anniversary gift. You don't sell or throw away anniversary gifts, especially when they're Teddy bears.

So I imagine when Kyle packs up to go south and leave all of this behind, the Teddy bear will be sitting beside him in the car.

It's going to be easier for me, hopefully. As I write this, She who is thankfully, gratefully, blessedly, still with me, has all of her grandparents' and mother's iconic dinnerware spread out on the dining room table.

We're not going south. We don't really care for south, can't afford Manhattan anymore, anywhere below that is politically unsavory.

So we're not going anywhere, but taking advice from Steve, we're preparing for the day when one of us has to have an "estate sale," alone.

So we started with the glassware. We took pictures of all of it, the Havilland gold-rimmed dishes, the Wedgewood, her mother's endless collection of ruby glass, and emailed it to the daughters. Who wants what? The replies came fast. No takers. There is no place in shaky Los Angeles for fancy dinnerware. They'd like my clocks, my paintings, but they have no room for oriental rugs or more furniture and basically, they really "Don't want to talk about it."

"You should have an estate sale," one suggested. Yes, I already had that advice.

No, we don't want to talk about it either. Nobody does. The very idea is upsetting.

So back into the breakfronts it all goes. The glass doors will close, and hopefully another year or five or ten will pass without one of us having to watch strangers prowl through the house, picking at things, sniffing at prices.

"How much for the Teddy bear?" someone will ask.

I don't know if She will sell it, she's pretty tough with money. I won't.

If the day comes and I, the impatient one, is still standing, I'll sell everything for a buck, the dinnerware, the silver, the dog dishes, bird cage and all, and then I'll just walk away. No, I won't sell the damn bear. I'll leave it sitting in the window, the one facing the moonrise.

About the Author

J.P. Devine, a former New York and Hollywood actor, painter and dancer, who worked with Bob Newhart, Jerry Lewis, Johnny Carson, Ricardo Montalban, and Zero Mostel, gave up those lucrative art forms and took a vow of poverty to become a freelance writer. All because a tarot card reader in Hong Kong in 1953 told him he would become famous in "letters" late in life. Author and friend Ray Bradbury told him at age 37, that that was late enough. Go forth.

Jeremiah Patrick Devine, the descendant of four Irish immigrants is the husband of Katherine Joly Devine, father of two daughters, Jillana and Dawn, and an Old English sheep dog, Jack, who may or may not be alive when I get the Pulitzer.

www.ingramcontent.com/pod-product-compliance
Lightning Source LLC
Chambersburg PA
CBHW071652090426
42738CB00009B/1495